*School, Family, and Neighborhood:*
*The Theory and Practice of*
*School-Community Relations*

# School, Family and Neighborhood: THE THEORY and PRACTICE of SCHOOL-COMMUNITY RELATIONS

EUGENE LITWAK
and
HENRY J. MEYER

Cheryl Elise Mickelson,
*Research Associate*

Columbia University Press
New York & London 1974

Library of Congress Cataloging in Publication Data

Litwak, Eugene, 1925-
    School, family, and neighborhood

        1.  Community and school.  2.  Home and school.
I.  Meyer, Henry Joseph, 1913-     joint author.
II.  Title.                 Dec. 2, 1974
LC215.L52      370.19'31      73-17274
ISBN 0-231-03354-0

*To the parents, students, and staff of
the Detroit public schools*

# ✣ PREFACE AND ACKNOWLEDGEMENTS

This book is addressed both to social practitioners and to social scientists. It is intended primarily to offer guidelines to practitioners concerned with local school-community relations of educational institutions. Practical suggestions are offered, sometimes in prescriptive language, as proposals for action rather than as rules. The arguments behind the practical suggestions and our analyses of linkages between complex social organizations and community primary groups based on sociological theory should be of interest to social scientists.

As a practical problem and as a theoretical problem, the management of relationships between schools and their families and neighborhoods has not heretofore received much systematic attention. Practitioners usually offer examples from their practice but provide few guiding principles. On the other hand, social scientists tend to consider the antithetical rather than the complementary relations of bureaucracies and primary groups. We hope this attempt to analyze school-community linkages will stimulate practitioners to conceptualize their experiences and social scientists to elaborate their theories.

Chapters 1 through 4 are theoretical and general, suggesting a frame of reference within which practitioners may place problems they face and their efforts to deal with them. Chapters 5 through 12 are pragmatic, at times almost like a "cook book" in the approach to specific mechanisms of school-community linkages.

Practitioners may find the presentation of the first set of chapters more general than they are accustomed to. Social scientists may find statements in the later chapters too narrow or too dogmatic. The former can supply the content of specific situations in their own schools and communities and modify the stated principles accordingly. The latter can view examples and suggestions for action as propositions rather than as facts or established generalizations. From either viewpoint, we hope the result will be the posing of significant hypotheses to be tried by practice and tested by research. Our aim is to be provocative.

Since the book is intended for the training and use of practitioners, we have stripped away much of the format of traditional academic presentations. Documentation has been limited to references that stimulated the development of our ideas. We attempt to be somewhat formal and paradigmatic in our analyses. We hope that our compromise has produced a book that practitioners and social scientists will find useful.

The content as well as the form of this book developed through interaction and critical stimulation between practitioners and social scientists. We recognize with deepest appreciation the many persons in the Detroit public schools and at the University of Michigan who contributed to the ideas which the authors alone must take responsibility for expressing. The general idea of a balance theory of coordination between bureaucracies and community primary groups began to develop before we came to think of it in terms of school-community relations. Our colleagues and students in the School of Social Work at the University of Michigan—particularly those associated with the doctoral program in social work and social science—were challenging and creative critics. When we began to work with Carl Marburger, Director, and William Rasschaert, Evaluator, of the Great Cities School Improvement Project of the Detroit public schools, we saw that their demonstration project (one of the Ford Foundation "grey areas" projects) provided an empirical experience for which our theories supplied some conceptual illumination. From their professional insights, these educators were attacking educational problems of the central city by attempting to devise ways of bridging the gap between school and home. To examine the feasibility of research useful to the Great Cities Project and pertinent to our theoretical interests, we met almost weekly with Dr. Marburger and Dr. Rasschaert. They seemed to find in the theories a rationale for and a stimulant to their practical objectives. We most gratefully acknowledge our debt to them not only for the hard criticism to which their experience subjected our ideas but for their creative modification and extension of the theories. From these sessions emerged a number of "working papers" that were the initial basis for the present volume.

From these discussions and papers, we developed a research proposal, ultimately funded by the U.S. Office of Education and reported as Project No. 5-0355, Contract No. OE-3-10-033, under the title, *Relationship between School-Community Coordinating Procedures and Reading Achievement*, December, 1966. Part of the research was conducted as a project of the Detroit Area Study, Department of Sociology, the University of Michigan. In preparation for this research we spent several months observing and talking to faculty and students in four Detroit schools. John Leggett assisted in this field work and provided much fine observational data. The research project involved systematic surveys of children, mothers, school neighborhood residents, and teachers of eighteen elementary schools. During the course of the research, Dr. Samuel Brownell, then Superintendent of the Detroit Schools, provided both encouragement and cooperation. We had the able assistance and the benefit of stimulating ideas from Oliver Moles, Donald Warren, Shimon Spiro, David Hollister, and J. Allen Winter.

Concurrent with the research, we met about twice a month for one-and-a-half school years with the first school-community agents employed to implement the Great Cities Project in seven schools. The format of these discussions was our presentation of theoretical propositions to which the practitioners would react with supportive and contradictory reports from their current experience. From this interaction we found an acceptable way of stating general guidelines. Those to whom we are especially indebted for contributions that are the basis for chapters 5 through 12 are Lorraine Aldridge, Eleanor Barnwell, Frances Couzens, Betty Deshler, Betty Hogan, Ian McPherson, Lucius May, Louis Monacel, David Neiderhauser, Larry Power, Eleanor Sadowski,

Clarence White, and Roselyn Yergen. Omission of others who participated in this exciting collaboration is a fault of our records and not a lack of appreciation.

The task of recording and summarizing the materials of these "seminars" was carried by Cheryl Mickelson. Her work was so fundamental to the form and content of chapters 5 through 12 that acknowledging her collaboration in the book is scarcely adequate. We bear responsibility for subsequent changes.

The first "School-Community Manual," a mimeographed volume composed mostly of Cheryl Mickelson's summaries of the seminars in Detroit, was used and subjected to criticism and suggestion by our colleague, John Erlich, and the social work students he was training in the practice of school-community work. The substantial collaboration of Jack Rothman and John Erlich is gratefully acknowledged in the chapters they contributed to. A second draft of the "School-Community Manual" was mimeographed, and included early versions of several of the theoretical chapters. We wish also to thank Richard English for assistance with this stage of the evolution of the book.

Marian Iglesias typed most of the earlier versions from which the book emerged. We thank her for her skill, endurance, and patience. The manuscript for the book was typed by Katherine Schoenfield, and we thank her, too. Suzanne Meyer made many editorial suggestions, and she was a zealous proofreader. More intangible contributions were made by Eleanor Litwak, and Nora, Ezra, and Nathaniel, to the work of their husband and father. We cannot thank our wives, Eleanor Litwak and Suzanne Meyer, enough.

For exceptional encouragement, advice, and tolerance, we thank John D. Moore, Executive Editor, Columbia University Press. We are also indebted to Judith Richman, who compiled the index at the final stage of publication.

This book was created by those we have named here—and the children, parents and teachers of Detroit to whom we dedicate it. They are not responsible for what we have written, including many controversial and perhaps erroneous statements. We want

very much to give them credit without implying that they share
our views.

September, 1973

EUGENE LITWAK
HENRY J. MEYER

# ❉ CONTENTS

# Part One

## School-Community Relations
## Theoretical Framework

# 1 ❋ Local School-Community Relations: An Overview

Educators and other professionals on the staffs of schools—social workers, psychologists, nurses—face many practical problems when they decide to develop a systematic program to relate their particular school to the local community. What kind of program should be started? How can the program be implemented in the midst of the many other activities that crowd the school day and the school year? For what new duties must personnel be found? What does a school-community worker do?

It is necessary to place these problems in perspective. What do we mean by a school's "local community"? And what do we mean by a "program of school-community relations?" "What is the purpose of a program of school-community relations?" We summarize, in the first four chapters, the theory that underlies the discussion in later chapters of practical strategies for dealing with problems of local school-community relations.

## What We Mean by a School's "Local Community"

For our purposes, the core component of the "local community" of any particular school consists of families of children who attend it and their immediate neighbors. Sometimes a single high school will serve an entire small city so that its local community becomes, in effect, coterminous with the territory covered by the school system. Specialized schools—such as vocational schools or schools for handicapped children—may draw their children from the total area of the system. There is always a geographical aspect, but the families served by the school, wherever they live, constitute the "local community" that we are primarily concerned with.

1

Our interest in local school-community relations concentrates on the school families and their neighborhoods for several reasons. First, these are the main social settings outside the school for the children whose benefit is the ultimate justification for a school-community program. The family has direct influence, and the family's economic and class circumstances affect opportunities and motivations. The neighborhood usually bounds the meaningful social world of the younger school child, locating his playmates and friends. The older child, more mobile and independent, enlarges his spatial world to respond selectively to his circle of peers who, nevertheless, often live in and use the facilities of a limited territory. A second reason for concentrating on school families and neighborhoods is that they are more directly accessible to school personnel and are most likely to be directly concerned with the school.

We use the term, "school-community relations," rather than the narrower term, "school-family relations," because we want to consider the broader context of the social world within which school children live. Furthermore, we want to keep in mind the fact that school families themselves are subject to wider influences which must be recognized in a program of school-family relations. However, some of the larger societal elements that can be major factors in education can only be summarily discussed in this book.

## What Should Be the Purpose of School-Community Relations

It is inevitable that relationships of some sort will be established between the school and its local community as we have defined it. Even if the principal and staff of a school attempted to ignore school families and neighborhoods, they would nevertheless be defining a relationship with them. What the school does may be as minimal as the routine communication of the child's progress, necessary contact about attendance, illness, or "trouble," the occasional PTA meeting. Or it may be an elaborate plan of work on many fronts with school parents and others from the local area. A school may be said to have a "program" of school-community relations, by our definition, when some deliberate effort is made on the part of the school or of the school families to affect their relationships to one another.

## The Purpose of a School-Community Relations Program

The purpose of a school-community program falls within a school's more general educational goals. To simplify the problem of stating these goals, we may describe them, in ideal terms, as the enhancement of conditions leading to maximum learning in the sense both of academic achievement and of socialization contributing to successful life experiences. We are aware that there are different views of what these abstractions mean. Furthermore, in each actual situation one must determine whether or not the school seeks these objectives and is in a position to pursue them. Our general working assumption will be that the purposes are honestly sought both by schools and families, but we will not ignore the contrary assumption. In the language sometimes used by educators, the direction of the school's professional effort is to increase each child's "educational motivation and achievement" and to help him develop qualities of "good citizenship." The objective of a school-community program is, therefore, to contribute to these purposes.

Obviously, many crucial activities of the school other than its school-community relations affect the children's education. Relations between school and families are of great importance but by no means exclusively determining. A school-community program developed without concomitant attention to curriculum, teaching styles and methods, special services, and many other features of the total school should not be expected to produce miraculous results, or even to have visible effects. Indeed, we do not believe that a good school-community relations program can be developed without implicating most of the other features of the total school effort. On the other hand, we believe that a school will fail to be maximally effective if it neglects its local school-community relations.

These relations may be conceived in terms of the "distance" between the school and its families and neighborhoods. A school-community program is intended to affect this "distance" in some way. What that distance should be depends on the viewpoint taken with respect to the importance of the "community" for the school's objectives. We may outline at least three points of view among educators, acknowledging that our descriptions are over-simplified.[1]

1. *"Closed-door" position.* This viewpoint takes its name from the general view of some educators that community involvement is extraneous, if not injurious, to the education of the child. The basic assumption is that schools can best handle within their walls all the major problems of education. Therefore, community participation should be kept to a minimum. The presence of parents in the school will hamper the educator in the performance of his duties. Lacking professional training and having strong emotional ties to the child, the parent will inhibit the use of professional judgment. This approach is consistent with some sociological theories that have dealt with relationships between large-scale bureaucratic organizations and family and neighborhood groups. Thus, Max Weber points out that strong family systems tend to undermine the development of rational bureaucracies based on merit.[2] Talcott Parsons implies that families and large-scale bureaucracies must keep their distance if each is to operate efficiently. [3] The viewpoint of the traditional French and German school

1. These positions are described in Eugene Litwak and Henry J. Meyer, "Administrative Styles and Community Linkages of Public Schools: Some Theoretical Considerations," in Albert J. Reiss, Jr. (ed.), *Schools in a Changing Society* (New York: The Free Press, 1965, pp. 51-53.

2. T. Parsons, *The Structure of Social Action* (Glencoe: The Free Press, 1949), pp. 542-52; Max Weber, *The Theory of Social and Economic Organization,* A.M. Henderson and T. Parsons (trans.), (New York: Oxford University Press, 1947), pp. 354-58.

3. T. Parsons, "The Social Structure of the Family," in Ruth N. Anshen (Ed.), *The Family: Its Function and Destiny* (New York: Harper, revised, 1959), pp.260-63; George A Theordorson, "Acceptance of Industrialization and its Attendant Consequences for the Social Patterns of Non-Western Societies," *American Sociological Review,* 18 (October 1953),

systems illustrates this position, which is often associated with a curricular emphasis on the "3 R's." From this position, a school-community relations program will be effective if it maximizes social distance between the family and the school.

2. *"Open door" position.* In contrast is the "open door" position. It assumes that many of the basic educational processes take place outside the school building, in the family, peer group, and neighborhood. Furthermore, the motivation necessary for learning in school has its source in the everyday life of the child. This necessitates intimate school-community contacts. Although few sociological theorists have expounded this approach, practitioners in many fields are actually working to induce closer contacts.[4] Most major cities implement programs designed to increase contact between schools and families. An extreme example is that of a school installing washing machines and cooking facilities so that families in need might use school facilities for their everyday living needs. The "pupil centered" philosophy of education is often associated with this position. From this viewpoint, the effective school-community program will produce closer contact between the family and the school.

3. *Balance theory.* A third position recognizes some validity in both the "open door" and "closed door" approaches. It asserts

---

pp. 480-81.

4. For example, the U.S. Employment Service has helped State agencies expand services beyond filling job vacancies with available job seekers to identifying actively unemployed segments in the community and reaching out to bring them into the agency for employment, counseling, and training. See Joseph M. Becker, William Haber, Sar A. Levitan, *Programs to Aid the Unemployed in the 1960's* (Kalamazoo, Mich.: W. E. Upjohn Institute for Employment Research, 1965). In education, see Gene C. Fusco, *School-Home Partnership in Depressed Urban Neighborhoods* (Washington: U.S. Office of Education, Department of Health, Education, and Welfare, 1964). In delinquency programs, see *Reaching the Fighting Gang* (New York: New York City Youth Board, 1960). In social work agencies, see Harold B. Sharkey, "Sustaining the Aged in the Community," *Social Work,* 7 (January 1962), pp. 18-22; Berta Fantl, "Preventive Intervention," *Social Work,* 7 (July 1962), pp. 41-47; Berta Fantl, "Casework in Lower Class Districts," *Mental Hygiene,* 45 (July 1961), pp. 425-38. For a summary of literature and consideration of theoretical issues, see Eugene Litwak, "Voluntary Associations and Neighborhood Cohesion," *American Sociological Review,* 26 (April 1961), pp. 258-66. Among organizational theorists who might conceivably argue for the merger of bureaucratic and primary groups are: Warren G. Bennis, *Changing Organizations* (New York: McGraw-Hill, 1966) and F. J. Roethlisberger and W. J. Dickson, *Management and the Worker* (Cambridge, Mass.: Harvard University Press, 1939).

that both intimate and distant school-community relations must be balanced in different degrees under different circumstances to optimize educational objectives. This approach notes two kinds of errors which a school-community program can make. It can bring the schools and community so close together that professional standards are seriously weakened; and it can keep families and schools so far apart that lack of coordination causes contradictory influences to emanate from both sides. To avoid these errors the balance theory argues that optimal social distance is a determinable point between the extremes of intimacy and isolation. At such a point the schools will be close enough to coordinate activities with families but not so close as to impair the performance of professional educational tasks.

The balance theory approach implies that the kind of linkage between the family and the school should depend on whether the social distance between them is too great or too little. For example, a majority of parents in a northern urban school may be southern rural migrants who are suspicious of the school and do not see value in education. At another school in the same system a majority of parents may be professional persons who place excessive emphasis on academic achievement, scrutinize the school too closely, and intrude in the teacher's actions. Still another school might have both kinds of parents. In the first case, the balance theory approach would suggest the need for linking procedures to close the distance, in the second case to increase social distance, and the third case would require the operation of both types of program. Under this approach, the effective school-community program is one that can produce the desired balance implied by these examples.

Each of these positions has its appeal and probably some validity. We adopt the balance theory because it seems most inclusive, fits the experience of educators in more complex urban settings, and because it rests on a more general theoretical analysis of the complementary functions of primary groups and of bureaucratic organizations in the achievement of social goals.[5]

## The Balance Theory of Coordination

The balance theory of coordination underlies our discussion of problems and strategies of school-community relations. Therefore, it will be useful to consider here the essential reasoning behind that theory. It can also be applied, we believe, in other areas.

*Expert and nonexpert tasks in education.* In our view, education requires the performance of two general tasks: (a) Those which require specialized training and equipment, and (b) those which can be handled by persons on the basis of their ordinary experience and socialization. The two types intermingle but for purposes of exposition we may treat them as though they were easily identified and quite different. The analysis can apply to tasks that fall between the extremes.

The professional educator can easily point to tasks that require specialized training or equipment and hence cannot be effectively performed by the average parent. For example, parents rarely have sufficient knowledge to teach such high school subjects as mathematics, chemistry and geography. They seldom have the professional knowledge and skill required to teach a large group of first-grade children how to read and write while maintaining order in a classroom. The typical home will not have the libraries, laboratories, gymnasiums, and other physical facilities found in schools. Aware of such needs, some teachers may think all aspects of education require professional training. They may overlook the fact that the educational process depends also on tasks handled in the everyday activities of families. Some are obvious. Families provide adequate food, clothing, rest, and perform many other nonexpert tasks. Many tasks of more subtle character, while per-

5. E. Litwak and H. J. Meyer, "A Balance Theory of Coordination Between Bureaucratic Organizations and Community Primary Groups", *Administrative Science Quarterly*, 11 (June 1966), pp. 31-58.

formed by nonexperts, play crucial roles in education. For example, family members play a key role in "teaching" the child the basic language necessary to enter school at all. The contribution this makes to schooling is evident when children enter school from non-English-speaking families, such as Puerto Rican immigrants in New York during the 1950s and 1960s. Linguistic differences in the use of English by different social classes, racial, and ethnic groups have attracted attention, highlighting the fact that schools must take such variations into account.[6] The task of basic language teaching falls primarily outside the province of the specialist.

Nonexperts perform many other educational tasks. Parents and older siblings often act as tutors supplementing the school. The family plays an important role in educational motivation in a variety of ways. It provides supervision of home study, inculcates values that affect attitudes and behavior in school, exposes children to significant models, and in many other ways makes them ready for school. The family sustains or dampens interest in the more formal learning of the classroom. The professional educator becomes most aware of these socialization functions of nonexperts when they are not performed, or performed with results that the usual approaches of the school are not prepared for, so that the work of the teacher becomes difficult or impossible.

A breakdown of the educational process can also occur, of course, from failure of the expert to do his job. In the late 1960s and early 1970s, when it was obvious that the public educational system was markedly less effective for the poor, attempts to assign responsibility produced a major dispute between professional ed-

6. There has been increasing emphasis in the last ten years on the view that linguistic differences in social class and ethnic groups are sufficiently great so that they place at a disadvantage those who do not adhere to the standards used in a given school. Unfortunately because these differences are masked under a common language designation (i.e., English in the United States) the differences are often not recognized as such and the student is diagnosed as backward. Some experts have sought to combat this kind of inadvertant bias by refering to local linguistic differences as a different or second language to make the school staff sensitive to the potential bias they might have against students who come from different social classes and different ethnic groups than they do. One of the first works to point this out was that of W. Lloyd Warner, Robert J. Havighurst, and Martin B. Loeb, *Who Shall be Educated?* (New York: Harper, 1944). For more recent discussions, see F. Williams (ed.), *Language and Poverty* (Chicago: Markham, 1970).

ucators and communities of poor parents. The educators often argued that inadequacies of poor families were mainly responsible; spokesmen for the community tended to blame the professionals, charging discriminatory maldistribution of resources and irrelevance or indifference in educational programs. Such charges were most forcefully stated by urban black communities which demanded changes in the educational system—decentralized school administration, black teachers for black students, stress on curriculum useful in the situation of black persons, and more.

We need not take sides in this argument to establish the basic point it illustrates: that the process of education requires both technically trained experts and the nonexpert members of families and other groups in the community. In the heat of argument, extremists have said that teachers can be dispensed with altogether and their tasks taken on by ordinary citizens with some extra training. The other extreme has argued that a good teacher has sufficient skills to produce disciplined and educated students if only allowed by the family and community to do so. Those with more moderate views would probably accept our position that education of the child in contemporary American society requires close cooperation between expert educators and primary group members of community groups.

This viewpoint may seem almost self-evident. But less obvious are the special, and largely exclusive, contributions made from each side of the equation.

An expert brings to a situation specialized knowledge and resources that depend generally on economies of large scale. A mathematics teacher in a high school brings to his or her students a specialized knowledge of mathematics and how to teach it, as well as the setting of a building and its facilities in which to teach. It is expedient to instruct fairly large numbers of students in one place and at one time. To understand what the nonexpert brings to a situation, we must understand the circumstances under which specialized knowledge is not useful or useable and when small-scale economies are more effective than large-scale economies.[7]

7. E. Litwak and J. Figueira, "Technological Innovation and Theoretical Functions of Primary Groups and Bureaucratic Structures" *American Journal of Sociology* 73 (January

*Theoretical Framework*

*Limitations on the use of expert knowledge.* One type of task the expert can contribute very little to involves situations so unpredictable that there is no time to make the expert or the resources he needs available. If a tornado strikes a community most persons trapped in dangerous situations are rescued by their neighbors before firemen and doctors can arrive.[8] These experts are better trained for rescue work but the necessity for immediate action outweighs the value of their superior knowledge. A child psychiatrist may be more expert in handling a child's feelings in a traumatic situation, such as the divorce of his parents, but the psychiatrist is rarely available over an extended and continuous period, and someone without training must serve. Teachers in school often find that their expertise cannot be made available when needed because of the demands on their time from other children. Compared to parents, the teacher actually has little personal contact with any individual child, especially over an extended time. Even if the teacher is better equipped than the parent to handle certain problems of behavior, this is often impractical. A pupil-centered approach advocated by some would provide more opportunity to supervise children, but it is unimaginable that this could equal the everyday supervision the parent can give. When tasks are unpredictable, exceedingly widespread, or extended through time, the contribution of the expert is likely to be limited.

In another type of situation it is less efficient to use experts than nonexperts. Many tasks do not require specialized training, and to use an expert to perform them would be both wasteful and cumbersome. The treatment of children's minor wounds and injuries is such a task. Basic knowledge is quite sufficient in most cases, and there could never be a sufficient supply of trained personnel for such purposes anyway. Providing supplementary help to elementary school children is another example. Most American parents have at least a high school education, and can help their

1968), pp. 468-81; E. Litwak "Extended Kin Relations in an Industrial Democracy" in E. Shanas and G. F. Streib (eds.), *Social Structure and the Family: Generational Relations* (Englewood Cliffs, N. J.: Prentice Hall, 1965).

8. W. H. Form and Sigmund Nosow *Community in Disaster* (New York: Harper, 1958), pp. 54-82.

children learn to read. Probably a trained reading specialist could do better, but this is usually not necessary. The parent may be able to help because he or she knows the child better and can take into account such idiosyncratic circumstances as the special meanings the child denotes to particular sounds.

Both types of tasks discussed above as instances when experts are more limited than nonexperts relate to availability of persons to do the tasks and accessibility to those for whom the tasks are to be done. A third, and very important, reason why some tasks are better done by nonexperts is that technical knowledge does not yet exist for them or is inapplicable to them. The common cold and the minor variations in mood that often affect a child's interest and behavior in school are examples. What to do about such situations is likely to depend as much on everyday experience as on training.

Tasks for which technical training is inapplicable often involve questions of values. The setting of basic educational goals is perhaps the clearest instance of a task where the knowledge of the professional educator may be less effective than that of the citizen-parent. Decisions intended to reflect community values require expression of these values in some way. In many instances experts are actually distrusted as spokesmen, an educational situation that has been institutionalized in the United States in the tradition of citizen governing boards. We are likely to see the issues as "political," meaning thereby that values and not technical knowledge should determine decisions. Should educational systems and religion be kept separate? Should schools undertake children's sex education? If funds are cut back, what part of the educational program should be reduced: physical education, social studies, college preparation, or what? If funds are increased, what should be added? Answering these questions does require some technical knowledge but they fundamentally involve value judgements. Insofar as the educational system is expected to reflect community values, community members rather than professionals are usually better able to say what these values are.

We have suggested three kinds of circumstances where the nonexpert can serve faster and more flexibly than the expert: in situations which are so unpredictable that there is not enough time to bring in the expert; in situations where the knowledge of the ordinary citizen is as great as that of the expert; and in situations where there is no expert knowledge. In general, we may say that all three of these situations involve *nonuniform tasks*. Situations where expert knowledge and economies of large scale make a difference may be said to involve primarily *uniform tasks*.

*Complementary contributions.* We can now restate the original proposition. The basic educational process requires experts to handle uniform tasks and nonexperts to handle nonuniform tasks. If either element breaks down, the process suffers. If we do not have competent experts or if experts seek to monopolize all nonuniform as well as uniform tasks, or if the nonexpert tries to handle the uniform tasks by himself, the educational process will be impaired.

This abstract proposition must be qualified to fit the real situations that educators and community members deal with. First, it is often unclear whether a given task is essentially uniform or nonuniform. Most tasks include both characteristics. Most situations faced by teachers, for example, involve both uniform and nonuniform tasks which in realistic terms cannot be divided between expert and nonexpert persons. Problems of discipline that might ideally be better handled by parents may arise while the teacher is teaching reading and hence must be handled by the teacher. A child may ask for help with homework which the parent tries to give to the best of his knowledge. It is particularly important to recognize that teachers and other experts often have to act in two different capacities on the job—sometimes dealing with uniform and sometimes with nonuniform events—so as to understand the potential usefulness and the limitation of community intervention in the school activity. There is often room for argument about what part of the school's activity is primarily uniform and calls for expert performance and what part primarily calls for the contribution of the nonexpert. However, such a determination must be made if community intervention is to facilitate and not impede education.

For our purpose of analyzing underlying theory it is

adequate to think of the teacher as an expert who takes major responsibility in education for the uniform tasks and the parent as nonexpert who can better perform and take responsibility for most of the nonuniform tasks. The balance theory sees the essential problem as one of appropriately linking the school as the primary locus of experts, with families as the primary setting of nonexperts so as to achieve the best form of cooperation.

*The influence of setting on communication between experts and nonexperts.* Our analysis suggests that experts in the school and nonexperts in the community should be in communication with one another. However, differences between these two settings require that communication linkages should not bring them into such close contact that they impair the social structures that are required to sustain each. The generic organizational form necessary for efficient performance of uniform tasks by specialized experts is what sociologists call the *bureaucracy*, or complex organization, whereas the generic organizational form of the family and most community groups is called the *primary group*. These structures are in many ways contradictory in their dominant social features, although many forms of social organization have features of both. The members of a bureaucracy (for example, teachers, principals, social workers, secretaries) are chosen and promoted on the basis of their knowledge, ability, and achievement. Members of primary groups (mothers, fathers, sisters and brothers, relatives) are born into the group. When brought in otherwise, by marriage, choice, or residential propinquity, they are assumed to be members because of personal qualities and not achievements. Primary group members are not supposed to be excluded on the basis of inability to do a particular job. If a wife is a poor cook or a son does not do well in school they are not excluded. In contrast, a bureaucracy is "inefficient" if its members perform poorly. Bureaucracies stress specialization and large-scale economies which generally have limited areas of interest (for example, education, treatment of illness, or manufacture of a product), and in those areas participants tend to become specialists, with equipment and facilities developed for their work. The primary group with its generally small size cannot have such specialization of functions or acquire, with its necessarily limited resources, large-scale facilities. The family may have a division of labor between husband and wife, but within a broad separation of roles each will have many overlapping tasks (for example, the woman is mother, housekeeper, cook, purchaser of food and goods, liaison with maintenance personnel, tutor to the children, companion to her husband, practical nurse). Parallel lists can be made for each family member. Furthermore, the family has legitimate voice in such spheres as health, education, religion, leisure, and morality, whereas the bureaucracy generally has legitimacy limited to a single or a few areas of social life. The complex organization thus tends to stress few goals and to focus specialists on them, whereas the primary group tends to stress multiple goals and to require generalized concern with them. Relationships between members of the family, and to a considerable degree of other primary groups, are valued for themselves. Relationships between participants in a bureaucracy are essentially instrumental, that is, used in the common work for the organization's purposes. Teachers become counselors or assistant principals when it is useful to the school and if they are qualified. Such shifts do not occur in families. The norm of interpersonal relations in the family is love and positive affect. In bureaucracies, friendship is tolerated only to the point where it interferes with organizational efficiency (for example, by favoritism).

The contrasting qualities of bureaucracies and primary groups as ideal types need not be further elaborated. It is sufficient to point out that professional expertise is maintained in social organizations that stress achievement, instrumental, specialized, and impersonal relations, whereas the generalized qualities of the nonexpert are maintained in social organizations that stress the opposite characteristics.

Problems could arise for each if these two forms of organization are brought too closely into contact. This is well illustrated when parents expect their child to get special privileges and better marks because the teacher is a relative or close friend of the family. Such primary group expectations may interfere with the exercise of proper professional judgement, just as nepotistic practices in employment or promotions may allow less competent persons to be selected. Contact that is too close can lead to impairment of primary group support for the child when, for example, parents over-identify with the limited objective of the school and allow school performance to control the child's treatment at home. It is not unusual in communities where families of professionals are dominant to find children who show in their behavior the results of pressure related to such a breakdown of the primary group. However, it must be remembered that too great a separation of school and family, as we have pointed out, is equally serious, since it limits the essential contributions of the bureaucratic and the primary group forms of organization to the education of the child.

In sum, organizational settings of bureaucracies and primary groups present two dangers for appropriate communication between persons in the community and experts in the school. If they are too close their antithetical structures may lead to reduction of effective contributions of expertise or of primary group support. However, if they fail to communicate, the contributions of both cannot be brought to the common educational purpose. The former point is often stressed by educators who feel it necessary to resist encroachment of community demands to participate in school affairs, while the latter is often stressed by community members who seek greater participation.

*Communication for balance.* This analysis leads again to the balance theory, suggesting that communication between school and community should seek to achieve some midpoint of social distance—close enough so that they can coordinate their activities but sufficiently distant so that their structures do not interfere with one another. Sometimes, therefore, communication procedures that bring school and community closer are desirable and at other times such linkages should serve to separate them. If the distance is already appropriate, communication linkages should maintain the balance. A school-community relations program must incorporate communication linkages that contribute to balance.

How this is to be done differs somewhat from the position of the school and of the community. The common problem of

optimum communication for the school whose target of influence
is the families and community groups is different from that of the
community whose target is the formal organization. The differences in function and in organizational structures previously discussed require different emphases and techniques. In this book we
will primarily consider how schools can build programs to reach
the community. Later in this chapter, however, we will also discuss the basic requirements for communities that try to reach and
influence the schools. In both instances, the kinds of linking mechanisms that are developed and their possible contributions to
achieving balance will be central.


## The School's Use of Linking Mechanisms

There are a number of linking mechanisms (also called
mechanisms of coordination, linkage procedures, or approaches)
that schools and other formal organizations have used to relate to
their local communities. These mechanisms are not necessarily
viewed by schools as communication linkages or as deliberate
components of a school-community program. We have given
names to practices observed or reported in the literature which
appear to serve such purposes. By examining them we are able to
consider some of the principles of communication and influence
they express.

*Description of Linking Mechanisms*

Eight mechanisms of coordination will be described as approaches a school or other formal organization can use in order
to reach and influence the local community.

1. *Detached worker.* An organization uses this mechanism
when it sends a professional person to enter the family or home
territory of those to be influenced so as to develop a trusting,
quasi-primary group relationship through which to bring the
group's norms and values into harmony with those of the organization. The professional person has considerable autonomy from

the organization in his work and participates directly in the family or group to be influenced. Most obvious illustrations of this mechanism are the street worker with delinquent gangs and aggressive casework of social agencies.[9] Some of the work of school-community agents in urban school programs, such as the Great Cities School Improvement Project of the Detroit Public Schools, exemplified this mechanism.[10] Teachers and principals who regularly visit their children's homes, school nurses and social workers, and other school personnel may also represent this approach.

2. *Opinion leader.* In this approach, a professional person from the organization makes use of natural or indigenous leaders in the neighborhood, through whom families and neighborhood members are influenced in their relationship to the organization. The natural leader has close relationships with those whom he or she influences, and the professional person hopes to make use of these established relationships by gaining the support of the natural leader and relying upon him to gain the support of the group for the organization. This approach has also been used in delinquency areas. In Chicago the area development program of Shaw-McKay made great use of local opinion leaders.[11] The schools have often used this approach in systematic recruitment of influential citizens to aid their millage campaigns.

3. *Settlement house.* This mechanism involves the provision of physical facilities and professional persons located in the home territory of those to be affected so that they are easily accessible. The aim of the settlement house approach is to provide a change-inducing milieu, and for this reason it is important to have a

9. For a description of the use of "streetgang workers" to deal with delinquent groups, see P. L. Crawford, D. I. Malamud, and J. R. Dumpson, *Working with Teenage Gangs* (Welfare Council of New York City, 1950); W. B. Miller, "The Impact of a Community Group Work Program on Delinquent Corner Groups," *Social Service Review*, 31 (December 1957) pp. 390-406; W. B. Miller, "Preventive Work with Street Corner Groups: Boston Deliquency Projects," *Annals of the American Academy of Political and Social Sciences*, 322 (1959), pp. 97-106.

10. See Carl L. Marburger, "Considerations for Educational Planning," in A. Harry Passow (ed.), *Education in Depressed Areas* (New York: Teachers College, Columbia University, 1963), pp. 303-321.

11. See S. Kobrin, "The Chicago Area Project: A Twenty-Five-Year Assessment," *Annals of the American Academy of Political and Social Sciences*, 322 (1959), pp. 19-37.

professional staff who can purposefully influence those who are to
be affected. The approach combines the traditional community
center with focused educational and therapeutic programs. It
has been used in the rehabilitation of delinquents,[12] and is
also illustrated by some "community school" programs where
more is intended than merely opening the school to the public
after school hours.

4. *Auxiliary voluntary association.* A voluntary association,
bringing together members from the organization and from the
community, can be established for linking the two groups.
Usually staff and leadership positions are not filled by professionals. Members associate by virtue of the interest of the
organization and are not independent of it. The best illustrations of this procedure for linking school and community are
parent-teacher associations and homeroom mothers' clubs. A
local block club would not be regarded as an example of the
auxiliary voluntary association linking mechanism because it is
independent of the school, unless it is organized and guided by
school personnel.

5. *Common messenger.* This mechanism uses common members of the organization and of the community group to be
affected as messengers to link the two. Individuals can be
common messengers in this approach only if they are regularly
members of both groups, more or less on a day-to-day basis.
As common messengers, they can communicate in both directions. For the school, the child is the most obvious example of
the common messenger, since he regularly comes and goes
between the family and the school. One reason frequently giv-
en for employing indigenous workers (that is, persons from the
population served by the organization) is that they serve as
common messengers although that term itself may not be used.
Another example is the parent who serves on a volunteer or
part-time paid basis as auxiliary school personnel assisting
teachers, working in lunch rooms, and similar capacities.

12. One partial illustration of this approach is the work at Provo described by L. T.
Empey and J. Rabow, "The Provo Experiment in Delinquency Rehabilitation," *American
Sociological Review,* 26 (October 1961), pp. 679-95.

Among other functions, members of local boards of education or advisory committees attached to a school also represent common messengers.

6. *Mass media.* In this approach, the organization tries to influence the members of the community by using public communication, that is, newspapers, television, radio announcements, leaflets, posters, etc.[13]

7. *Formal authority.* This mechanism is that of legal authority or the authority of well-established custom used by the organization to require members of the community to conform with the expectations or requirements of the organization. For the schools, the attendance officer may use formal authority, or the school principal may do so through his power to suspend or expel a student.

8. *Delegated function.* This is not a linking mechanism in the same sense as the others already described. Rather than linking the school and the community directly, this mechanism delegates responsibility to another organization, which must then link itself to the community groups the school seeks to affect. The other organization is assumed to have better access, greater expertise, or more appropriate facilities than the school. Hence, the school links itself to the community through that agency. Referral to medical agencies is a typical example.

*Some Principles for Deciding which*
*Linking Mechanisms to Use*

Identification of linking mechanisms is necessary as a first step toward the development of a program of school-community relations. A second step is to decide which mechanisms to use. This requires the determination of the goal of the program. Then, one must ask how each mechanism bears on the goal. To answer this question the effective principles embodied in the mechanisms need to be considered.

13. Elihu Katz and Paul F. Lazarsfeld, *Personal Influence* (Glencoe, Ill.: The Free Press, 1955): Carl I. Hovland, "Effect of the Mass Media of Communication," in Gardner Lindzey (ed.), *Handbook of Social Psychology* (Cambridge, Mass.: Addison-Wesley, 1954), II, 1062-1103.

*The choice of linking mechanisms depends on the goal of the school-community program.* From our earlier analysis we may recall that the goal of a program may be the reduction or the increase of social distance between the school and the community. Some mechanisms are more useful for one or the other of these purposes.

The point of view taken by the school will influence whether the objective will be primarily to close social distance, or increase it, or to do both, depending on the circumstances. We have mentioned that where the "closed door" position is adopted, the goal will usually be to increase and maintain social distance. Where the "open door" position is held, the goal will usually be to reduce social distance and maintain close relationships. Where the "balance theory" position is taken, the goal will be either to decrease or to increase social distance as an appraisal of the specific situation may require.

*Some communication principles as guides to selecting mechanisms.* It is useful to think of the linking mechanisms in terms of some of the principles that have been found to apply to other forms of communication.[14] What is required to communicate *from* the school *to* the family? What are the barriers to such communication? How can it be managed so as to bring the school and family closer together or to separate them further? Four principles are especially relevant to assessing the potential usefulness of the linking mechanisms:

1. *Principle of initiative to overcome selective listening.* In communication theory, this is the problem of gaining attention for the message. Research has established that only selected persons listen to communicated messages and that they listen selectively. Some people ignore the message, others listen to part of the message and ignore the rest. The school must sometimes persuade indifferent

14. Of the many discussions of mass communication theory, the following will be useful here: Carl I. Hovland, cited in note 13; Herbert H. Hyman and Paul Sheatsley, "Some Reasons Why Information Campaigns Fail," *Public Opinion Quarterly*, 11 (Fall 1947), pp. 412-23; Eugene Litwak, "Some Policy Implications to Communications Theory with Emphasis on Group Factors," *Education for Social Work*, Proceedings of the Seventh Annual Program Meeting (New York: Council on Social Work Education, 1959), pp. 96-109; Herbert I. Abelson, *Persuasion: How Opinions and Attitudes Are Changed* (New York: Springer, 1959).

or hostile families and neighborhood groups to receive its communication. The hostile or defiant family cannot be assumed to read information sent home, to join the parent-teacher association and attend its meetings, to take advantage of teacher-parent conferences, or to come voluntarily to the school when the child has a problem. The school must exercise great initiative to reach such families and other groups. In its repertory of linking mechanisms some must permit such initiative. Among possible mechanisms there will be variation on this dimension. An invitation to join the PTA represents little organizational initiative; sending a teacher or attendance officer to visit the family in its home represents great organizational initiative.

2. *Principle of intensity to overcome selective retention.* Even when persons have been confronted with a message they do not always accept nor retain it, and sometimes they distort it in keeping with prior attitudes. To meet this problem, the school must have among its linking mechanisms those that permit intensity of communication. Such communications take place in an atmosphere of trust, are prolonged, can be carried on in many different contexts, and offer opportunity for much interaction between the communicator and the person he is seeking to communicate with. Casual contacts or written communications have less intensity than protracted contacts and face-to-face communications. The opinion leader and the detached worker approaches permit much more intensity than the mass media approach.

3. *Principle of focused expertise to provide feedback and flexibility.* Many studies of communication have shown that feedback and technical knowledge of the communicator facilitate acceptance of the message, especially when the content is technical or complex. The communicator must be in a position to correct misunderstanding and to restate the message if it is to be successfully conveyed. Some communications from schools are simple, such as notices of a meeting or changed time for lunch hour; many are quite technical or complex, such as an explanation of the new mathematics or the rationale for a new grading system. The principle of focused expertise implies that the more complex the information the more contact is necessary between a professional and

the group to be affected. It is usually difficult to put complex or technical information in simple terms and an expert may be needed to convey its ramifications. Furthermore, the presentation of such information requires the communicator to take account of any special problems a given group may have in absorbing the information and to adapt the communication accordingly. Thus, immediate feedback and response are necessary. An expert in close touch with the group is called for.

The school must be in a position to bring focused expertise to bear through some of its linking mechanisms. A settlement house approach with classes for parents on how children learn provides a high level of focused expertise; a school newspaper (mass media) provides very little.

4. *Principle of maximum scope to reach the optimum number.* Sometimes communication is desired with a large number of persons, while at other times only a few individuals are the target. It is therefore important to consider whether a linking mechanism has wide or narrow scope. Mechanisms vary in scope within the same time and resource limits. Sending a person from a school to develop a trustful relationship with a family, as in the detached worker approach, would not reach as many families as sending a school-wide notice home through the children, as in the common messenger or mass media approaches.

Although these four principles by no means exhaust the relevant dimensions of communication, they are particularly pertinent ones. By using them we can re-examine some of the linking mechanisms to assess their power in the process of communication between school and school families.

*Linking Mechanisms Reexamined*

The mechanisms of coordination differ in the extent to which they embody the above principles of communication. Hence, they vary in inherent capacities to decrease or increase social distance between schools and primary groups. We may illustrate by analyzing three of the mechanisms in these terms:

1. *Detached worker—a mechanism useful for closing social distance.*
As a means of communication, the detached worker approach
has the following characteristics:

a. It permits great initiative on the part of the bureaucratic organization, since the organization sends the worker out
to meet face-to-face the people to be affected.

b. It involves intense relations between the professional
and the group to be affected since a strong emotional friendship is viewed as a major tool of change.

c. It entails focused expertise since the professional person participates directly with the people to be affected.

d. It has limited scope since one professional person can
deal intensely with only a limited number of people.

With the exception of scope, all characteristics of this
mechanism are highly useful for communication across great
social distance, that is, for closing social distance when the
organization must deal with hostile or indifferent families and
groups.

Thus, when a school seeks to communicate its goals and
programs to a hostile family, it must take the initiative, using
intensity of interaction to penetrate primary group boundaries,
and it must make use of focused expertise to effect changes in
social norms which are very complex. In northern urban communities migrant southern white families often seem to require
such an approach to convey the values of the school with
respect to the conditions for the educational motivation of the
children.

In terms of balance theory, this same mechanism must
be considered less effective for coordination where families are
over-identified with the school, and the bureaucratic organization does not have to take the initiative since the family will
approach the school on its own initiative. Intensive relations
are unnecessary since the primary group is already receptive
and intensive relations in such circumstances may, indeed,
evoke over-identification. Furthermore, the detached expert approach is extremely wasteful where families already identify
with the organization, since there are other procedures (mass

media and voluntary association) which can communicate to such families and reach many more of them without running the risk of too much intimacy for effective balance. The relationship between some suburban families and schools illustrates the limitation of such a mechanism.

2. *Mass media—a mechanism useful for increasing or maintaining social distance.* In a similar manner, we can examine the mass media approach:

a. It permits *little initiative* on the part of the organization, since its capacity to reach people in the community depends on their willingness to read the message, turn on their radios, television sets, etc.

b. It has *little intensity* for the people it reaches. The comparatively impersonal nature of mass media communications makes them easy to ignore. One can turn off the radio, throw away the message, and escape in many other ways from the communication.

c. It provides *little focused expertise.* There is no face-to-face contact between a professional expert and those persons the organization seeks to affect. If the message is not understood as it is first presented, there is no opportunity to modify it to fit the unique situation of particular individuals.

d. It has *great scope.* The techniques of mass media can address a message to a large number of people at modest cost.

The characteristics of this mechanism allow it to give a semblance of communication between the school and the family without much risk of affecting those whom it reaches. Because of its low initiative, intensity, and focused expertise, it is useful for disseminating simple, factual information to a large number of people in an impersonal manner. It is a useful mechanism for maintaining existing social distance, or for increasing social distance where relationships have become too intimate. In some suburbs, where parents are closely involved with the school and tend to disrupt professional activities by their too close scrutiny of the teacher, the use of communication via mass media may create a more distant and better balanced relationship.

3. *Common messenger—a mechanism useful both for opening and closing social distance.* Some mechanisms can be used either to open or to close social distance, depending on the particular manner in which they are used. The common messenger approach may illustrate this possibility.

a. It has *moderate organizational initiative* since the school is in constant contact with the family through the messenger.

b. It has *moderate intensity* since the messenger has continuous membership in the family to be affected.

c. It has *low focused expertise;* in fact, there is considerable opportunity for the message to become distorted.

d. It has *moderately high scope* since it is a technique which could be used to reach most parents in the school.

This technique can be described as an insulated form of communication when its mediated, arms's-length aspects are stressed. Contact between school and parents is indirect and the school has little control over what is actually communicated. Used in this manner, it is not likely to foster closer contact between the school and the family.

However, there are ways in which this approach can be used effectively as a first step in bringing about closer contact. For example, the child can be sent home with messages concerning school events of great importance to him and will therefore be motivated to gain his parents' attention and involvement. When parents become common messengers through serving as auxiliary school personnel, social distance may be lessened considerably. If the parent is interested enough to work in the school, he or she may be in an effective position to influence the family as a group, although this may vary with the issue involved.

The common messenger approach may also be useful for conveying some general communications regarding values and goals of the school. These messages may be unplanned and even unrecognized, but they may be very powerful in their long-run effect. Thus, the child may subtly affect the values of his parents by continuous expression of views to which he has been exposed at school.

*Summarizing Tables*

The relationship of each linking mechanism to the various principles of communication is summarized in Table 1. In general, those mechanisms with low initiative, intensity, and focused expertise are most useful for creating and maintaining social distance. Those with high initiative, intensity, and focused expertise are most useful for closing social distance and maintaining close relationships. Mechanisms with moderate initiative, intensity, and focused expertise, or with a low position on some dimensions but a high position on others, can be useful either to open or close social distance, depending on how they are used.

## Table 1

### Underlying Principles of Communication Related to Linking Mechanisms Between Bureaucratic Organizations and External Primary Groups, e.g., Between Schools and Families

| | PRINCIPLES OF COMMUNICATION | | | |
|---|---|---|---|---|
| *Coordinating Mechanisms* | *Initiative* | *Intensity* | *Focused expertise* | *Scope* |
| Detached expert | highest | high | highest | lowest |
| Opinion leader | low | highest | low | moderate |
| Settlement house | moderate to low | high-moderate | high | moderate |
| Voluntary association | lowest | moderate-low | moderate | high |
| Common messenger | moderate | moderate-low | moderate | high |
| Mass media | moderate to low | lowest | lowest | highest |
| Formal authority | high | low | high to moderate | moderate |
| Delegated function | high | high to low | high to low | moderate |

Table 2 summarizes the usefulness of the linking mechanisms in relation to the policy position taken by the school, that is, the "open door" position, the "closed door" position, and the balance theory position. The reader will recall that the "open door" position tends to lessen social distance, the "closed door" position tends to increase social distance, and the balance theory position leads either to the goal of closing and or creating social distance depending on the situation.

**Table 2**

**Comparative Usefulness of Linking Mechanisms for Three Positions on School-Community Relations**

| | | *"Open door" Position* | *"Closed door" Position* | *"Balance Theory" Position* |
|---|---|---|---|---|
| *Linking Mechanism* | *Goals:* | *Close social distance* | *Create social distance* | *Create and/or close social distance* |
| Detached worker | | very high | very low | very high when distance is to be decreased (e.g., community is hostile); very low when distance is to be increased (e.g., community too involved). |
| Opinion leader | | potentially moderate, e.g., when community is friendly, or when coupled with another mechanism (e.g., detached worker, mass media) used for recruitment. | very low | potentially moderate when distance is to be decreased through intensity; very low when distance is to be increased. |

## Table 2 (continued)

| | *"Open door"* Position | *"Closed door"* Position | *"Balance Theory"* Position |
|---|---|---|---|
| *Linking Mechanism* | *Goals: Close social distance* | *Create social distance* | *Create and/or close social distance* |
| Settlement house | high; potentially very high when community is friendly. | very low | high when distance is to be decreased through focused expertise; very low when distance is to be increased. |
| Voluntary association | moderate; potentially very high when community is friendly. | moderate | moderate when distance is to be decreased by scope; moderate when distance is to be increased. |
| Common messenger | low | high | moderate when distance is to be decreased by scope; moderate when distance is to be increased. |
| Mass media | low; potentially high when community is friendly and when coupled with an intense mechanism. | high | very low when distance is to be decreased; high when distance is to be increased. |
| Formal authority | very low | very high | very low when distance is to be decreased; very high when distance is to be increased. |

*Possibility of Constructing Other Linking Mechanisms*

It is quite possible to develop, theoretically, a number of other linking mechanisms in addition to those we have described. In Table 1, the reader will notice that the theoretical combinations of principles of communication with which we deal are far from exhausted. For example, no mechanism is clearly high on initiative but low on intensity and focused expertise, nor is there a mechanism which is clearly low on initiative while very high on intensity and expertise. Many other gaps can be noted. Mechanisms have been considered because they seem to have theoretical relevance and are also to be found in practice. We recognize that this listing may be far from complete. It is useful to note at least two other mechanisms which may be regarded as variations of those already described. These might be called separate mechanisms but we prefer to treat them as modified mechanisms used by schools in their relationships with the community.

1. *The modified detached worker.* The modified detached worker differs from the full-fledged detached worker essentially in that he has less autonomy from the organization. He may operate outside the organization to some extent, entering the home territory of those he seeks to affect, but there are organizational limits to the extent to which he can do this. As a consequence, the intensity of the relationship and the degree of focused expertise of the modified detached worker also tend to be reduced, although this is not necessarily so. He may maintain the highest level of intensity and focused expertise but reduce the number of people he contacts (reduced scope). Or he may maintain the scope of a full-fledged detached worker, but lessen the intensity and focus of the relationships. In practice, the modified detached worker approach is characteristic of the work of many school-community agents.

2. *Combined settlement house and voluntary association approach.* Characteristic of this approach is its combination of the focused change goals of the settlement house mechanism with the voluntary association as a means of reaching these goals. That is, focused therapeutic or resocialization goals are sought by means of

group programs conducted by nonprofessional staff. In the settle-ment house approach the professional person is viewed as impor-tant in achieving focused change goals. The after-hours programs of many schools combine settlement house and voluntary associa-tion approaches. This combination clearly means less focused expertise than in the settlement house mechanism, possibly less intense relationships, and probably greater scope. Increased scope is an advantage the combined approach has over the settlement house approach. With limitations on the number of professional staff available, therapeutic or resocialization goals might have to be abandoned altogether. Rather than do this, the goals are pre-served and an alternative means is sought to reach them. This approach is in fairly wide use although its effectiveness is not clear even theoretically.

*Sequences of Linking Mechanisms*

It has been seen that each mechanism is strong in some aspects and weak in others. In order to capitalize on the strong points of the various mechanisms, they can be used in sequence. For example:

1. *Detached worker, followed by settlement house.* The detached worker is an excellent first step for bridging the gap between the school and an apathetic and/or hostile community. However, since it is limited in scope, there are serious limitations on the number of people who can be reached by this approach alone. One solution is to begin with the detached worker approach and follow by using the voluntary association or the settlement house mechanism. The detached worker makes the first contact that forms a relationship with the people to be affected. As soon as possible, and on the basis of this relationship, people are transfer-red to a settlement house which has considerably wider scope.

2. *Formal authority, to detached worker or settlement house.* By the use of formal authority, the school has great initiative in making contact with hostile or deviant people. For example, it can send the attendance officer to the home to find out why the child is not in school. However, this approach lacks sufficient intensity to

bring about change in the goals and values of the people to be affected. The attendance officer may be successful in getting the child back to school on a particular occasion, but may make little impact on the orientation of the family which allows the child to skip school. In this situation, the original contact by the attendance officer could be followed up by a detached worker or by involvement of the family in a settlement house type program. Both these mechanisms have high intensity and, therefore, have greater potential to change the values and behavior of the people to be affected.

3. *Settlement house, followed by common messenger and mass media.* In situations where relationships have become too close, as may happen with the settlement house approach, greater distance can be created by shifting to mechanisms with less intensity. In this case, the mass media and the common messenger could be useful. By using the mass media, and the child as common messenger, the parents need not even enter the school building.

Sequencing of mechanisms is much more complex than these examples may suggest. How to move, for example, from an intimate relationship created by the detached worker or settlement house mechanisms to relationships defined more distantly in the voluntary association or common messenger approach is not always clear if one wants at the same time to avoid creating feelings of rejection, loss, or betrayal. The skill of the school-community worker will be taxed constantly by such demands even when the theoretical possibilities of sequencing are evident.

*Some Comments on "Using" Linking Mechanisms*

Our discussion of the nature of linking mechanisms and their utility for increasing or decreasing social distance between schools and primary groups must be understood as preliminary. They will be considered at length in subsequent chapters. However, it is necessary at this point to note that the effects of using any given mechanism will depend not only on its inherent qualities—as we have indicated—but also on the manner in which it is used. The inherent characteristics of a mechanism may be viewed as the potential that will allow it to be used more readily in one way than another. But these characteristics do not entirely control its consequences.

For example, the detached worker procedure has great potential usefulness for bridging social distance and bringing school and family closer together. It may also be used, however, to alienate families by strengthening negative attitudes and values. This is not a likely outcome because the professional person involved will promote the objectives of the school and not sabotage them, although the latter is always a possibility. Furthermore, quite unintentionally, a detached worker may generate resistance if he is not skillful, his efforts inadvertently increasing social distance. We would, nevertheless, expect any use of the procedure to have a more visible effect than a mechanism that was less intense, personal, and aggressive.

Another technique to note is the joint use of several mechanisms. We have presented the mechanisms as though they were separate so that their distinctive characteristics might be recognized. However, they are more likely to be used in combinations. Furthermore, some of the same activities of a school-community agent may in practice represent the use of several mechanisms. For example, the detached worker may affect a family not only for the purpose of changing its relation to the school but also to utilize its influence as potential opinion leader among other families.

It should be noted that all the mechanisms identified are not equally available to a school or to the school-community agent working in a particular building. Resources may be lacking to provide facilities and staff for a settlement house approach; time may be limited for detached worker approaches; rules of the school system may limit the type of communication through mass media. Furthermore, the way the building is run by the principal and the orientation of the teaching staff may affect whether particular mechanisms are used and how.

The description of the various linking mechanisms is in no sense a description of the role of the person in the school, such as the school-community agent, who has responsibility for school-community relations. One person alone could not possibly carry out the activities required in the settlement house approach, for example, and work in the community at the same time as a detached worker. Furthermore, there might be contradictions between various linking mechanisms if they were attempted within a single role; for example, between that of the detached worker and the use of formal authority. What is expected of those responsible for a program is that they be trained in diagnosing the situation so as to know which linking mechanisms will be appropriate. Individuals responsible for the program may, of course, carry direct responsibility for some part of the program, or they may personally initiate some aspect involving one of the linking procedures. They should certainly have training and experience in the use of each linking mechanism. But their work will be affected also by the success they have in bringing their colleagues in the building into a supporting relationship to their efforts.

## Some Issues Implicated by the
## School's Use of Linking Mechanisms

The discussion of mechanisms of coordination from the viewpoint of the school that seeks to conduct a program to influence families and neighborhoods may have given the impression that the goal is only to provide knowledge so that schools can manipulate families to their own ends. Questions of values, ethics, and democratic ideals are implicated in any activity involving the school and the community.

We have been made particularly aware in recent years that our public school systems, or the individual schools that compose them, are not necessarily in tune with the needs and demands of the people they presume to serve. The civil rights movement and national concern for education of the "underprivileged" have dramatized the racial, ethnic, and social class biases of many schools. School systems, and individual schools, become rigid and unapproachable in some instances, and a few may even be corrupt in the sense of deliberately blocking the public purposes for which they were established. Even under less extreme circumstances, it cannot be assumed that the interests of the school will be those of the community.

There are two aspects to this question. First, the basic *goals* of the school may differ from those of parents. For example, the school may stress academic objectives when families prefer vocational ones; or, conformity may be an objective of socialization in the school whereas innovative capacity may be desired by some families. The resolution of differences in goals is, and must be, a continuous process in the public school systems of a society with democratic ideals. Usually, public schools—like other public institutions in our society—pursue multiple goals and are subject to pressures in support of different goals from the political processes that control the public school system. These processes are not only formal ones operating through school boards and official control over financial resources and key administrative personnel; they also include the demands and influences of parents and citizens expressed both individually and through many voluntary associations. Professional educators must also take responsibility for expressing social ideals as the profession interprets them in addition to reflecting the viewpoints of their publics. Communication between schools and school families is a significant part of the means by which sufficient consensus may be achieved to guide school policy. There must be communication in both directions—from the school to the community and from the community to the school. The very concept of a school-community relations program implies this two-way communication.

A second aspect of the question of whether school and community have different interests concerns *means*. Because professional persons are experts in the means of achieving certain goals, they are expected to know more about teaching reading, about child development, learning, and other technical subjects than parents. But these means cannot be utilized without cooperation from nonprofessionals, especially those in families. Here again, two-way communication is crucial, and the links between school and family must allow for it.

We do not discuss the ways that families and other community groups may seek to influence schools in the same detail that we discuss how schools can influence the community. We assume that most educators, social workers, and other persons using this book will be interested in it as professionals in school systems concerned with school-community relations. They will therefore primarily want to understand how to work from a location within the schools. This does not mean, however, that even for this purpose they can be ignorant of how the community might from its side effectively influence the school. At minimum, this knowledge may help them as professionals if they try to correct any actions they find schools taking that violate ethical or democratic norms. Some understanding of school-community relations as viewed from the community's side is also necessary in order to deal with the problems a school must face under community pressure if the accepted purposes of the school are to be preserved. For these reasons, the following section of this chapter suggests without elaboration how the local community may use linking mechanisms to influence the school.

## The Community's Use of Linking Mechanisms[15]

Linking mechanisms by which the community reaches and tries to influence the school to some extent parallel the mechanisms of coordination already discussed. There are important differences, as one might expect, when the problem of achieving balance is viewed from the stance of the primary group rather than the bureaucracy. We first offer descriptions of some of the empirical ways community groups—particularly families in the local community of a school—try to influence complex organizations such as schools. Then we consider underlying principles that help to determine how and when it is useful to employ different mechanisms.

15. This section is based on more extended work by E. Litwak, E. Shiroi, L. Zimmerman, and J. Bernstein, "Community Participation in Bureaucratic Organizations: Principles and Strategies" *Interchange,* Vol. I, No. 4 (1970).

*Description of Linking Mechanisms*

1. *Advocate bureaucracy.* Primary groups may seek to communicate their viewpoints and to press for change in bureaucracies through another bureaucracy that will represent the primary community's interest. Thus, parents seeking to correct what they regard as improper acts of schools may hire a law firm to sue, or they may ask an existing advocate organization (for example, the NAACP or ACLU) to intervene on their behalf. This mechanism is the same in essence as that called "delegated function," but it takes on a different emphasis when used by the community. It makes a difference whether the bureaucracy used is one with which continuous, or membership, relations are established (such as labor unions, some ethnic associations, some political organizations) or if it is an organization (such as a law firm) that serves temporarily and for a limited purpose. How the advocate bureaucracy conceives of its function in the advocacy process is also important. For instance, does it primarily supply knowledge to its client, does it participate with and/or guide client actions, or does it act on its client's behalf? These and other differences are important when community groups use this mechanism in their strategy of influencing target bureaucracies. The details need not be elaborated here where our purpose is only to describe in general terms linkages from communities to schools.[16]

2. *Strategic influencers.* In a variation of this mechanism, the community may enlist the support of powerful or influential persons to advocate their cause. Members of the community, often

16. There has been a growing interest in the idea behind the advocate agency or professional. In its most popular fashion it has expressed itself in various "action lines" of newspapers where people are invited to express their problems in newspapers which seek to aid them in their dealing with various bureaucracies. The development of race relations commissions to aid people who have been discriminated against in housing or on the job would also be a case in point. R. Cloward's and R. M. Elman's "The Storefront on Stanton Street: Advocacy in the Ghetto" in G. A. Brager and F. P. Purcell (eds.), *Community Action Against Poverty* (New Haven: College and University Press, 1967) seeks to develop this idea in social work. It should also be kept in mind that some of the historical attempts to develop advocate agencies have been worse than failures in that they have been taken over and dominated by the very group they were supposed to fight. What we have in mind are Federal regulatory agencies which were often set up to be advocates for the consumer or larger public.

opinion leaders themselves, or community groups, may make contact with two types of strategic influencers who may help to change target bureaucracies. The *intra-system influencer* may be, for example, someone superior in line to the principal of a particular school within the school system or if not superior nevertheless of reference group significance to the bureaucratic personnel to be influenced. *Extra-system influencers* can be in many locations, the most obvious of which affect political or economic interests of the bureaucracy. "Going over the head" of those to be influenced is a familiar tactic, and the factors and circumstances that lead to its successful use or its failure deserve more consideration than we can give them here. It is sufficient to indicate that this analog to the opinion leader approach is a linking mechanism available to the community.

3. *Voluntary associations.* Community groups may use voluntary associations, rather than full-fledged bureaucracies, to press for their interests. They may be auxillary to the target organizations, such as Parent-Teacher Associations, or separated from them, as were parent's organizations developed in the dispute over racial integration in New York in the late 1960s.[17] They may be continuing associations turned toward the particular concern of the community group, or they may be temporary associations developed for the purpose at hand.

4. *Mass media.* The use of the mass media as a mechanism through which primary groups can influence bureaucracies is limited usually by lack of resources (money, personnel) for sustaining information or publicity programs. Therefore, this technique must be used through an advocate bureaucracy, in a discontinuous fashion, or by creating events that are "newsworthy" and hence reported through the regular institutions of the media. Although it can be used deliberately, the mass media approach is more often for the community a concomitant of other mechanisms. Since it cannot be closely controlled by the community but may have important consequences, it must therefore be carefully employed.

17. David Rogers, *110 Livington Street* (New York: Vintage Books, 1968).

5. *Ad hoc demonstrations.* Sometimes used as devices to attract attention and publicity for a cause (especially in the mass media), sometimes used to develop, sustain, or exhibit emotional solidarity, sometimes intended as a direct interruption of established practices by the target bureaucracy, *ad hoc* demonstrations constitute an influence mechanism available in some circumstances to community groups. Publicized marches, street mass meetings, sit-ins, disruptions of meetings, sporadic violent or destructive acts—all illustrate this mechanism. It involves attempts to direct collective behavior, and its initiation and outcome are often difficult to control.

6. *Sustained collective action.* Sharing only in superficial ways some characteristics of the *ad hoc* demonstration, this linking mechanism is characterized by a more sustained, systematic collective action against the target bureaucracy. Strikes, boycotts, harrassment, and the like require coordination but may serve at least two purposes for community groups: attraction of public attention to their cause and interference, usually through economic effects, with the functioning of the target organization when it depends, as most organizations do, in part on community use or support. Withholding of labor, trade, or participation can hurt the bureaucracy and influence it toward concessions sometimes indirectly as on the apportionment of state funds allocated to public schools on a pupil-count basis when parents keep their children at home. This approach assumes as a minimum a strong voluntary association or a very cohesive community primary group, (neighborhood, ethnic, or whatever), to provide the kinds of resources necessary to maintain a sustained and systematic community action.

7. *Common messenger.* Persons who are simultaneously members of community primary groups and of the target bureaucracy are in a position to serve as common messengers. Such persons are indigenous to the community in the sense that they share important characteristics (residence, ethnic or class status, kinship or other ties to the social network) with the population the bureaucracy is supposed directly to serve. How they participate in the bureaucracy will affect their potential for influence on behalf of

community groups. Common messengers can have more expanded and differentiated use by the community than by the bureaucracy. Therefore several forms of this linking mechanism will be noted.

   *a. Common messenger: employee.* Many service organizations have by conviction or formal requirement hired indigenous workers to facilitate understanding of and communication with the clientele they serve. Communities themselves have often demanded that indigenous workers be hired. Their influence differs if they are *expert* (teachers or other specialists) or lower skilled (cafeteria workers) and if they occupy positions of relatively high or relatively low power in the organizations. A teacher or social worker from the local community is an example of a high-powered indigenous *expert*, whereas a street-crossing guard is an example of a low-powered indigenous nonexpert. Sometimes the demand will be made that experts be employed who share major social characteristics of the clientele regardless of their membership in the local community. An example is the demand that black teachers be hired to teach black children. The underlying purposes of such proto-indigenous experts are the same as for local community members, but the community may have less control over them as common messengers.

   *b. Common messenger: unpaid participant.* School children and local community members who may serve on formally established school committees or local school boards are examples of unpaid participants in the formal organization of the school who may serve as common messengers for the purposes of community influence. Such unpaid indigenous participants may, like paid workers, be low-powered (school children) or high-powered (members of the local board of education). The extent of influence will depend on the formal power of the positions they occupy in the bureaucratic system. It will be lower, for example, for local board members if such important decisions as hiring and firing of principals and teachers is centralized for the whole school system. It will be higher if these decisions are delegated to local school boards.

   8. *Individual ad hoc contact.* The parent who contacts a teacher to complain, to inform, to get information, or for other purposes

illustrates this linking mechanism often used in communication from community to bureaucracy. The purpose of the contact (whether to a specific child or general), the timing of the contact (crisis situation or otherwise), the frequency or continuity of contact, the form of contact (in person, by telephone, or in writing), the location of the person contacted in the organization, and other features of this apparently simple mechanism all determine its effectiveness. Indeed, this approach could be elaborated into a number of subcategories, but for our purpose it is sufficient to present it as a single type of mechanism.

## Some Principles for Deciding which Linking Mechanisms the Community Should Use to Reach the School

The principles that govern communication from the community are essentially the same as those governing communication from the bureaucracy. The same basic problems must be faced. Selective listening, retention, and interpretation must be overcome, and appropriate persons in sufficient numbers must be reached. However, because the target of the community is a bureaucratic organization where uniform tasks predominate over nonuniform tasks (which are nevertheless of great importance), these principles require somewhat different interpretation. The problem of resources is different for the community and its groups. The mixture of uniform and nonuniform tasks in the bureaucracy creates more complex problems of diagnosis and strategy planning. Most of all, perhaps, the balance between too close and too distant is exceedingly delicate since the functioning of experts in bureaucracies is in some ways more vulnerable than the functioning of nonexperts in primary groups. These general statements may take on meaning if some of the points are elaborated.

*Selective listening.* Selective listening, as previously indicated, is the process by which persons systematically fail to hear messages contrary to their existing position. Overcoming selective listening requires great initiative on the part of the communicator, whose initiative is different if the target is a bureaucracy rather than a primary group, (a school rather than a family). For example, the bureaucracy can send one person who can encompass most primary groups, which are usually of limited size. A bureaucracy is often large, and one person from the community can rarely hope to make contact in reasonable time with a significant portion of its personnel. If the bureaucracy is resistant to change, it may be insufficient to reach the head of the organization. One might have to reach far down into the ranks to produce a change. For instance, it may be of small consequence for the community to succeed in affecting a change of school superintendent if the teachers in the system are unwilling to change.

One way of overcoming selective listening in a bureaucracy is to confront it with another bureaucracy or large-scale organization which has the resources, personnel, expertise, and aggressiveness to spread the community's message to all the places where it should be heard. Although the purpose and the underlying principle are the same when the bureaucracy uses a detached worker and the community an advocate bureaucracy, the mechanisms are clearly different.

*Selective interpretation.* This refers to several aspects of the situation that primary groups face when trying to communicate with bureaucracies. One aspect involves the differential receptivity and consequences that arise from the fact that bureaucracies require many of their personnel to perform both uniform and nonuniform tasks. Although the distinguishing mark of the school's contribution to education of children is its provision of expert knowledge and skills, nonuniform tasks for which nonexpert performance is suitable or necessary nevertheless form an integral part of the work of teachers and other school personnel. To the extent that schools resemble closed communities (that is, they incorporate a large part of the total lives of children for extensive lengths of time) their adequate performance of nonuniform tasks becomes as important as their performance of expert tasks designated as uniform. Classroom teachers must handle discipline, behavior idiosyncracies, and simple duties such as dressing, feeding, and comforting children. They cannot avoid in such situations, and in their expert performances as well, the intrusion of their personal value systems, often quite undeliberately. Since the school encompasses both uniform and nonuniform tasks, the community's message must be differentially conveyed and interpreted in ways the community desires. For example, a message from nonexpert parents presenting teachers with a demand with respect to such expert tasks as techniques of teaching reading or chemistry would be interpreted as irrelevant and not taken seriously. If the community seeks to change the behavior of experts, it must itself focus expertise on the target organization. An advocate expert, perhaps backed by an advocate bureaucracy, is required. On the other hand, where nonuniform task performance is unsatisfactory and the community seeks to change it, there is no reason why nonexpert parents cannot themselves intervene to express their own views and demands and to insist on changes without consequences damaging to the children's training. Such primary group intensity may be quite effective and mechanisms providing this should be used. Of course, the intertwining of uniform and nonuniform tasks, the complexity of factors within the school that affect teacher conduct, and various sets of potential reactions to any given community action all make the problem more complicated than our discussion of it conveys. The point is, however, to suggest how communication principles must be analyzed from the community viewpoint.

*Scope.* The problem of scope is similar for the community and the bureaucracy. However, the choice of wide vs. narrow scope might vary. Because most bureaucracies are exposed to public view, they can lose public support if shown to be violating community norms, and may be induced to change. Community groups in such circumstances might use mechanisms of wide scope, communicating not only to personnel of the bureaucracy but well beyond them. This might be so, for example, in instances of overt racial discrimination by a school in a northern city where the black community is sufficiently powerful to make its displeasure known and effective. On the other hand, groups in the community sometimes seek to change bureaucracies in ways that differ from prevailing views of the wider community. Parents of children

in a public school may be a minority in a community with a
majority of nonschool families and parochial school parents.
Their efforts to seek more funds to expand educational programs
may not be generally favored. Communication mechanisms of
narrow scope would be preferable here in order to reduce visibility
of a campaign which would not have support of the wider community. Parents seeking sex education in the schools in an unfavorable community climate are another example. Of course, an alternative to limited scope in such circumstances is wide scope educational or propaganda efforts to change community opinion. The
point is that tactical decisions with reference to scope are necessary on the part of the community trying to influence the bureaucracy.

*Some Community-Based Linking Mechanisms Reconsidered*

In the above we have indicated four major underlying principles by which to judge whether a given mechanism of communication should be used by the community to influence the bureaucracy: sender initiative, primary group intensity, focused expertise, and scope. The linkages described and others that might be
observed could be evaluated in terms of these underlying dimensions. Sequencing of linkages and their clustering could be guided
by the principles to assess potential impact of community effort in
any given situation.

Before using these dimensions for a schematic assessment of
linking mechanisms, it is useful to examine several mechanisms in
some detail so that the kind of analysis behind our assessment can
be understood. We shall examine the advocate bureaucracy, mass
media, and the common messenger who is a high-powered indigenous nonexpert such as a member of a local school board chosen
from the local community.

*Advocate bureaucracy.* (a) It would rate high on sender initiative since it can bring large resources to bear on the target bureaucracy, and it is oriented toward putting pressure on opposing
organizations. (b) It is low on primary group intensity since it is
itself a bureaucracy and does not include community primary

groups as such. It only represents them. (c) Its potential is high
for focused expertise since this is the strength of such an organization. However, the actual rating on this dimension would depend
on whether the expertise available was most suitable at any given
stage in the process of trying to influence the target bureaucracy.
Thus, a community group might hire a thoroughly competent law
firm to assure that black history be included under the law requiring high schools to teach American or state history. The same law
firm may not have the expertise to judge whether the textbook
adopted did more than comply technically with a legal decision
so as to satisfy community concerns that generated the demand
in the first place. (d) This mechanism can have moderate to high
scope, depending on the size and resources of the advocate bureaucracy employed and its tactical procedures.

*Mass media.* (a) This is a mechanism with moderate community initiative. Most target bureaucracies must react in some way
to public attack in the press or through other media. However,
since the media seldom follow up situations in great detail, this
mechanism seems to have less sender initiative than, for instance,
an advocate bureaucracy. It could be high on this dimension in
a circumstance, for example, where the target bureaucracy is very
vulnerable to public pressure, for example, a school system just
before a school board election. (b) Mass media is low on primary
group intensity. Not controlled by community primary groups,
the media will not necessarily voice primary group sentiments and
viewpoints. (c) Communications through the mass media can develop moderate levels of focused expertise, as when reporters take
the time to research a situation and present its technical aspects.
But the functions of the press, radio, and television keep the mass
media from sustaining the level of focused expertise of, for example, the advocate bureaucracy. (d) Mass media is a mechanism,
however, capable of very large scope.

*Common messenger: high-powered unpaid participant.* How does
this variant of the common messenger approach rate on the underlying dimensions when the person involved is a member of a
local school board chosen from the community? With respect to
initiative, such a person may be rated moderate. The indigenous

school board member can indeed reach key personnel in the school by virtue of his position of power. However, his knowledge by which to judge whether his message is honestly and accurately responded to is limited. He might insist that black history be considered a suitable educational topic but be unable to know whether technical objections to its introduction (for example, lack of suitable teaching materials and teacher preparation) are justifiable. On the other hand, greater initiative on behalf of the community can be generated with respect to matters where nonuniform, nonexpert tasks are at issue. This approach is very high on primary group intensity since it offers a direct channel of powerful influence on issues which concern community groups. The mechanism is low on focused expertise for the reasons noted above. But the power of the position of a school board member may be such as to call for outside expertise. Hence we would rate the mechanism low to moderate on this dimension. Scope is more moderate for this approach, being generally limited by the size of the community represented so far as funneling pressure and being bounded by the limits of the bureaucracy subject to jurisdiction of the local school board.

From these analyses it is seen that the capacity of linking mechanisms initiated by the community varies. It is also affected by specific factors in the concrete, empirical situation. Nevertheless it is possible to make provisional, general ratings of mechanisms on the underlying dimensions. Such an assessment is presented in Table 3.

**Table 3**

**Ratings of Community-Initiated Linking Mechanisms on Underlying Dimensions**

| Selected Types of Linking Mechanisms and Examples | Underlying Dimensions | | | |
| --- | --- | --- | --- | --- |
| | Community initiative | Primary group intensity | Focused expertise | Scope |
| *Advocate bureaucracy:* Community employs law firm or is represented by established organization (e.g., NAACP) | high | low | high | moderate-high |
| *Facilitative bureaucracy:* An organization provides information to or on behalf of community | moderate-low | low | high | moderate-high |
| *Strategic influencers:* Persons within the target bureaucracy and capable of influencing bureaucracy are used | moderate | low | high-moderate | low-moderate |

| | | | | |
|---|---|---|---|---|
| *Voluntary association:* Ad hoc or continuing auxiliary or independent membership organization | moderate-high | moderate | low-moderate | moderate |
| *Mass media:* | moderate | low | moderate-low | high |
| *Ad hoc demonstrations:* Mass meetings, marches, sit-ins, disruptions, etc. | moderate-low | moderate | low | high-moderate |
| *Sustained collective actions:* Organized strikes, boycotts, etc. | moderate-high | moderate | low-moderate | high-moderate |
| *Common messenger:* | | | | |
| a) Employee – high-powered indigenous expert, e.g., teacher who is member of community | high | high | high | low |
| b) Employee – low-powered indigenous nonexpert, e.g., teacher aide from local community | low | high | low | low |
| c) Employee – proto-indigenous expert, e.g., black teacher not from local community | high | moderate-high | high | moderate-low |
| d) Unpaid participant – high-powered indigenous nonexpert, e.g., community member of local school board | moderate-high | high | low-moderate | moderate |
| *Individual ad hoc contract:* | low-moderate | high | low | low |

## Table 4    Illustrations of Linking Mechanisms
## Community Groups Might Use to Influence Schools

|  | *Outside Community Supports Local Community Group* | |
|---|---|---|
| *Type of Task* | *Target bureaucracy is friendly* | *Target bureaucracy is hostile or indifferent* |
| (a) Uniform or expert's task, e.g., developing content for a black history course already decided on | 1. *Low sender initiative, low primary group intensity, high-focused expertise, moderate scope.* E.g., small group of parents meet appropriate teaching and administrative staff to make known their interest in content and confidence that educators will develop suitable content. May offer to obtain expert aid from competent facilitative organization such as faculty of university. Give public credit to school. | 2. *Moderately high sender initiative, moderate to low primary group intensity, high-focused expertise, high scope.* E.g., Parents press for participation of advocate, broad based organization, such as NAACP, in selecting personnel involved in developing course content, such personnel to be educational and subjectmatter experts. Strong publicity to community group's cooperation. |
| (b) Nonuniform or nonexpert's task, e.g., agree to include sex education in curriculum | 1. *Low sender initiative, moderate primary group intensity, low focused expertise, high scope.* E.g., make known by ad hoc contact and mass media that inclusion has wide support and address appeal to local and central levels. Expect school to respond to expressed interest. | 2. *Moderate sender initiative, high-primary group intensity, low-focused expertise, high scope.* E.g. Through mass media, demonstrations, and similar mechanisms, press target school to recognize demand as not technical but one of values which are made visible by these methods. |
| (c) Uniform (expert) and nonuniform (nonexpert) task requirements equally important, e.g., adopt employment system for competent teachers sharing community's values | 1. *Mix of mechanisms best achieving combination of (a) and (b).* E.g., assure by ad hoc contact and low-powered common messenger that school's judgment of teacher competence acceptable. Offer assistance to identify positive values of prospective teachers. | 2. *Mix of mechanisms best achieving combination of (a) and (b).* E.g., short circuit local school with facilitative advocate and influencers to higher location with strategy of 1. but where mass media coverage can follow. |

| *Target bureaucracy is friendly* | *Target bureaucracy is hostile or indifferent* |
|---|---|
| 3. *Moderately high sender initiative, moderate primary group intensity, high-focused expertise, low scope.* E.g., support autonomy of professional staff to decide teaching content and with minimum public attention offer to obtain outside facilitative expert assistance. | 4. *Very high sender initiative, high to moderate primary group intensity, high-focused expertise, low to moderate scope.* E.g., in this maximally adverse situation, local community must in effect substitute its own or imported advocate bureaucracy with experts to develop course content (and perhaps teach it). Requires great resources and sustained efforts, perhaps staged through program to achieve nonuniform task of gaining outside community support or friendship of target school. |
| 3. *Moderate sender initiative, high primary group intensity, low-focused expertise, low scope.* E.g., by direct contact with school personnel, ad hoc group of parents with minimum publicity convey aims and indicate local community will constitute protective enclave for cooperative school. | 4. *High sender initiative, high primary group intensity, low-focused expertise, very low scope.* E.g., by high-powered common messenger and individual and small group ad hoc contact insist that community decision govern through local school board if available or community voluntary association; use covert pressure so as to avoid mass-media coverage until one is in a position to build one's own organization and use systematic boycotts, strikes, etc. |
| 3. *Mix of mechanisms best achieving combination of (a) and (b).* E.g., use low scope mechanisms avoiding publicity to strengthen and supplement if necessary expert autonomy of local school as judge of teacher competence and use ad hoc contacts buttressed by strategic influencers for protective insulation of local school. | 4. *Mix of mechanisms best achieving combination of (a) and (b).* E.g., unpublicized use of advocate bureaucracy and high-powered indigenous expert with multiple ad hoc contacts and sustained collective action if necessary, being sensitive to reactive damage in lowered school performance as resistance. |

*Community-Initiated Linking Mechanisms and Balance Theory*

The potential of various linking mechanisms for reducing or increasing distance between the community and the large-scale bureaucracy is reflected in the ratings of Table 3. The concept of balanced distance is equally applicable for optimizing the educational goals of both community and school. Therefore, the selection, sequencing, and combination of mechanisms should be adapted to the actual situation with this in mind. With our present state of knowledge the development of a community program to affect school-community relations will involve complex assessments, value judgements, and much trial and error. Without elaborating them here, we can suggest on the basis of balance theory some general factors that need to be taken into account.

A key determination will be whether the desired changes involve essentially uniform or nonuniform tasks carried on in the school. The conceptual distinction between such tasks blurs in most realistic situations. Furthermore, multiple and related changes will usually be sought rather than a single change. Nevertheless, sensitivity to the type of tasks to be affected is necessary to avoid consequences that may run counter to desired purposes. In the language of balance theory such consequences reduce chances of achieving a balanced distance. Mechanisms that reduce distance so that community inputs can become operative with respect to nonexpert performance may, if not carefully used, impair needed expert performance. For example, to press for black teachers so as to express community values about racial identity and pride might result in reduced technical quality of teaching unless the community is also sensitive to qualifications of teachers. Mechanisms that may reach the school (for example, ad hoc demonstrations or sustained collective actions) but lack focused expertise must be coupled with mechanisms (for example, some form of advocate bureaucracy) that provide this input.

In the achievement of balance another important factor is the extent and nature of the distance between school and community. Is the target bureaucracy friendly (that is, close in values, trust, and receptivity) to the purposes of the initiating community group, or is it hostile or indifferent? Does the larger, outside community within which the school and local community groups operate tend to support the initiating community group or does it not support that group's values, aims, and interests? Mechanisms must be chosen and adapted to the existing situation.

Other factors also affect the strategy and tactics a community group can successfully use if it initiates an effort to influence the school. Among such factors are: the level of resources available to the community group, such as financing and number and qualifications of manpower and the breadth and depth of commitment among the local population; the structural characteristics of the social system of the school bureaucracy, for example, whether it is unified or vulnerable because of internal conflicts, and the level of its resources available for change or resistance to change; the availability of allies to the community group in the form of supporting organizations and persons; legal constraints and opportunities available to the community groups. The list can easily be extended, but to understand how a school-community program initiated from the community might look, we can illustrate by considering in simplified form the three factors discussed above: type of task (uniform or nonuniform), extent of support from the outside community (supporting or not supporting), and one expression of distance (target bureaucracy mainly friendly or mainly hostile or indifferent).

Table 4 suggests some desirable features of community-initiated efforts to influence a school: (a) to develop content for a black history course (uniform or expert task) satisfactory to community views, assuming the decision to have such a course has already been made; (b) to agree to include sex education (or black history) in its curriculum (nonuniform or nonexpert's task); and (c) to adopt a system to insure employment of competent teachers whose views of classroom discipline and value orientations are consonant with those of the community (equally uniform and nonuniform task). For each of the tasks, possible approaches are suggested in situations in which the outside community supports the objective of the local community and the target school is on the one hand friendly and on the other hostile or indifferent. Finally, the contrasting circumstance is assumed: that the outside community does not support the local community and the target school is either friendly or hostile or indifferent.

In this table, every aspect of the problem for the community group has been simplified. It is particularly difficult to convey in such compressed form the difficulties in assessing types of tasks and favorable or unfavorable orientations of schools and communities. Furthermore, the manner of use as well as the type of mechanism has an additional effect in real situations. An especially important aspect that cannot be adequately summarized in brief illustrations is the need to be sensitive to reactions from the school bureaucracy so as to adapt tactics to changing circumstances. This is certainly necessary also for the school from its side when it conducts its school-community program. From the community's side flexibility is even more important because it risks not only losing its special purpose but also damaging the effectiveness of the school in its primary area of contribution, namely the performance of specialized uniform educational tasks that require professional expertise otherwise unavailable to the community.

This last consideration has led us to observe two institutional deficiencies in our society that impair effective inputs from the community to the common purpose of educational effectiveness. One is the general unavailability of what we have called advocate bureaucracies independent enough of special interests to serve the general community. The second deficiency is the lack of mediating and adjudicating institutions to temper the unintended damaging effects on both sides. Programs initiated from the community in our society are especially likely to generate conflict. Grievance handling and dispute settling procedures—perhaps mechanisms to be used by and on behalf of the "public"—in community areas such as education and race relations are not yet well developed. The experience acquired in other areas, such as industrial relations, may provide useful ideas that can be adapted to community-school relations.

## Conclusion

Whether the development and management of a school-community relations program is viewed from the side of the school or from the community, the central requirement should be kept in mind. Education—at least in democratic societies—depends on a complementary relationship between forms of social organization that can facilitate inputs of expert knowledge, on the one hand, and inputs of more generalized support on the other. Performance of what we have called uniform tasks of experts is enhanced by the location of educators in complex, formal organizations. The primary groups of the community—family, neighborhood, peer group—sustain the noninstrumental, personalized, inclusive relations that allow nonexpert, nonuniform tasks to be done. Therefore, a balanced distance between these complementary but partly antithetical forms of social organization should be maintained for maximum educational advantage. A program of school-community relations must in some manner attend to the problem of distance and therefore with procedures for affecting it.

The linking mechanisms described serve to decrease or increase the distance. The principles involved in the mechanisms involve ways of communicating with or influencing others so as to meet problems of selective listening, selective interpretation, technical complexity, and scope or numbers reached. We have suggested that the same principles operate in different ways when the targets of influence are primary groups of the community or persons in the school bureaucracy. In presenting these differences we may have given the impression that school-community programs are essentially contests. This is not so, although adjustments and adaptations that will inevitably be necessary usually create some sense of loss or gain in those involved. Conflict will occur over immediate issues and, perhaps, more basically when the values and goals of school and community members seriously differ. Our analysis does not lead to judgments as to which side is right or wrong or should win. Such judgments must be made but they will have to be made from different premises. Our purpose in this chapter has been to suggest why it is important to be concerned with school-community relations and to establish a framework in which to consider the elements that constitute a program that can deal with such relations.

# 2 ❦ The School as a Social Organization: Administrative Style of the School and Linking Mechanisms[1]

The central purpose of those responsible for school-community relations, as the previous chapter has indicated, is the development of a program for the school that will be able to utilize appropriate linking mechanisms in order to achieve the optimum relationship between school, families, and neighborhoods. In order to do this, the existing situation in the local community must be appraised and diagnosed, as must the existing situation in the school. In this chapter we shall analyze administrative styles that may be found in different schools and relate these styles to the use of various mechanisms of coordination. In chapter 3 we discuss career orientations of administrative and teaching staff that may affect its operation as well as consider problems of changing the school's social system.

Our analysis will be presented from the viewpoint of those persons in the school who are primarily responsible for initiating or conducting a program of school-community relations. Such

1. This chapter is based on Eugene Litwak and Henry J. Meyer, "Administrative Styles and Community Linkages of Public Schools: Some Theoretical Considerations," in Albert J. Reiss, Jr. (ed.), *Schools in a Changing Society* (New York: The Free Press, 1965), pp. 49-98.

responsibility may rest with different persons in different schools: the principal or an assistant principal, a school committee, one of the nonteaching professional staff, such as the school social worker or school nurse, or a person especially employed for the purpose. The specific location will make some difference but some considerations will be basic. To simplify our discussion we shall use the term *school-community agent* as a generic designation for the person or persons who may have primary responsibility for the school-community program.

## Why the School-Community Agent Must Understand the Social System of the School

The school is the base from which the school-community agent operates. Each school building develops its own pattern to some degree and this specific pattern must be learned. The social system of the building will affect the kind of work the school-community agent can do, the linking mechanisms that can be used, and the activities that can be developed. Can programs be operated with some independence or will they be circumscribed by administrative rules? Can teachers be expected to cooperate in activities that involve parents or do they keep their distance? Is the orientation of the staff toward the "closed door" or the "open door" position with respect to its views of school families and the "outside" community? Do opinions of teachers count for much or does the principal dominate the building? Such questions as these make it clear that the social character of the building is of considerable importance for the work that can be done.

The school-community agent will have to base upon his analysis of the social climate of the school a number of important decisions as he develops his particular role. Should he be primarily oriented to the school building or toward the community? This involves more than personal preference. In some building situations the community agent may find that he must first work within the school to change its understanding of school-community relations and only then shift more of his attention to external activities. Or he may decide that the school is receptive enough for him to use a range of linking mechanisms at the outset. Or, in some circumstances, he may discover that the school cannot form constructive links with the community and is unwilling to change, so that the community agent must either abandon his purpose entirely or utilize school system and community influences to encourage change in the school. The community agent must also decide where to begin his work. Does he build on what the school may have been doing—such as its parent-teacher organization, or its newsletter to parents—or start something different? He must size up the school as a going social system to answer such questions.

Finally, the school-community agent must understand his school in order to interpret it to the community—to the families and pertinent people in the neighborhoods. It is obvious that the distance between school and families cannot be bridged when families hold unrealistic views of the school any more than when the school holds unrealistic views of the families.

## Types of Administrative Styles

The administrative style of a school involves more than the form of management or leadership exercised by the principal. We use the term here in a broad sense to refer to the total social structure of the school whether it be determined primarily by the principal, or by other factors emanating from the larger school system or from the staff in the building.

Our purpose is to find some general bases on which to describe different school administrative styles that are empirically observable so that we may consider how these different styles affect linkages to the community. In the literature on the sociology of organizations, various concepts are used to describe what we call "administrative style." Some writers refer to "process oriented" vs. "goals-oriented" organizations;[2] others use such terms

2. James G. March and Herbert A. Simon, *Organizations* (New York: Wiley, 1958), p. 29.

as "democratic," "autocratic," and "laissez faire";[3] or "bureaucratic" and "nonbureaucratic"[4] or differentiate between "therapeutic" and "custodial" styles of organization.[5]

## Basic Dimensions of Bureaucratic Organizations

The terms noted above suggest that different emphases have been placed on common features of formal social organizations. It is therefore useful to look for basic dimensions of organization which may vary and provide a clue to differences.[6] One set of dimensions may be derived from the earliest and most familiar analysis of bureaucracy as a social structure—that of the German sociologist Max Weber.[7] Weber was portraying a particular kind of formal organization but the characteristics he identified may be viewed as dimensions that can be expressed in varying degrees or amounts and hence to characterize other kinds of formal organizations. The major dimensions may be summarized as follows, naming the dimension first and then indicating contrasting expressions of it.

1. *Authority structure: hierarchical or collegial.* How is control over its members exercised in the organization? One principle is that of a hierarchy of authority, with orders originating in higher levels and ultimate power vested in the executive. Military organization and most businesses illustrate this arrangement of authority. A contrasting principle stresses the mutual approval of members of the organization as colleagues having relatively equal power and exercising authority through some form of collective expres-

---

3. Most of these stem from the discussion by Ronald Lippitt and Ralph White. See *Group Dynamics: Research and and Theory* (2nd edition), D. Cartwright and A. Zander (Evanston, Ill.: Row, Peterson, 1960), pp. 527-53.

4. *From Max Weber: Essays in Sociology,* H. H. Gerth and C. Wright Mills (trans. and eds.) (New York: Oxford University Press, 1946), pp. 196-203.

5. M. Greenblatt, "Implications for Psychiatry and Hospital Practice: The Movement from Custodial Hospital to Therapeutic Community," in *The Patient and the Mental Hospital,* M. Greenblatt *et al.* (eds.) (Glencoe, Ill.: The Free Press, 1957), pp. 611-20.

6. The following discussion of administrative styles is in part a summary and in part an elaboration of an article by Eugene Litwak, "Models of Bureaucracy Which Permit Conflict," *The American Journal of Sociology,* 57 (September 1961), pp. 177-84.

7. *From Max Weber,* cited in note 4, pp. 196-203.

sion. Groups of professionals—such as doctors working together in a clinic—often exhibit this collegial form of authority structure.

2. *Division of labor: specialization or generalization.* To get the work done, does the organization depend primarily on a high degree of specialization for limited tasks to be performed by individuals or categories of members, or is each member or category of members expected to be competent to do most tasks?

3. *Interpersonal relations: impersonal or personalized relations.* Between members of the organization, do relations tend to be primarily formal, limited to the work to be done, essentially businesslike, or are they more likely to be warm, include personal as well as work interests, and hold friendliness to be important? Does one or the other of these emphases characterize relations between levels in the organization—such as the principal and teachers—as well as relations between people on the same level, such as among teachers?

4. *Performance guides: delimited, a priori rules; or, internalization of organizational goals; or, ad hoc determination of duties.* What system is generally used in the organization to decide what work is to be done and how it is to be performed? Three different principles may be noted: (a) work is predetermined and rules about how to do it are established in detail so that most questions that come up can be handled by checking the rules; (b) understanding and acceptance of the goals of the organization are stressed and members decide the best ways of getting the work done by considering what is best for the organization; (c) in the absence of predetermined rules or agreed-on clarity of the organization's goals, individual members use their own judgment about what to do and how to do it.

5. *Goal or policy setting: separation or merging of policy and administrative decisions.* How are the general policies and goals of the organization set? Are policies determined first and then carried out by administrative actions, or does the organization tend to let administrative decisions determine what the policies will be?

6. *Personnel assignment: on basis of merit or on bases irrelevant to organizational goals.* When persons are hired, assigned to various duties, transferred and promoted, or dismissed from the organiza-

tion, is the controlling principle the competence and capacity of the persons to do what the organization requires? Or, do other factors dominate personnel decisions, such as nepotism and personal friendship, prejudice for or against certain groups of people, political advantage or pressure, and the like?

*Descriptions of Types of Administrative Styles*

Using these dimensions, a number of administrative styles of schools may be described by noting how they express each dimension in the complex patterns that make up their formal social organizations. The descriptions will be "ideal types"—that is, abstract delineations more extreme in feature than those usually found in the empirical world. We may expect real schools to approximate one or another of the types rather than to correspond to them. The purpose of the descriptions is to serve as reference points for observing actual schools rather than as portraits of them.

1. *Rationalistic administrative style.* The kind of bureaucracy Max Weber analyzed most fully can be described on the dimensions as follows: hierarchical authority, specialization in the division of labor, impersonal relations, a priori rules, separation of policy and administration, personnel assignment on the basis of merit. This same characterization also fits the custodial emphasis in prisons or mental hospitals, the traditional form of German and French school organization, "scientific management" in industry, and what Simon has called "process" styles of administration. The term we use is "rationalistic administrative style."

2. *Human relations administrative style.* If organizations are characterized by opposite poles of these dimensions (except personnel assignment), we find: collegial relations, generalization in division of labor, personalized relations, internalized organizational goals, merged policy and administrative decisions, personnel assignment on basis of merit. Such an organizational style in industrial research has been called "human relations"; in education it has been associated with "progressive education"; in study of treatment organizations it suggests "therapeutic milieu"; it

resembles what Simon calls the "goal oriented" administrative approach; and it suggests what is sometimes implied by "democratic" group atmosphere. We call this the "human relations" style.

These two administrative styles seem to represent opposites, stressing contrasting poles of each dimension except that of personnel assignment on the basis of merit. Both styles seem to be empirically visible among public schools. But this does not exhaust either the logically conceivable or the actually existing types that result from variations in position on the basic dimensions.

3. *Compartmentalized administrative style.* Another administrative style seems particularly pertinent to educational organizations. It combines features of both rationalistic and human relations styles, side by side in the same organization. In schools, scheduling of classes, fixing of hours to be devoted to subjects, keeping attendance and grade records, building maintenance, and similar functions seem often to be run on a rationalistic basis, whereas classroom teaching, motivation and management of individuals and groups of children, communication and relations between teachers, and similar activities may be characterized by a human relations style. Other examples of such a mixed administrative style can be seen in hospitals, in colleges and universities, in large law firms, in industry, and elsewhere. It may be argued that most organizations to some degree take this form, but some organizations, it seems to us, exceptionally exemplify it.

Organizations incorporating contradictory rationalistic and human relations elements can—and usually do—develop internal mechanisms to accommodate or compartmentalize their contradictions, although all sources of internal strain are rarely eliminated. This has not been fully studied, but the compartmentalized administrative style appears, from preliminary analysis, to develop mechanisms, such as differential assignments of persons to roles, serial role performance by the same persons, temporal and spatial segregation of role performance, translator and other communication roles, evalution groups, and other arrangements.

It is possible to derive many other types of administrative style by combining the basic dimensions in different ways, but we will not go into this logical exercise here. We will note three additional forms, however, that appear commonly in our observations of public schools. Two of these styles are variations of the rationalistic organizational form and the third of the human relations form.

4. *Autocratic administrative style.* The autocratic administrative style has the attributes of the rationalistic organization except that a priori rules are not operative to restrain and delimit the duties, powers, and privileges of superordinates, especially—in the school—those of the principal. Hence, the executive of the organization has considerable power to define what is legitimate activity in an arbitrary, and often personal, manner. There are always some restraints on even an autocratic principal, and this administrative style reflects the degree of personalized direction rather than implying absolute control.

5. *Paternalistic administrative style.* This variant of the rationalistic administrative style reverses two of the dimensions: it does not have a priori delimitations of duties—especially executive duties—and it adopts personalized rather than impersonal relations between organizational members. It may often appear that the executive of the organization—the principal—is genuinely concerned with his staff as persons and with their performance. However, as in the autocratic type, arbitrary power remains with the superordinate to define the work situation and task assignments.

Both autocratic and paternalistic administrative styles tend to put the full burden of decision making and the determination of merit on the executive, often on the principal of the school. No organizational guarantees deriving from other members of the organization provide support for legitimate organizational goals. Such centralization of decision making may well lead to clogged communication channels and slowed-down decision processes. On the other hand, these administrative styles may function efficiently and effectively when the executive is able, has integrity, and is strongly committed to organizational goals consonant with those of the other members of the organization. In the school system, the concept of the principal as the "captain of his ship" is close to what is implied by both of these administrative styles.

6. *Laissez faire administrative style.* This type of bureaucratic form is a variant of the human relations administrative style. We call it laissez faire. It has the characteristics of the human relations style except that performance determinants are neither a priori nor internalized but rather individualized on an ad hoc basis. As a consequence, members of the organization may make contradictory, uncoordinated determinations both of goals and performance duties. One teacher might stress drill, another life experiences. Having a generally decentralized system of goal determination and of authority, and utilizing personalized relationships between members of the organization, the laissez faire bureaucratic form may well produce scattered islands of effort. Some teachers may be successful, others not, but the school as an organization is unlikely, we hypothesize, to have or achieve organizational objectives. It has been observed that this situation sometimes obtains during the preretirement years of a principal who has "given up" and whose school had previously taken the form of an autocratic, paternalistic, or even rationalistic administrative style.

7. *Nepotistic administrative style.* Although any administrative style is subject to restatement in terms of the nonmerit characterization of the dimension concerned with assignment of personnel, a pervasive infusion of nonmerit criteria may produce a form distinctive enough to justify a special designation. This administrative style we call *nepotistic*, although the term is not entirely apt. Selected and rewarded regardless of performance on bases irrelevant to the achievement of organizational goals, personnel are members of the organization because of such personal or status considerations as friendship, race, religion, social class, and the like. Since organizational objectives have not governed their membership, benefits of the job may take precedence over performance. Some school administrators have called teachers with such orientations "mercenaries": they have given up (or never had) educational goals and are interested only in the money they earn. Principals, too, are sometimes so oriented. When this style pervades the school, decisions and task performances are likely to reflect personal convenience not identical with effective education.

Although we have discussed administrative styles without

specific attention to students as members of the organization, it is apparent that they are affected by the administrative style of their school. We will not develop this point here, noting, however, that nonmerit styles applied to students may reflect conscious or inadvertent race and class biases both in educational materials and teaching styles as well as in evaluations of abilities and student achievement.

*Summary table of types of administrative style.* In Table 5 we summarize in abbreviated fashion the characteristics of each of the administrative styles with respect to the dimensions of organizational structure. We have indicated the greater likelihood that autocratic, paternalistic, and laissez faire styles will be subject to nonmerit assignment of personnel by noting this as an alternative for these styles. We have also represented the "nepotistic" administrative style by noting that it is dominated by its nonmerit handling of personnel. Styles other than those in Table 5 are readily conceivable, and some are empirically observable, particularly forms intermediate to the ones described. It is a task of further research to see whether these types are the major ones to be found and, indeed, how meaningfully the actual social structures of schools fit any of these types. We believe that the styles noted are visible among the schools of most large school systems and will be recognizable to most educators or students of social organization.

## Administrative Style and Organizational Effectiveness: Some General Criteria

It should be recalled that the purpose of describing administrative styles of schools is to allow us to consider what advantages or difficulties the different styles offer for developing school-community relations programs using various mechanisms of coordination. We must ask first, however, whether different administrative styles can be found to be more effective in accomplishing some rather than other tasks involved in balancing school-community relationships. We will take the polar positions on the dimensions of organization and consider under what conditions they contri-

**Table 5　Administrative Styles as Defined by Dimensions of Organizational Structure**

| Dimensions of Organizational Structure | Administrative Style | | | | | | |
|---|---|---|---|---|---|---|---|
| | Rationalistic | Human relations | Compartmentalized | Autocratic | Paternalistic | Laissez faire | Nepotistic |
| Authority structure | hierarchy | collegial | hierarchy and collegial | hierarchy | hierarchy | collegial | (Any combination of dimensions) |
| Division of labor | specialist | generalist | generalist and specialist | specialist | specialist | generalist | |
| Interpersonal relations | impersonal | personal | impersonal and personal | impersonal | personal | personal | |
| Performance guides | a priori rules | internalized goals | a priori rules and internalized goals | ad hoc rules | ad hoc rules | ad hoc rules | |
| Goals or policy setting | separation of policy and administrative decisions | merger of policy and administrative decisions | both merger and separation of policy and administrative decisions | separation of policy and administrative decisions | separation of policy and administrative decisions | merger of policy and administrative decisions | |
| Internal mechanisms of isolation | none | none | present | none | none | none | |
| Personnel assignment | merit | merit | merit | merit and nonmerit | merit and nonmerit | merit and nonmerit | nonmerit |

bute to effective organizational action, thus attaining some basis for evaluating any given administrative style that is an expression of the various dimensions.

1. *Hierarchical vs. collegial authority structure.* Any large organization requires some process whereby all members can have sufficient common directions to achieve some coordination. Otherwise, the organization could not achieve any of its goals. Where the tasks to be performed by members of the organization are essentially repetitive and unambiguous, simple guidelines can be provided almost by rule to give sufficient direction. Where tasks are not repetitive, however, and where the situations are ambiguous, simple guidelines cannot be created in advance. Under these circumstances, some system must be provided to insure that decisions will be made and accepted. Such a decision-making system is generally called the authority structure, some sort of which is necessary for coordination in any large organization.

As mentioned in chapter 1, we will use the concept of "uniform" and "nonuniform" tasks or situations to refer to the general contrasting conditions that may face organizations. However, in chapter 1 we were speaking about extreme forms of nonuniformity which generally could best be handled by community primary groups. Now we are speaking about moderate forms of nonuniformity, that is, those for which some expertise is required and which must be carried on within the boundaries of the organization. In short, uniformity and nonuniformity are opposite ends of a continuum rather than a dichotomy. As suggested in chapter 1, where an organization must face many types of tasks or many ambiguous and unanticipated situations, we will say that it is characterized by "nonuniform tasks" in contrast to an organization characterized by "uniform tasks" where relatively familiar and continuous demands tend to face it. We do not imply by this terminology that uniformity or nonuniformity inhere necessarily in the task, or that tasks retain this character indefinitely. Some tasks may be treated by custom as simple and repetitive although they express conditions of great complexity. For example, checking student attendance is often considered routine in the school although absenteeism is a problem of complex character. Sometimes, a new technology becomes available and its use can change ambiguous and nonuniform tasks to uniform ones. For example, the use of group diagnostic examinations to detect hearing and vision deficiencies greatly changes the nature of one kind of possible problem the school may have in assessing factors affecting school work. With complex and multiple goals, it is likely that schools will face both uniform and nonuniform tasks and that these will change. We would expect that elementary schools which have to pay heed to the socialization of the children would face nonuniform tasks in greater proportions than secondary schools that can devote relatively more attention to subject matter.

When considering whether the hierarchical or collegial principle works best with uniform or nonuniform tasks, it should be noted that both principles accept several assumptions. The first assumption is that uncertainty about what can be done is not so great as to preclude some kind of decision and the establishment of some general way to meet the situation. For example, although classroom discipline problems vary greatly and can hardly be handled by simple rules, some general guidelines or policies can be established. If every instance had to be decided separately, the decision making system would be overloaded, causing delay, confusion, and uncertainty. A second assumption is that those responsible for making decisions for the organization will have competence by virtue of training or experience to make those decisions. This does not necessarily mean that they have professional competence but only that their capacities will be acknowledged to constitute legitimate bases for authority. In a hierarchical system, competence for decision-making is assumed to be greater at the top than in the lower levels, but if this is not so the organization may be deprived of the best possible direction. In a collegial authority structure, the collective wisdom of the members is assumed to be most competent, but if, for example, particular individuals are more competent than others, the organization is likewise deprived of the best decisions. (In collegial situations, such a circumstance is sometimes recognized by acknowledging a colleague as "first among equals.") A third assumption follows from the others: that the nature and variety of tasks are sufficiently limited so that

persons at the top of the hierarchy or those composing the collegium can possess the necessary competence to make appropriate
decisions. If the organization, in fact, faces many tasks, each requiring different types of competence, multiple hierarchies or
collegia may be required.

Collegial structure has some obvious advantages over hierarchical structure in nonuniform situations; the collegium can
assign to each member the responsibility most appropriate to his
special competence. Thus, the organization can approach the
ideal of permitting its most expert persons to make decisions for
it. But collegial structures have some equally obvious disadvantages: much communication is required and the time necessary to
reach decisions is relatively long. Where there are predominately
uniform tasks, or relatively few decisions to be made, a more or
less permanent authority hierarchy is likely to be more efficient
in reaching effective decisions.[8]

2. *Specialization vs. generalization in the division of labor.* In an
organization the virtue of specialization is obvious: A person can
become more knowledgeable and skillful from practice when he
does one job rather than many. However, there are circumstances
when specialization is not a virtue. Where the task is constantly
changing or not well standarized, specialization may be dysfunctional because the specialist may be trained for an obsolete task.
Or, his training may become obsolete as the state of knowledge
about the task changes. This is not merely a matter of wasted
resources; frequently the specialist persists in using his obsolete
specialized expertness so as to block the progress of new skills. In
short, specialization may become a vested interest.[9]

What the generalist lacks of the specialist's expertness he
gains presumably in acquiring principles applicable to various
tasks. The risk of dilettantism, of being a "jack of all trades," is

8. For circumstances where hierarchy does not permit commitment to decisions, see
March and Simon (cited in note 2), p. 81.
9. For some of the weaknesses of specialization, see Harold L. Wilensky and Charles
N. Lebeaux, *Industrial Society and Social Welfare* (New York: Russell Sage Foundation, 1958),
pp. 235-65. For an illustration of movement from specialization to generalization, see R.
A. Cohen, "Some Relations Between Staff Tensions and Psychotherapeutic Process," in
*The Patient and the Mental Hospital* (cited in note 5), pp. 307-308.

compensated for by adaptability to changing tasks and new skills and knowledge. It is significant that progression up the administrative ladder in hierarchical organizations is accompanied by increasing generality of skill and knowledge, of transferability, and of responsibility for a wider range of decision-making. In part, this is a function of job demands at higher levels, where decisions have to be made about many different operations and their coordination, and where ambiguities and uncertainties about these decisions are more frequent. As the tasks become less uniform specialization becomes less useful and generalization more desirable.

3. *Impersonal vs. personalized relations.* The value of impersonal relations among members of a bureaucratic organization, according to some students of bureaucracy, rests in protection of rationality against extraneous personal demands, such as friendship, especially in such matters as evaluation of work and devotion to functional tasks. There is some evidence, however, that in situations of ambiguity individuals need personalized support if they are to work efficiently. Thus, Blau points out that in a group where individuals could not assess the right decision to make they confided in other members of their group who could understand their uncertainty without using it to evaluate them invidiously.[10] Others have held that where interpersonal skills are intrinsic to the job—as in military combat teams, or in psychotherapeutic treatment—personalized relations are necessary.[11] Such relations are exposed to the risk of irrationality (favoritism, nepotism, etc.) which may in part be avoided by internalization of the concept of merit, by seeking some objective measure of output, or by separating evaluation from administration.

We would argue that from the viewpoint of administrative effectiveness the maintenance of impersonal relations would be

10. Peter M. Blau, *Bureaucracy in Modern Society* (New York: Random House, 1956), pp. 63-64.

11. Edward A. Shils and Morris Janowitz point out that a sense of primary group loyalty may be so strong among combat troops that it is given greater weight than the risk of death. See "Cohesion and Disintegration in the Wehrmacht in World War II," in *Public Opinion and Propaganda*, Daniel Katz *et al.* (eds.) (New York: Dryden Press, 1954), pp. 91-108.

desirable where there are relatively uniform tasks but less effective where the organization faces nonuniform and ambiguous situations.

4. *A priori rules vs. internalized goals vs. ad hoc delimitation of duties.* Max Weber's analysis of bureaucracy noted the necessity of a priori rules that, among other effects, delimited duties and privileges of individuals in organizations. This facilitates coordination as well as specialization: where standardized decisions can be anticipated by rules there are minimal demands on hierarchical decisionmaking or personalized adaptability. This argument presupposes a preponderance of uniform tasks. Where tasks are nonuniform, they cannot be governed by a priori rules, for the rules would be too numerous to remember, would risk inappropriate application, or would overload the system of authority.

One alternative in the face of nonuniform situations is to encourage internalization of general policies at all administrative and operational levels of the organization. When confronted by unanticipated or ambiguous events, members of the organization can then make judgments based on their understanding of organizational policy, goals, and values. The difficulty with this solution to the problem of coordinating behavior is that the means to achieve internalization of goals and policies are uncertain and those now available require stability of personnel and considerable investment of time and effort. Professions like social work and medicine, which involve many nonuniform tasks for which a priori rules cannot be relied on, require long and expensive training and socialization periods before it is assumed that internalization of necessary principles has taken place. For the relatively uniform tasks of an automobile assembly line, in contrast, such a lengthy process would be unnecessary, as well as exorbitantly expensive.

An alternative to a priori rules and to internalization of policies is the expediency of ad hoc determinations of duties as situations arise. In effect, this leaves to the best judgment of members of the organization what they should do. If this judgment is guided by policy or organizational precedent, it is tantamount to internalization of policy; if it has no guide at all or only that of

idiosyncratic experience, it can lead to anarchy. It is most obviously useful when goals and values are well understood and accepted
but when neither rules nor policies can be established. This can
occur in new organizations, or for new directions in old organizations, where goals are known but means are uncertain. In these
circumstances it is useful or necessary to give individuals wide
discretion. This is typically the arrangement in professional organizations, such as law firms and group medical practice, or
when professionals practice within organizations. Thus, a social
worker with street gangs employed by a community organization
agency follows few specific rules in order to gain the trust of a
delinquent gang and redirect its activity; the process is professional if not artistic, and he must make decisions and adaptations as
he proceeds. Similarly, the psychotherapist can seldom be governed by a priori rules; his tasks are too ambiguous and his technology too uncertain. In such circumstances ad hoc determination
of duties guided by general internalized policies may be the only
reasonable arrangement. The risks are, of course, large; in
particular, there are minimal bases for organizational evaluation
of judgment and performance.

In general, it would appear that a priori rules are most
useful when the organization is faced primarily with uniform
tasks. Internalization of policies and ad hoc determination of
duties are preferable, or necessary, when the organization faces
primarily nonuniform, ambiguous situations.

5. *Separation vs. merger of policy and administrative decisions.* To
deal with changing demands on the organization as a whole, Max
Weber concluded that effective bureaucracies must separate goal
setting, or organizational policy, and administrative practice. Top
management should decide what the organization *should* do, while
administration consists of those decisions which best implement
given policy. The previous line of reasoning should make our
conclusion clear: such a separation is most effective when organizational tasks are primarily uniform. When the organization faces
nonuniform tasks, goal setting and goal implementation through
administrative decisions would seem to be more effective if
merged.

6. *Merit vs. nonmerit evaluation of personnel.* All organizations must have criteria as well as procedures for evaluation of personnel. Evaluation is intrinsic to processes of recruitment, training and socialization, job assignment, and the provision of monetary and other rewards. Evaluation is implicated in the motivational system of the organization as well as in its system of membership maintenance. It would seem obvious that effective organizations must require evaluation of personnel to be based on performance in terms of organizational tasks and goals. This is the definition we give to "merit" as a basis for evaluation.

The use of nonmerit—that is, organizationally irrelevant—bases for evaluation of personnel is risky, although the results may or may not reduce organizational effectiveness. Nepotistic recruitment, for example, is an uncertain organizational principle even though the boss's son may on occasion also happen to be the best man for the job.

Problems with the merit principle arise not from its desirability but from its application. What criteria of merit can be applied? Without developing the argument here, we suggest that when the organization primarily faces uniform tasks, adherence to rules and policies is a meaningful criterion of merit. For organizations that deal with ambiguous tasks, however, such a criterion is less applicable or not applicable at all. In this situation, merit can be assessed only in terms of output or outcome variables. If these are themselves uncertain—as they often are in education, treatment, and social service organizations—adherence to a preferred ideology within the organization is often substituted.[12] But this is a poor substitute criterion, often, in effect, constituting nonmerit evaluation.

*Summary of Bases for*
*Evaluating Administrative Styles*

Accepting the foregoing analyses of dimensions of bureaucratic organization, it is fairly obvious how the types of adminis-

12. This point is discussed in reference to "people-changing organizations" by Robert D. Vinter, "Analysis of Treatment Organizations," *Social Work*, 8 (July 1963), pp. 14-15.

trative style described earlier can be evaluated. The human relations type would seem to be the best style when organizational tasks are nonuniform and ambiguous. The rationalistic style operates best when tasks are relatively uniform. The compartmentalized model is most suitable when both uniform and nonuniform tasks face the organization. Administrative styles accepting non-merit personnel assignments are likely to be less effective than those based on merit. We would expect autocratic and paternalistic styles to work better for uniform tasks and to work more poorly for nonuniform tasks. The laissez faire style, if effective at all, should work better for nonuniform situations. We cannot conceive of situations where the nepotistic administrative style would necessarily work effectively.

## Which Administrative Styles Are Best for Public Schools?

This question can be properly answered from the previous analysis only if we have additional information about the uniformity and nonuniformity of tasks faced by the school, if we know the nature of the school's goals, and if we can estimate the school's flexibility as an organization. Furthermore, we would need to make some evaluation of the effectiveness of the school—how well it educates its students. Such information is rarely available in clear, adequate form, nor has there been sufficient research to permit confident discussion about schools in general. We can, however, make some assumptions that seem plausible in the light of general experience in schools, and thereby pursue an analysis that may be helpful by suggesting some of the things that enter into the question.

Contrasting assumptions have sometimes been made about the nature of the educational process. A "three R's" approach implies that the process is basically made up of fairly uniform tasks. Children are assumed to have fixed capacities ("IQ's don't change") and there are standard ways of motivating students. Drill with predetermined materials is the pedagogical task and standardized examinations assess academic achievement. Nonpedagogical tasks of the teacher and the complement of school personnel fall into comparable uniform patterns. In contrast, a "pupil-centered approach" conceives of the chief problem as motivation, and hence education must be highly individualized. In order to learn, the child's individual experiences must be tied to the learning situation which, in turn, must be tailored to each child's unique life situation. Hence, materials and manner of teaching must be extremely varied to fit variable and changeable requirements. No single standard of achievement is meaningful; motivation and growth cannot be reduced to common scores.

If these deliberately exaggerated characterizations are considered, the first is obviously made up of what we have called uniform tasks, for which our analysis prescribes a rationalistic administrative style. The second requires a human relations style to deal with its extremely nonuniform tasks. Whether these extremes are ever to be found in fact, and whether maximum effectiveness is achieved by the theoretically congruent administrative style, are, of course, matters for empirical determination. Observation suggests that approximations of each approach may be found, but are not typical among schools.

More typical and more plausible is the supposition that educational and socialization tasks of the public schools are both uniform and nonuniform. Not only are the housekeeping aspects of the school likely to be amenable to routine but certain educational aspects as well. Thus, scheduling and distribution of time to different subjects, some common evaluation standards, and even some teaching techniques may be conceived of as uniform tasks. In fact, some standard patterns emerge and new procedures and techniques may convert nonuniform into uniform tasks. On the other hand, schools must deal with problems of motivation and socialization which are not uniform. The art of teaching and the management of the school so as to facilitate education demand far more than science and technology can now make predictable and standard. This is the condition for which our analysis asserts the appropriateness of the compartmentalized administrative style. It permits rationalistic management of the routine components in the work of teachers and other persons in the organization while providing a human relations style to operate with respect to nonuniform components. In a sense, this is the meaning of the assertion that the administrative style should allow the teacher in the school to act as a professional.

As earlier indicated, a compartmentalized administrative style requires internal mechanisms to manage the potential conflict between rationalistic and human relations components. The teacher as well as the organization must be protected against accepting either extreme as an exclusive approach. If, for example, the teacher is (or thinks he is) required to emphasize clerical and other routine aspects of the job, this emphisis may well pervade classroom teaching so that order and control become more important than learning and socialization. Orderly records, neat rooms and neat children, and adherence to schedule may displace adaptability to individual differences and variability in teaching techniques. On the other hand, total neglect of routine in the interest of variability may well make the management of some essential organizational tasks impossible. This dilemma is critical for the school as a social organization, and its resolution requires deliberate attention.

Although we suspect that the compartmentalized administrative style is generally more appropriate for public schools, we are not unaware that different emphases within this form are probably required for different age-grade levels in the present structure of school systems, and perhaps also for different social class backgrounds of present school populations. Secondary school levels may tip the balance toward the rationalistic style because socialization is less central and knowledge transmission more capable of standardization. In elementary schools the balance tips toward the human relations style. Similar reasoning would suggest that low-income populations, with less effective educational motivation than populations of higher educational background, would respond to greater emphasis on the human relations component of the compartmentalized administrative style.

To summarize, Table 6 suggests the kinds of tasks for which each administrative style is deemed most suitable.

Table 6   **Compatibility of Administrative Style
With Organizational Tasks**

| Administrative Style | Kinds of Tasks | | |
|---|---|---|---|
| | *Uniform* | *Nonuniform* | *Both uniform and nonuniform* |
| Merit: | | | |
| Rationalistic | very high | moderately low | moderately high |
| Human relations | moderately low | very high | moderately high |
| Compartmentalized | moderately high | moderately high | very high |
| Merit and nonmerit: | | | |
| Autocratic | low | extremely low | very low |
| Paternalistic | very low | very low | very low |
| Laissez faire | extremely low | very low | very low |
| Nonmerit: | | | |
| Nepotistic | lowest | lowest | lowest |

## Administrative Styles and Linking Mechanisms

We may now consider how various school administrative styles are related to the different linking mechanisms described in the previous chapter as major instruments of a school-community program.

### Dimensions of Bureaucratic Structure and Linking Mechanisms

We have viewed linking mechanisms as activities of the school and, as such, they will be affected by the administrative style of the school. The use of a given linkage mechanism will be facilitated or limited to the extent that the linkage is consistent with the bureaucratic principles expressed in the administrative style. By consistency we mean the extent to which both the linking mechanisms and the administrative style stress such common dimensions as hierarchy or collegial authority, impersonal or personal relations, etc.

Two aspects of the idea of consistency deserve consideration here. In the first place, if the requirements for using a particular linking mechanism contradict the dominant bureaucratic principles of the administrative style, it is unlikely to be put into use regardless of its potential utility for linking the school and community. For example, a school with rigid rules and strong hierarchical authority structure operating on an impersonal basis (that is, a rationalistic style) is not likely to give much consideration to a mechanism that is highly personal and dependent on autonomous and flexible activities of the school-community agent. Such a mechanism (for example, detached worker) is likely to be ruled unacceptable and hence not even tried. In the second place, if an inconsistent mechanism is tried, internal friction is likely to develop which may well lead to the diversion of energy and attention away from organizational goals, including those of school-community relations. Some of the practical implications of the need for consistency between linking mechanism and administrative style are obvious: the school-community agent should initiate his efforts in such a way that the whole program is not jeopardized at the outset; he must sometimes work to change aspects of administrative style before mounting a school-community relations program using the full range of mechanisms. It is important to be able to recognize compatibility between administrative styles and mechanisms.

*Linking Mechanisms and Administrative Styles*

In Table 5 we identified a number of administrative styles of schools in terms of the ways they embody dimensions of bureaucratic organization. We also noted the compatibility of the different styles with uniform or nonuniform organizational tasks, or with both uniform and nonuniform tasks at once (Table 6). We may now ask what the different mechanisms of coordination require in dimensions of organization and uniformity or nonuniformity of task.

1. *Some mechanisms are clearly more consistent with human relations than with rationalistic administrative style.* Thus, the detached worker requires decentralized rather than hierarchical authority, internalization of policy rather than a priori rules, generalized rather than narrowly specialized assignment of duties, merger of policy and administrative decisions, and probably personalized rather than impersonal relations within the organization. In general, the tasks of the detached worker tend to be widely varied, unpredictable, and nonuniform, the types of tasks congenial to the human relations administrative style. Only this style—or its embodiment in the compartmentalized administrative style—could permit the autonomy, flexibility, and adaptability required of the detached worker's role. These are inconsistent with rationalistic styles, whether merit or nonmerit. In one school that was observed, a school-community agent seeking to use the detached worker approach was prevented from doing so by the insistence of the principal that he sign out and indicate precisely where and how long he would be in a predesignated place, and that he "clear" all plans before meeting with groups of parents or others in the community.

The settlement house mechanism is similarly more consistent with a human relations administrative style than with a rationalistic one, since it requires personalized relations and adaptability in performing the various tasks of working with groups from the community in the school building or in other facilities. What is to be done is not only varied but professional discretion is also necessary, the tasks likely to be nonuniform and changing as classes, groups, and programmed activities develop.

The opinion leader mechanism would also appear more consistent with human relations than with rationalistic styles since extraorganizational procedures—such as unscheduled contacts, attendance at community organization meetings, and the like—may be necessary to reach opinion leaders and to convey to them desired kinds of information. Such activities are less likely to develop in a hierarchical, rules-oriented, impersonal structure. However, since the opinion leader may be a conveyor of information whatever its source, and may be reached in a variety of ways that are less personal, this mechanism may also be used consistently with rationalistic administrative styles when operating in conjunction with other mechanisms, such as mass media and formal authority.

Human relations organizational structures are particularly able to utilize the detached worker, the settlement house, and probably opinion leader linking mechanisms more consistently than other organizational structures.

2. *Some mechanisms are clearly more consistent with a rationalistic administrative style.* Formal authority and mass media both lend themselves to hierarchical control and executive management. They tend to be impersonal, and do not conflict with a priori definitions of organizational tasks by rules or with specialized job duties. The tasks required when using these mechanisms are, compared to the other mechanisms, relatively uniform. It is likely that emphasis on the human relations style—personalized, decentralized, stressing general rather than specialized skills, and so forth— would actually impede the most effective use of these mechanisms. We have already noted that the opinion leader mechanism, also, may in some circumstances be consistent with the rationalistic administrative style.

3. *Mechanisms available generally to both rationalistic and human relations styles.* The other mechanisms are not so readily seen as more consistent with human relations or with rationalistic styles. *How* they are used would seem more affected by administrative style than *whether* they can readily be used. Thus, a parent-teacher association (auxiliary voluntary association) may be instituted and operated from the top of an authority hierarchy or from a more general collegial inclination. In schools where the principal controls with an iron hand, he often "has a PTA" and "runs it." On the other hand, in schools where highly decentralized and personal relations prevail, the faculty may encourage and develop room-mothers' clubs and other auxiliary associations.

The common messenger mechanism, likewise, lends itself to formal or informal use, under strict rules, general policy, or wide discretion.

The operation of delegated function as a mechanism— referrals to agencies and invitiations to organizations to work with the school, for example—would also seem to depend on how delegation was accomplished, what functions were delegated, and which other organizations were used. These might be affected by the organizational structure of the school as well as by its definition of goals and objectives, but any of the administrative styles we have identified would seem capable of using the mechanism.

4. *Consistency of mechanisms with compartmentalized administrative style.* Since the compartmentalized administrative style contains both human relations and rationalistic components, it is obviously in some degree compatible with all of the mechanisms. This is not to say that this administrative style will automatically adapt to any mechanism. Indeed, special adaptations will probably be required in the component that is least consistent with the mechanism used. For example, the detached worker approach may be compatible enough with teachers as to those aspects of their work they define as individualized and not subject to standard procedures, such as the health or dress of particular children or their home study situations. But it may be viewed as incompatible with aspects of their work such as instruction in reading, marking grades, or reporting the child's progress and standing to parents. If the detached worker approach concerns itself with the latter, strain may well be generated. However, the fact that other aspects tolerate or support the approach will probably mean that the strains are minimal compared to the situation in a noncompartmentalized administrative style. None of the mechanisms can be essentially inconsistent with the compartmentalized style as they can be with other administrative styles.

Just as the compartmentalized style was noted to be most compatible with both uniform and nonuniform tasks, so it is most compatible with all the mechanisms of coordination and hence the most useful for developing a school-community program using the entire battery of mechanisms to promote optimal balance. This does not mean, however, that the other styles preclude all school-community programs, but only that the range of available mechanisms will be narrower.

It is true, however, that the research necessary to substantiate our assessments of consistency is incomplete and therefore they must be taken as tentative and merely plausible in the light of our observations. With a similar qualification we suggest a ranking of the combinations of administrative styles and linking mechanisms in terms of their likely capacities to carry out comprehensive school-community programs successfully.

We would rank highest the *merit* styles—compartmentalized, rationalistic, and human relations—utilizing *consistent* mechanisms. The human relations style would rank highest where the school's major problem is closing distance, the rationalistic organization would rank highest where the school must open distance, and the compartmentalized would rank highest where the school serves a mixed community, that is, needs both to close and open distance.

We would rank next the rationalistic and human relations styles, but utilizing *inconsistent* mechanisms.

Finally, the nepotistic style would rank lowest since it is *nonmerit* and could be *inconsistent* with all mechanisms as well.

## Implications of Administrative Style for the School-Community Agent's Strategy

The purpose of the foregoing anlaysis has been to provide a perspective from which to view the general social structure of a school. We now consider in conclusion some implications of the analysis for the school-community agent's work strategy.

### How to Use the Conceptual Types of Administrative Styles

The several types of administrative styles that have been described are intended to be suggestive, not definitive. They should be thought of as "ideal types," or "models," against which a particular school can be "tested" to gain a sense of its relevant basic social structure. Two points should be kept in mind: (a) a school will rarely "fit" a type exactly and therefore the school-community agent should be sensitive to variations or styles that are not yet identified; (b) a school's administrative style should not be assumed permanently fixed and unchangeable. The school-community agent should use his assessment of administrative style to judge the most promising possibilities for effecting a program, which may well involve both adaptation to the existing situation and efforts to modify it so as to enhance the possibilities. He should be prepared to reassess administrative style as it changes and adapt his program accordingly.

There are other important aspects of school social structure in addition to its general administrative style, particularly the organization of school staff around various career orientations. These will be discussed in the next chapter, and must also be considered when planning strategy.

*How to Size Up Administrative Style*

Short of an extensive research project, the predominant administrative style of a school can only be tentatively estimated. The following suggestions may facilitate such an estimation.

1. Keep in mind the dimensions of organization. Look for evidences of how authority is exercised, the extent of specialized or generalized work functions, the extent of impersonality, and other features that will give a sense of how the school operates. Remember that it is the social system that is to be appraised, not the "personalities" of principal and staff. There is often a tendency to ascribe the way things are done in a school building to personality—"the kind of person so-and-so is"—but the community agent should watch carefully what happens in relationships between persons, in their interactions.

Some of the things that might be noted can be mentioned:

a. *Authority structure—hierarchical or collegial.* How are decisions reached? Does the principal tend to decide most things himself or does he usually consult with teachers? If he does consult others, is it usually one or two favorites, a special clique, or those who are most likely to be involved in the results of the decision? Are there working committees, not just proforma ones? Does the principal's office have to clear most of the things teachers want to do?

b. *Division of labor—specialization or generalization.* To what extent are teachers expected to pitch in on various jobs that come up in addition to their usual assignments? Do they tend to say that some things are "not my job"? Are many different things that come up—such as trouble in the halls, the complaint or question of some parent, a child who seems to be getting too little sleep, and the like—viewed as the principal's responsibility rather than part of the daily work of the classroom teacher?

c. *Interpersonal relations—impersonal or personalized.* Is there much mixing between teachers and the principal, among teachers themselves, at lunch and other nonwork occasions? Are there social events involving school people that are not "duty parties"? Are first names generally used in private conversation? Do there appear to be genuine friendships among the staff? Are there likely to be spontaneous "bull sessions" after school, sometimes including the principal? Are teachers and administrators likely to know something about each other's families?

d. *Performance guides—a priori rules; internalized goals; ad hoc judgments.* Does there seem to be a clear rule for almost everything? Are supplies requisitioned for unlimited purposes or must teachers exercise considerable discretion in how they use supplies? Are teachers comfortable about making decisions when something new comes up without finding out how it is supposed to be handled? Do most of the staff simply do what they think best in a situation without much concern for what others are doing? When new things come up—such as discussion of student grades at conferences with parents—does the principal or a faculty meeting usually decide in considerable detail how it is to be handled, or is its general purpose discussed and teachers left to work out how they will carry out the purpose?

e. *Goal or policy setting—separation or merger of policy and administrative decisions.* Does there tend to be a fairly clear set of goals formulated from above, or do the customs of the school seem to define what its goals are? Is there much talk of the principal's "policy" as compared to "the way he expects things to be done"?

f. *Personnel assignment—merit or nonmerit.* Do new assignments tend to go to "favorites" or "uncooperative teachers," depending on whether the assignments are desirable or undesirable? Are men or women favored? Is there evidence of covert or unconscious racial, religious, or ethnic bias in assignments and rewards?

2. When looking for indications of how the school operates as a social system along the dimensions, remember to look at all key structural relationships: the interactions of principal and teachers; of teachers with one another; and of both with the children.

3. As the community agent begins to work, he can use his own experience in the school to gain insight into its administrative style. What are the restrictions and expectations he finds at the outset? How do principal and staff respond to his suggestions? As a participant observer, he can often acquire a sense of the working system.

4. It will be helpful for the community agent to find the opportunity to talk about "school tradition," not only with administrators in the building (principal and assistant principal) but also with "old timers" among the teachers and the nonteaching staff. The school secretary can often give valuable insights into how the school operates, and so can the custodian. Observing and talking to new teachers will provide further understanding. And the community agent should not forget that the students themselves can often provide clues to the system if they are watched and listened to.

5. Since the administrative style of a building will be a matter of relative stress on the various dimensions, it is often useful for the community agent to compare his school with others. He should try to visit other buildings, particularly those with a "reputation" for being "different" from the one where he works.

The kinds of understanding of the school as a social organization that this chapter is intended to promote should help the school-community agent maintain perspective so that he can determine what kinds of changes in organizational structure are necessary to his school-community work or, alternatively, what are the limits the administrative structure puts on the type of school-community linkages which can be used.

# 3 ✤ Administrative Style and School-Community Imbalance: Some Strategies for Changing Organizations

An understanding of social distance between the community and the school must recognize that factors arising in either the school or the community may be involved. In this chapter we first examine briefly some general factors in administrative styles of schools that may create an imbalance in their social distance from the community. This leads us to consider some implications of the organizational theory presented in chapter 2 for strategies of changing administrative styles of schools. The major emphasis in this book is on how schools can reach out and effect changes in the primary groups of their local communities. However, persons within the school—administrators, principals, teachers, school-community agents, and others—concerned with school-community relations may find it desirable, or even necessary, to bring about changes in the school to facilitate their program. We shall not try to present an inclusive theory of deliberate organizational change, but only one sketch in broad strokes some organizational imperatives that we believe should be taken into account.

Thoughout this chapter we take the stance of a change-agent with known goals that he or the population wants to achieve. We speak, therefore, in terms of actions he "should" or "must" take to serve his purposes. In order to expose the theoretical argument, as well as to suggest appropriate change strategies, we shall also present our analysis as though the administrative styles of schools have been deliberately established and can be deliberately changed. The many factors and conditions that determine administrative style in the empirical complexities of actual situations will be largely ignored. Nevertheless, we think the theoretical analyses presented may enhance understanding of principles that are applicable when adapted to realistic situations.[1]

## Administrative Styles and Social Distance from the Community

From the analysis in chapter 2 we can derive the ways different administrative styles can cause imbalance between schools and communities. For example, where the population is hostile to, suspicious of, or uninformed about education, some form approaching a human relations administrative structure will be needed to narrow the gap between school and community. In these circumstances, if the school has a rationalistic structure, or if it is deliberately changed in that direction, this is an effective cause of school-community imbalance. On the other hand, if the school takes a human relations organizational form in a situation where the community is over-involved in educational practices, such a form would also be responsible for creating an imbalance in social distance. If merit criteria were compromised by an administrative style that accepted incompetent or biased teachers, responsibility for school-community imbalance would again lie with the organizational structure.[2] As a final example, if a school

1. Excluded from our analysis of change are the larger social forces in society. There is every reason to believe that major changes in income distribution or major advances or declines in the economy would have an enormous effect on schools. We set aside such factors in order to highlight the factors that must also be considered and which are more immediately accessible to change agents. Moreover, we do not analyze the psychological or interpersonal elements of change, although such factors can influence the school independently of social structure. A practitioner who engages in any kind of change effort should surely have some knowledge of these factors if he hopes to involve and influence his colleagues. Analysis of these factors should be additional to those dealt with in this chapter. Following are references the reader might examine for alternative ways of looking at organizational change: Neal Gross *et al., Implementing Organizational Innovation: A Sociological Analysis of Planned Change in Schools* (New York: Basic Books, 1971); Mathew B. Mills, *Innovation in Education* (New York: Bureau of Publications, Teachers College, Columbia University, 1964); Jerald Hage and Michael Aiken, *Social Change in Complex Organizations* (New York: Random House, 1970).

2. An early and clear statement of inadvertant bias by teachers against low-income

faced a mixed situation in the positions taken by persons and groups in the community—some families over zealous about education and some hostile—both rationalistic and human relations structures would contribute to imbalance. According to our theory, optimal balance would be best served by a compartmentalized administrative style.

These hypothetical possibilities have their counterparts in popular discussion. For instance, a major theme running through the complaints of black communities about schools in central districts of large cities in the late 1960s was lack of local community control. It was argued that school systems must be broken down into smaller units which could be more flexible in dealing with the special needs of the local population. The idea that local units are required to deal with idiosyncratic events suggests that the total school system should move from a rationalistic to a more human relations type of structure to deal with nonuniform events.

On the other hand, in the 1950s there were campaigns in various communities to do away with "progressive education" and return to the fundamentals of reading, writing, and arithmetic. A candidate won the top educational post in the state of California using the "three R's" theme as a major plank in his platform. In Wisconsin, a local community insisted on reviving the nineteenth-century *McGuffey Reader* as a symbol of traditional elementary education, thereby rejecting "progressive," pupil-centered approaches preferred by the professional educators. Translated into the language we have used to describe organizational structure, these community voices were saying that the schools followed the human relations model excessively and defined their tasks too much as nonuniform when the community wanted a return to a more rationalistic structure and a redefinition of the educational task as a more uniform one.

families was made by W. Lloyd Warner, Robert J. Habighurst, and Martin B. Loeb, *Who Shall be Educated*(New York: Harper, 1944). See also Kenneth B. Clark, "Educational Stimulation of Racially Disadvantaged Children," Martin Deutsch, "The Disadvantaged Child and the Learning Process", Vernon F. Haubrich, "Teachers for Big-City Schools," all in A. Harry Passow (ed.), *Education in Depressed Areas* (New York: Bureau of Publications, Teachers College, Columbia University, 1963); and Frank Reissman, *The Culturally Deprived Child* (New York, Harper, 1962).

More recently, a major complaint raised against some school systems by the black community has been that the teachers are racist and prevent their children from getting a proper education. To accuse a school of being racist is translated into our theory by saying the school is administered on a nonmerit basis. A similar view has been expressed by social researchers who have suggested that teachers (as well as other middle class professionals) often mistake cultural differences for innate intellectual abilities. Thus, many children are inadvertantly labeled as "unintelligent" when the fact is that their values or language skills are different from those of the middle class teachers. To use an analogy, it would be like calling a French child stupid because he did not speak English and consequently performed poorly on I.Q. tests given in English.

It should also be recalled that when school administrative styles are incongruent with community interests and viewpoints, the schools are unlikely to be able to use those particular linking mechanisms most needed for closing or increasing social distance. Thus, administrative style can be a source of imbalance and it can also impede programs in achieving balance.

## Two Types of Changes in Administrative Style

Two assumptions can be made that create different general situations requiring different types of change strategies. First, it can be assumed that an existing administrative style is essentially appropriate to the community situation but that it is necessary to make some changes that will improve its operations. For example, introduction of new textbooks that more closely reflect community viewpoints may be desirable. Under a second assumption, the existing administrative style of the school may be inappropriate to the community situation and therefore the change required is a fundamental one. One administrative style must be replaced by another. For instance it may be desirable to change from a rationalistic to a human relations form (for example, from a form supporting a three-R's approach to a pupil-centered approach) or from a human relations to a rationalistic form (for example, pupil-centered to programmed learning). Our organizational theory suggests certain broad principles of change in both these cases which we will highlight.

*Improving Administrative Style*

*Rationalistic and human relations structures.* In some situations improvements, but not basic changes, are sought in an administrative style. For instance, a school might be considering the introduction of a new textbook or whether there should be advanced classes in English or the hour that teachers should leave the building. It would be our hypothesis that changes of this type are best initiated from the top of a rationalistic organization and communicated downward in a fairly formal manner to those below. In contrast, we would argue that in a human relations structure such changes are best achieved when introduced at a colleague level and in a less formal manner. The character of these formal or informal methods will depend on the complexity of the pattern, practice, or situation to be changed.

To make this point clear, let us consider simple and complex changes. Suppose in a rationalistic organization a simple change has to be made (such as a new rule that all teachers must remain in the school at least ten minutes after their last class has been officially dismissed). This change can be easily communicated by a written memorandum from the superintendent of schools which is in turn sent to all teachers in the system. Similarly, if the board of education decides that a certain history textbook will be used in all schools in the system, a memorandum to this effect can go to all school principals and the change can take place with great speed and effectiveness. We are assuming, of course, a neutral or favorable view of the desired change throughout the organization.

If the change is more complex, even under this same assumption, the rationalistic system might require additional procedures. If the system is to change from a common attendance schedule to split sessions (that is, different students attending at different times), a teachers' meeting, in addition to a written notice, may be necessary to explain the ramifications of the change. However, this meeting would need to be informational only, with a person fully informed of details of the change responding to questions about the plan. If the change to be made is exceedingly complex, the teachers might need a longer training workshop or similar mode of learning about the change. For instance, teachers who had to learn the "new math" or "new physics" often went to summer institutes or classes to learn about and understand fully the complexities of the new content and teaching methods. The central point is that in all these examples the necessary level of communication can be determined in a rationalistic structure by persons in the hierarchy of decision-making and information about the changes generally transmitted in fairly formal fashion.

Our theory suggests that making effective changes in a human relations context would be different. Members of the staff would play a greater part in making the initial decisions. There could be more informal modes of communication to convey the new requirements. In a human relations context the question is likely to be not which textbook all teachers must use but rather how to find textbooks to fit different student needs. This process requires face-to-face discussion and exchange of experiences between staff members, a sharing of what may have worked well for them in the past. Exchanges of experience are verbal ways of trying to introduce persons vicariously into actual experiences. The more complex the change being introduced into a human relations structure, the more it becomes useful or necessary for success to use simulated experiences (role playing, practice sessions under supervision, or similar procedures). These intermediate methods of communicating what the change requires involve a knowledgeable communicator to whom the learners relate in a quasi-apprenticeship manner. On the most complex level actual apprenticeship learning procedures may be necessary. Thus, if a new way for the teacher to develop a student's self-confidence is to be introduced, the leader might first find it necessary to give a role-playing demonstration, next provide a real demonstration, and then act as supervisor to the group of teachers under an actual teaching situation. This type of simulation and apprenticeship is necessary for transmitting very complex behaviors because it is often impossible to state all the contingencies. But it is possible to observe learners in actual situations and judge whether or not they are being successful.

In contrasting rationalistic and human relations structures in their characteristic manner of dealing with simple and complex changes, we have illustrated the point previously made in chapter 2 that the former is better adapted to uniform and the latter to nonuniform tasks. This suggests that change of structure may be called for in some degree if the nature of the new task strains the structure, a problem we shall discuss in a later section of this chapter. Partial or ad hoc changes may be attempted, however, by a change-agent in recognition that the hierarchical structure of the rationalistic style needs modification in a participative direction when complex changes are desired and, conversely, the human relations style needs modification in the hierarchical and formal direction when simple changes are to be introduced.

With respect to any changes intended to improve the functioning of administrative structure, however, our theory suggests that the change-agent should utilize the existing system of the school. Thus, changes in a rationalistic system can be introduced from above and in a relatively formal manner. Changes in the human relations structure should be introduced by more informal procedures that involve members of the organization in colleague relations.

*Laissez faire organizational structure.* The theory developed in chapter 2 leads us to suggest that other administrative structures present different problems for those seeking to improve them by introducing changes. A laissez faire structure will generally require methods with wide scope, simultaneous use of formal and informal approaches, and possibly some means of adjudicating disagreements. Individual teachers and other staff tend to go their separate ways in a laissez faire system. Therefore a change strategy needs wide scope to reach everyone. The process cannot make use of the ongoing organizational structure to spread change because laissez faire structures have weak forms of coordination.

This contrasts with a rationalistic structure where change can be initiated through the higher echelon and passed down through channels, or the human relations structure where any member of the organization can reach all others through regular collegial contacts. A laissez faire organization can be further complicated when some individuals have varying forms of relations to one another. It would be necessary to vary the tactics of change for each orientation, thus using a multitype approach.

If the laissez faire organization contains several cohesive groups within the school staff who are in conflict, there is a further complication. If the change will not affect the position of any of the groups, it is only sensible to try to present the change as serving the needs of all the groups. However, in conflict situations it is wise to anticipate some controversy and to introduce the change, including some adjudication procedures to settle disputes that may arise. For instance, one could propose some simple rule such as a majority vote, some third party arbiter, or other procedure for deciding functions that might otherwise disrupt the staff.

In a laissez faire system, where one group is more powerful than another, it would make sense to have the more powerful group see the change as its project in order to promote its adoption within the school. When one must utilize a low-powered group to introduce change, still other strategies are suggested (for example, methods with low scope). However, since there are many different contingencies, we will not go into details of change strategies, instead suggesting here that general strategies of change can be derived from the theory of organizational styles.

One general precaution is advisable in any consideration of the laissez faire model. Most organizations have elements that can be characterized as laissez faire to the extent that school staffs have cliques or groups within them that hold different educational philosophies or viewpoints, particularly about teaching methods. A "realistic" formulation might propose that one should use rationalistic change processes in a rationalistic organization, but these should be moderated by laissez faire considerations insofar as elements of laissez faire appear within the organization. Similar formulations would apply to human relations organizations as well as the other types.

*Compartmentalized organizational structures.* The compartmentalized organization poses the problem of using several different change strategies simultaneously. In a compartmentalized organization members often fail to understand that two quite different styles of administration are necessary and desirable so long as they are properly insulated from each other. Failure to appreciate this often appears as a dilemma. It is expressed by teachers in terms of demands on them to keep fairly standardized records of grades, attendance, and promotions while at the same time dealing with highly unstandardized tasks in the classroom such as motivating children, maintaining classroom discipline, and developing specialized curricula for different children. Some teachers, not recognizing the need for rationalistic procedures in the first case and human relations procedures in the other, will feel strain from having to choose between images of themselves as clerks or professionals. They may be torn by the feeling that they should have autonomy to handle all matters and the demands of the larger system to coordinate standardized items required for centralized decisionmaking. Without understanding that both roles are legitimate, each having its own time and place, one teacher might decide that her job is basically to keep good records and hence put little effort into classroom motivation of children; another teacher might decide that the main job is to teach children and hence neglect records; yet another teacher, feeling torn by demands seen as opposite, might escape the strain by seeking a transfer.

The dilemma that confronts the change-agent in such situations (if our theory is correct) is the need to use rationalistic change tactics when dealing with the uniform elements of the job and human relations tactics when dealing with nonuniform elements, and in such a way that they are not confused or resented by the staff. Thus, to use discussion groups rather than a written memorandum when one wants to get a slightly different attendance form used would involve both an unnecessary waste of time and might in addition lead to inaccuracies, some teachers getting one interpretation and some another. On the other hand, a simple memorandum to the school staff suggesting that teachers pay more attention to what children have to say as a method for increasing student motivation would be wasteful and not as effective as informal teachers' meetings and other group sessions.

This is not merely a matter of using inefficient forms of change in compartmentalized organizations. It may also result in some persons in the organization thinking others are being given more advantages. Thus, those in the school who deal with uniform problems (payroll, student records) might feel that teachers are getting special privileges because they have gone on a "retreat" to discuss new methods of assessing teachers' value orientations. Their feeling of resentment can be exacerbated by their false view that all members of the organization should have the same administrative structure.

Discussion of the compartmentalized organization highlights the problem of using multiple change strategies already mentioned when we considered laissez faire structures. In addition, the theory implies that compartmentalized organizations will have somewhat unique change problems which focus on the mechanisms by which diverse structures are kept separated but coordinated with each other.

*Authoritarian administrative style.* Our theory suggests that the authoritarian structure, like the rationalistic one, can best introduce change from the top. However, there is a major difference derived from the fact that the head of the authoritarian organization has enormous discretion, that is, he is not governed by a priori delimitations of duties and rights. Given this characteristic, two variations in change strategies can be suggested. First, successful change techniques must appeal to the individual tastes of one person and, as a consequence, the change-agent must use skill in assessing and in handling this key person. The handling of personality factors is important in all change processes, but it is especially so when so much of the success or failure of the change effort depends on one person. In the rationalistic structure, the organization systematically seeks to eliminate personality differences, by stressing impersonal relations and rules. In human relations structures, personality differences are to some extent controlled by the constraints of group decisions and the efforts to inculcate common values. Much weaker organizational constraints operate in an authoritarian structure and it is important for change-agents to know the personality of the authoritarian leader very well.

A second factor is especially important in authoritarian structures. We would expect support of change efforts not to be very stable. Since changes can occur at any time, depending for the most part on the whims and fancies of one person, we hypothesize that support for change will be less stable than where changes become part of the a priori rules, as is the case in rationalistic organizations, or part of the group norm, as is the case in human relations ones.

*Changing Administrative Style*

Sometimes changes demanded are more drastic, that is, for change from one administrative style to another. Such recent demand that schools be decentralized and put under local community control to avoid racism and to give greater attention to the local culture is often translated to mean that the schools should shift from a rationalistic to a human relations approach.

We are aware, of course, that the same language can be translated differently. The community members may be asking for a change in the *basis* of nonmerit practices, seeking to substitute bias toward a particular group rather than a merit system. "Local community control" may mean simply a larger (or controlling) voice in allocation of resources with little concern about the form of administrative style used in the school. The demand to return to the "fundamentals" may express concern to reduce costs. We do not suggest that these popular expressions reflect an understanding of the relationships of organizational structure and educational interests. We do suggest that in many instances a response by the school to the grievances would require a fairly fundamental change in organizational structure.

In this section we point out some of the implications of our theories of organization for strategies that may be useful in changing administrative style. We shall concentrate on changes from rationalistic to human relations forms and on the reverse, from

human relations to rationalistic forms. In general the same principles apply that we have discussed with regard to changes *within*
organizational styles. The difference is that we must apply them
in a different context.

   *From rationalistic to human relations structure.* Over the last four
decades the movement from rationalistic to human relations
structure has been urged by practitioners and social scientists in
many different fields. For instance, in industry, beginning with the
early Hawthorne studies,[3]   the move was away from scientific
management (rationalistic) to human relations. In the field of
penology the move has been from custodial (rationalistic) to rehabilitation (human relations).[4] In the treatment of mental illness
the movement has been away from custodial (rationalistic) to
milieu or treatment orientation (human relations).[5] In education
there has been a cyclical movement. The early "progressive education" concept assumed a human relations structure, as does the
more current "pupil-centered" approach. An earlier stress on a
"three-R's" approach and an emerging interest in programmed
learning seem to imply a rationalistic structure.

   In the shift from a rationalistic to a human relations administrative style, the requirement of the latter that the staff internalize the goals of the organization as the primary basis for guiding
their task performances presents an especially difficult problem to
one who seeks to promote such a shift. Related to this is the
problem arising from the lack of fixed routines or detailed rules
and procedures. This makes it difficult to provide more than
general training for the staff before they begin to work, leaving

   3. F. J. Roethlisberger and W. J. Dickson, *Management and the Worker* (Cambridge,
Mass.: Harvard University Press, 1939) and William F. Whyte, "Human Relations—A
Progress Report," *Harvard Business Review*, 34 (1956), pp. 125-32.
   4. The move from custody to rehabilitation is noted in passing in the following works:
David Street, Robert Vinter, and Charles Perrow, *Organization for Treatment* (New York:
The Free Press, 1966); Richard H. McCleery, *Policy Change in Prison Management* (Govern-
mental Research Bureau, Michigan State University, 1957).
   5. Harvey L. Smith and Daniel J. Levinson, "The Major Aims and Organizational
Characteristics of Mental Hospitals," in Milton Greenblatt, Daniel J. Levinson, and
Richard H. Williams (eds.), *The Patient and the Mental Hospital* (Glencoe, Ill.: The Free Press,
1957), pp. 3-9; David A. Hamburg, "Therapeutic Aspects of Communication and Administrative Policy in the Psychiatric Section of a General Hospital," in *ibid.*, pp. 91-108.

details to be learned on the job or in training situations simulating the job since so much of the work requires special decisions adapted to the particular problem presented. Meeting these problems involves expensive procedures that are often of uncertain effectiveness and generally not adapted to handling large numbers of persons.

Before discussing these problems, we should note that the initiation of a change from rationalistic to human relations style must come generally from someone fairly high in the hierarchical authority structure of the rationalistic structure or from a location outside the particular school organization in a position of authority. It is unlikely that a staff member, such as a school-community agent, can do much unless the principal or a higher administrator in the school system wants to move in a given direction. Staff members can, of course, encourage the principal's interest in change or they may go around him to higher authority. We shall assume in the following discussion, however, that the principal favors the change, as is often so, particularly when a new principal is brought in, itself a recognition that change is desirable. The problems of internalization of goals and retraining of staff have to be faced by the principal as change-agent and by those on the school staff working toward the same end.

Let us explore first the problem of internalization, by which is meant bringing the staff members to the point where the values, attitudes, and norms of the school become part of the individual's own system of behavior when working as a member of the organization. This process, for purposes of simplification, is referred to as the "internalization of values."

There is no way to "require" an individual to internalize values of an organization or to know if he has done so unless one is in a position to observe whether his actions reflect such internalization. Thus, in a pupil-centered approach the teacher is supposed to have the best educational interest of the child in mind rather than a fixed method or theory of teaching. Within this context there is freedom to alter the curriculum, classroom procedures, and teaching materials as one sees fit. It would be very difficult to observe the procedures, much less to supervise them, since the very freedom given to the teacher makes it difficult to have enough continuous contact to evaluate the work. The larger the staff, moreover, the greater the difficulty.

As a consequence, there are in general only two ways in which the change-agent can be sure that teachers have internalized the desired values: by providing an intensive resocialization process, or by being in a position to select personnel known already to hold such values. Probably, a combination of both of these is needed. However, each of these processes involves problems.

Currently there are no rapid, efficient ways to change deeply held values through resocialization.[6] If a person grows up with racist values, for instance, and the goal of resocialization is to make him nonracist, this change would be very difficult and could be accomplished, if at all, only with enormous expenditures of time and effort. This makes it exceedingly costly to resocialize persons who have deep-seated resistances to the goals demanded. Practitioners who tried to move from custodial to human relations models in prisons often found that the custodial staff had value positions antithetical to those required for rehabilitation, believing that prisoners were persons who threatened society and should be punished. In part, their initial efforts to change these values faltered because the discussions and training programs held for the staff were not effective enough as socializing influences.[7] Lengthy and intensive training is required to change basic values,

6. We are pessimistic about the capacity of current practices to bring about fundamental changes in values to a measurable extent or in reasonable time. The efforts of various professional groups to produce change in deviant behavior, such as delinquency, classroom unruliness, and the like, are not encouraging. One study bearing on this issue is by Henry J. Meyer, Edgar F. Borgatta, and Wyatt C. Jones, *Girls at Vocational High: An Experiment in Social Work Intervention* (New York: Russell Sage Foundation, 1965). Successful efforts at complex personal change usually involve long-term and continuous contact where the recipients have themselves already expressed a desire to change (for example, Alcoholics Anonymous, Weight Watchers, etc.) or situations where the target of change has been in a totalitarian setting where his behavior can be monitored twenty-four hours a day, such as in a concentration camps or the reported "brain washing" carried out by Koreans on American soldiers. See, for instance, Bruno Bettelheim, "Individual and Mass Behavior in Extreme Situations," *Journal of Abnormal Social Psychology*, 38 (1943), pp. 417-52. When new technology or new knowledge enable the change agent to speed up the process without engaging in totalitarian behavior, we would have to modify our position.

7. See Richard H. McCleary, *Policy Change in Prison Management*.

usually in a new setting where the individual can acquire different significant others (that is, people who they use as ideal types) and lose the influence of earlier ones.

Resocialization is much easier and attainable if the staff to be trained already holds the values which the human relations bureaucracy seeks to stress. In that case it might be sufficient merely to state the school's new goals and perhaps discuss them in several in-service workshops. For groups between these two extremes, one would need somewhat more intensive experience than the first but less intensive than the second. For instance, one might hold a summer workshop using more intensive group experiences, such as T-groups. This in turn might be buttressed by continuing the retraining process in an apprentice-type relationship where staff members work with a teacher who has internalized the values.

We would suggest that unless the change-agent properly assesses the degree of value internalization of the staff and carries out a resocialization program that fits the assessment, his efforts at change will be unlikely to succeed. Otherwise, what will usually happen is some superficial ideological changes, with the basic work activities remaining unchanged.

Such a consequence would not be the most serious result of a failure of resocialization when changing to a human relations structure. A greater danger is that incompetency may be encouraged by reducing direct supervision of the staff without providing the alternative mode, that is, internalization of organizational values. As a consequence, restraint may be removed from incompetent teachers, who may then do what they please. Thus, where one moves toward a human relations structure without proper resocialization one can easily end up with a laissez faire or nonmerit system. If the majority of the staff are only interested in their pay checks and not in teaching, this consequence is almost bound to arise.

A second way to acquire proper staff in a human relations structure is to hire persons who have already internalized the desirable values. Such a selection process cannot be used for quick changes where the existing staff is very large and many of them hold unacceptable values.

Selection processes are also limited by our inability to readily

select the desirable persons and also by legal or institutional restraints on hiring and firing of staff members. We do not often
have tests that accurately measure degree of internalization of
desirable values. Hiring criteria are often set by civil service or
state education departments, and they rarely include requirements concerned with internalized values other than loyalty to the
government. In many large cities, teachers are protected by both
civil service and by contracts with unions that would, under-
standably enough, object to any process that sought to eliminate
teachers on the ground that they did not have the right value
orientations. These same institutions, it should be noted, serve also
to protect teachers with desirable values when they are already
employed and threatened with dismissal. We do not imply that
the limitations on arbitrary hiring and firing are undesirable.
Indeed, they are probably necessary to protect the very autonomy
required for teachers in a human relations structure. The point is
that selection is a limited means of changing the value orientations
of the staff of a particular school in a short time. For any single
school within a system where staff is expanding and transfers to
other schools can readily be made, selection can be used with some
effectiveness, even though it is difficult to be sure about internalized values in the process. In some schools, the principal takes a
very active part in selecting replacements so as to add the kind of
teachers he needs to change his organizational style.

The conclusion to be drawn from discussion of problems
faced in attempting to facilitate change from a rationalistic to a
human relations administrative style is that such a change is
exceedingly difficult. The basic requirement is that the human
relations staff must internalize the educational goals and values
of the organization. Unless the situation is such that most of the
staff of the target school with a rationalistic structure already hold
such values, the costs of changing values with a reasonable ex-
penditure of effort and in a reasonable length of time are very high
and the outcome quite uncertain. Less than adequate resocialization may produce laissez faire or nonmerit administrative structures that can be educationally less desirable than the rationalistic
style they replace.

*From human relations to rationalistic structure.* The change from a human relations to a rationalistic structure is rarely discussed explicitly by organizational theorists.[8] However, changes in this direction are necessarily taking place, even though they may be described in different terms. Thus, a term such as "automation" generally implies that a system has moved to a more rationalistic structure than before. For instance, the payroll department of a school system after the installation of a large computer operation would generally be seen as more rationalistic. The introduction of programmed learning and teaching machines might well require a more rationalistic school structure because the teaching activities involved often need to be at least somewhat standardized and rules established to cover many of the contingencies that arise.[9]

In a school operating under a human relations administrative style the staff are generally accustomed to considerable autonomy in decision-making and to comparative freedom from supervision over daily work activities. The problem for a change agent is to prepare such a staff to accept greater supervision from superior authority and to follow prescribed rules for their work. In addition, this usually means that their work will be more observable and more readily available for evaluation.

The content and operations of many tasks for which a rationalistic structure is appropriate can usually be described and explained in detail. Hence, formal training sessions are often appropriate. A classroom procedure can be used to show twenty or thirty teachers how to operate a teaching machine, how to score the children's performance, and how to spot breakdowns in the

---

8. Indirectly, the problem is often involved in studies of the effects of automation. As an example, see Floyd Mann and L. R. Hoffman, *Automation and the Worker: A Study of Social Change in Power Plants* (New York: Holt, 1960). See also Herbert A. Simon, *The Shape of Automation for Men and Management* (New York: Harper and Row, 1965), Chapter III.

9. Some part of the teaching activities can be taken over by machines and become more rationalized. What in fact happens to the over all school structure depends in part on how the school then uses the teacher. If the number of teachers is reduced or the teachers are replaced by employees primarily equipped to handle the more mechanical tasks (taking care of the machines, checking attendance, etc.), the structure will be more rationalistic. If the school retains or increases the number of teachers and frees them to handle the more idiosyncratic aspects of teaching, it may develop a compartmentalized organizational structure.

system. The rules and requirements for using the machines can be explained and teachers judged on their compliance. Those who perform well can be recognized and rewarded and those who do not perform well can be corrected. It does not necessarily follow that the purpose of introducing teaching machines— presumably to increase learning by the students—will be achieved thereby, but insofar as proper use of the new method supports that purpose, it can be assured. The problem will not be in the task or in learning it but rather in having the staff accept the necessity for rules and standards externally imposed on their work performance.

Resistance to accepting such changes is likely to be generated by the nature of the human relations structure itself. It tends to foster autonomous persons, capable of making their own decisions, and responsive more to colleagues than is true in other structures. If staff members are adapted to these norms, they can readily organize formal as well as informal opposition if they feel the changes are not proper. Furthermore, accustomed to providing their own justifications for the way they have been working, the staff of a human relations organization can often advance persuasive arguments against innovations requiring more rationalistic arrangements. The change-agent may need to provide for extended discussions about the change and to allow acceptance of the innovation to come gradually if he is to avoid fatal opposition by collective action, individual noncompliance, or outright sabotage.

There is another potential source of resistance to which the change-agent should be sensitive. Americans in general who reach higher levels of education—particularly college and professional training—often come to identify discretion and autonomy as indicators of high-status jobs. Some school teachers and other staff accustomed to the autonomy of a human relations structure may feel their prestige threatened by loss of autonomy. They may consider the job itself reduced in status. This is a potential factor of unknown strength most likely to appear when teachers have strong professional self-identifications and least important when teachers are "careerists," that is, look on their jobs not as professional but primarily as a source of income.

A related point is that generally the greater the discretion permitted in a job the higher the formal educational requirement for it. If discretion is reduced as rationalistic organization is developed, the staff may face a type of technological over-education. That is, their professional skills are no longer necessary for the new jobs. Even displacement may be feared. The change-agent should be alert to this sense of threat to job security and, indeed, realistically plan for any contingencies that result from the shifted demands of the job.

It is evident from the considerations noted that there can be serious dangers in moving prematurely from a human relations to a rationalistic administrative style. The shift is hard to reverse.

If we designate gross categories of teachers by their orientations toward their jobs, we may note that a very large group, the "careerists," probably would object very little to the change toward rationalistic structure so long as their jobs were not threatened or substantial work added.[10] They would also be least likely to resist change and least successful in doing so. The greatest threat to them would be more visibility to objective evaluation, invading, perhaps, even the classroom, their safest haven for shaping the work to their convenience. A second group of teachers, those ideologically convinced that a "traditional" educational approach is better, would obviously welcome a more rationalistic structure. There are likely to be few such teachers, however, who remain in a school with a human relations structure. The teachers who can be called "missionaries," those with ardent dedication to education and teaching, would be likely to accept any change they came to believe advantageous in improving education.[11]

10. By "careerist" we mean a person who is basically interested in only the money earned and the time spent on the job and not in the purpose of the work, whether the child is learning or not. The typology of teachers is adopted from Harold L. Wilensky, *Intellectuals in Labor Unions* (Glencoe, Ill.: Free Press, 1956).

11. By "missionary" we mean a teacher whose identification is not with the teaching profession but solely with the children. Anything that would help the children learn is supported no matter how it might affect teachers as a profession. For instance, "missionaries" would be willing to support a policy calling for indigenous workers to replace trained teachers on an elementary school level if they felt this would help children learn better.

This would be the point for leverage in gaining their cooperation. Pupil-centered teachers and those operating in personalistic, nepotistic ways would probably be most opposed to the change. The former would object on ideological and philosophical grounds. The latter would object because a reduction in individual discretion would reduce also their chances for personal prejudices to operate.

To summarize, moves toward rationalistic structures and away from human relations structures can often be facilitated by rewards and penalties since tasks for the new form lend themselves to visible and more or less objective evaluation. Unlike the contrary move (from rationalistic toward human relations), winning cooperation is less necessary. However, the staffs of human relations organizations are often capable of organizing resistance rapidly and effectively, including counter ideological objections. They may also be very sensitive to the threat to their prestige and status which they may feel from a reduction of discretion in their jobs.

*Changing other organizational styles.* To move autocratic, laissez faire, or nepotistic structures toward a human relations style would involve much the same considerations as those discussed for moving a rationalistic structure. There would be some differences. Initial recruitment or attention-getting devices would involve getting approval from a single person in the autocratic structure; it would mean reaching almost every individual separately in the other two structures. The problems of resocialization and selection would be especially acute in nepotistic structures since biases contrary to those for which human relations structure is generally preferred in a school would have to be resocialized. The problems of changing each of these three structures to rationalistic ones would involve many of the same considerations as moving from a human relations to a rationalistic form. However, it should in general be much simpler to move from an autocratic to a rationalistic structure than to make any of the other shifts.

The one organization form which has somewhat unique problems is the compartmentalized organization. In this organization the chief problem arises when members of the organization do not recognize the legitimacy of two different types of administrative styles. Such recognition must be achieved. In addition, it is necessary to develop some mechanisms of isolation to keep the two different components separated while they work along side each other. However, within these qualifications the major problems of shift are usually the same as those already mentioned with respect to changing rationalistic and human relations styles.

## Organizational Opposition

The change-agent must face the fact that staffs might be differentially organized in their determination to resist change. At one extreme, the teachers might have a very tight friendship constituting the work group within the school and, in addition, belong to a powerful union joining them with other teachers in the city and to workers outside the school system. At the other extreme, the change-agent might be faced with a teaching staff which has almost no real interpersonal ties and no formal organized memberships. They may be indifferent to or even dislike each other. It is clear that the change-agent would have to employ a different strategy in the two cases. In the second case there is no need to gain agreement from the group as a group. Individual consent or reward and punishment can be used. In the first case the change-agent generally must gain some agreement from the entire staff before making a change effort or prepare for a major power struggle at the bureaucratic level—for example, between the school and the teachers' union. The ingredients of change and resistance become interorganizational rather than interpersonal and strategies have to be adjusted accordingly. The types of problems which arise are in part analogous to those discussed when the community intervenes in the school. In part they are analogous to interorganizational problems. We elaborate in chapter 12 on delegated function. It is brought to the reader's attention at this time so he can be alert to such factors if he seeks to promote change in administrative styles.

## Community Pressures and Organizational Change

Before concluding this chapter on organizational structures and social distance between school and community, we may briefly note how the various types of administrative structure seriously affect the type of linkage by which the community can reach them. From the discussion in chapter 1 of linking mechanisms from the community to the school, and from our previous discussion in this chapter, it can be expected that the same essential logic applies. For instance, the rationalistic structure is one in which the community most needs to use an advocate expert as a means of communicating with and influencing the school. The rationalistic structure implies more specialization, more rules and technical procedures. Therefore, experts are needed to understand the bureaucracy and to penetrate it with information, requests, or demands. A single decision, for example, about introducing materials on ethnic groups may involve teachers, principal, area specialists, perhaps even central officials of the school system and the school board. In contrast, many aspects of such a decision in a human relations structure, especially with a child-centered approach to education, rest with the teachers individually or in collegial interaction. No specialized knowledge of organizational structure is needed to make contact. Whoever is reached in the organization will understand the problem since all staff in human relations organizations tend to do the same thing—that is, they are generalists. In addition, the collegial decision process does provide a means to spread the message throughout the organization.

In contrast to either of the polar cases, the laissez faire style generally requires that the community use linkages of wide scope since little coordination or communication can be counted on. For a school with an autocratic administrative style, mechanisms that allow focus on the key administrator are necessary. In a structure dominated by nepotistic relations, other mechanisms will be called for, probably those going outside the target school to the total school system or to the larger community and adapted to the conditions found there. These comments should by now be familiar to the reader as derivations from the organizational theories we have been using throughout this chapter. What must be pointed out as different is whether an attempt should be made to use the internal structure of the school or an outside group as the vehicle for introducing change, or whether the community should intervene directly or through an advocate, and whether it should direct its attention to the top of the organization or the staff.

For instance, if one wants to increase the emphasis on vocational teaching, does one rely on the staff or bring in outside experts? In part the answer to this question depends on how close the staff and community are. If they share common viewpoints then the community has only to make its wishes known and the staff can undertake the development. In the language of our linkage theory, we are saying that the community can use a relatively passive mechanism with low bureaucratic resources. However, if the organization does not share common views with the community, the community may have to depend on outside resources to produce changes, and the linkages will involve high initiative and high bureaucratic resources. The exact form these linkages take will depend on the structure of the organization as well as on the nature of the innovation. Where the change involves nonuniform tasks, such as setting basic school policy on racism or sex education, the community groups can interfere directly. When dealing with technical issues like up-to-dateness of course content, the community must rely on an advocate expert. In the case of rationalistic organization, changes involving nonuniformity must be aimed at the top where they are customarily handled. The technical changes must be aimed at the staff who customarily perform them. In a human relations, laissez faire, or nepotistic organization, both types of changes must be aimed at the staff. In an authoritarian organization both types of changes must (initially) be aimed at the top. We need not repeat what has been discussed elsewhere about problems of the community influencing the organization. Our purpose is served here by illustrating the manner of analysis useful to follow when thinking about community strategies for changing school administrative styles.

## Summary

We can now summarize the key points of our discussion of how organizations create distance from the community and some problems of changing administrative styles. Imbalance can be created by failure of the school to acquire and use the technical expertise and marshal resources that are the hallmark of the bureaucracy, whatever organizational form is taken. Our focus has been, however, on imbalance caused by inappropriate administrative styles. Where the community is already too distant, maintaining a rationalistic structure is responsible for imbalance. The converse holds when human relations structure encourages overinvolvement. Incompetent and biased teachers, and other forms of nonmerit structures, may be responsible for imbalance. Social distance is a product of conditions in the school as well as in the community.

From the perspective of our organizational theory, attempts to introduce changes within rationalistic structures should be initiated at the top and formal modes of change used. Attempts to introduce changes in a human relations structure should be initiated with the collegial group and informal, apprenticeship-like experiences emphasized. To move a rationalistic structure toward a human relations structure requires that the staff internalize the values of the organization. This entails difficult programs of socialization, training, and selection. The change of a human relations structure to a rationalistic one basically involves persuading persons to accept and adhere to rules in a fairly formal situation to which they are unaccustomed. Finally, community groups must vary their linkage strategies depending on the types of organizations they confront.

# 4 ✤ Primary Groups and School Linkages: Family and Neighborhood Forms

In this chapter we describe some typical family and neighborhood forms that may characterize the community situation faced by a school undertaking a school-community program. We also outline some strategies of linkage involved. Since a bewildering combination of elements goes into defining family and neighborhood situations, all possible cases cannot be considered. Instead, general principles that practitioners can adapt to particular circumstances are suggested.

To develop diagnostic categories of families and neighborhoods we use three underlying dimensions. Primary groups are classified in terms of their values, knowledge, and structure-resources. A family in which these elements are positive for education is considered to be at optimum distance from the schools. A family in which they are negative is considered to be at an extreme distance. Excessive emphasis by the primary group on these elements may represent the over-close condition. In general, the family that is too close requires the school to use linkages that are passive, with low intensity and low focused expertise. The family that is distant requires linkages with high initiative, high intensity, and high focused expertise. Similiar considerations will be developed from the community's point of view.

## Family Forms and School Linkages

### Variations in Values and Attitudes

To illustrate how variations in values and attitudes of families create the need for schools to utilize different linking proce-

109

dures, we pose contrasting conditions. How do requirements for linkages differ when family values are antithetical to those of the school and when they are harmonious? Values antithetical to the school's will not necessarily be the same in different communities.

*Education, per se, as a value.* The most universally recognized value with respect to education is that education itself is necessary. Should children go or not go to school? How important is education for children, and how much schooling should they have?

In the United States until very recently education has been as sacred as motherhood. Very few citizens would openly minimize its importance.[1] In studies of low-income neighborhoods where children generally performed least well by educational criteria, most parents expressed high educational aspirations for their children.[2] Some families, however, had little interest in education and revealed low aspirations. Most identifiable among these were white transient families from the southern Appalachian region. By "transient" is meant families who came to the North primarily to earn enough money to enable them to return and live more comfortably in their home communities in the South. These families had no long-run educational goals for their children. They wanted to take them back to grow up and remain in the southern rural communities.

Another type of family is one which recognizes education as an important goal but the family situation dictates that it be given a secondary place. Thus, the mother whose husband is sick and who does not have enough money to buy food and pay the rent might encourage an adolescent child to drop out of school and take a job. Older people with no children in school or those retired on a fixed income and squeezed by inflation may give education a low priority by voting against school millage increases. In contrast are those families who give education a high priori-

1. Recent criticisms of formal education question this value, on the ground that education has become a status symbol rather than a necessary base for a productive life. Some writers suggest that educators are putting too much stress on education today. See Ivar Berg, *Education and Jobs: The Great Training Robbery* (New York: Praeger, 1970).

2. E. Litwak and H. J. Meyer, *Relationship Between School-Community Coordinating Procedures and Reading Achievement* (Final Report Project No. 5-0355, Contract No. OE-3-10-033, Office of Education, Bureau of Research, HEW, December 1966), pp. 175-207.

ty, and see education as the chief vehicle for social mobility. Even more extreme are the families for whom education has become such an overwhelming goal that most other family values are sacrificed for it. Parents in such families might express excessive interest in their child's education by applying pressure on the teacher to give high marks to the child so that he can get into the "best" university. These parents often put enormous pressure on their children as well as on the school.[3]

The hypothesis is that the less the family stresses education—for whatever cause—the more the school must develop linkages that allow initiative to the school and provide a high degree of intensity. High initiative is necessary because a negative or indifferent value orientation will make families passive and unlikely to come to the school. High intensity is necessary because changing basic values generally requires intensive contact over prolonged periods of time.

*Family attitudes towards staff and teaching philosophy.* Even if education is valued, family attitudes toward curriculum and teaching methods may lead to conflict between the family and school. There is a wide range of such attitudes, depending on particular circumstances. The relevance of this point is made clear by some recent controversies.

One of the most serious charges against school systems has been on the issue of race. Many black families have attacked the schools for being racist, finding evidence of racism in the low level of employment of black staff, attitudes of white staff toward black children, and lack of instructional material on black culture. Education as such is not attacked, but the school staff, the school curriculum, or both. School staff in such situations may take the opposite view, that is, black families are racists and their proposals damaging to education.

White parent groups have reacted by attacking school staff and curriculum. They are hostile to the school because, they claim it now favors black families, overlooking black childrens' offenses

3. For a classic discussion of the variety of ways teachers from the schools show favoritism toward wealthy children, see August B. Hollingshead, *Elmtown's Youth* (New York: Wiley 1949).

while punishing white children for the same offense. Some white families believe black children have better chances now of getting into colleges than white children.[4]

It should not be assumed that parental objection to educational policy is limited to the race issue. There is much controversy between schools and families over teaching philosophy. The development of "progressive education" or "pupil-centered education" was viewed by some as "communistic," "immoral," or just "bad education." When the controversy is intense, superintendents, principals, and teachers have been fired. Recently, the issue of sex education in public schools has led to disputes between school staffs and communities, as well as between segments of the community.

A continuing source of conflict between the schools and some elements of the public has been the issue of religious education in the schools—its lack or too great emphasis on it. Some parents have sought to prevent the schools from offering prayers, while others have sought to introduce prayers. Some parents have sought to eliminate Christmas celebrations in schools, others to encourage them.

A more subtle basis for evaluating schools has been that of social status. Families might approve of education but reject the school in their neighborhood because they feel superior to many of their neighbors. We found evidence for this in a low-income racially mixed neighborhood.[5] White families tended to have minimal contact with the school, not wanting to associate with black parents or black school personnel. Their concept of improving the educational milieu for their children was to leave the neighborhood. It was not education or the school personnel per se they objected to, but associating with lower-status people. It was not necessarily a question of race, upwardly mobile black families avoiding association with black lower-status families, as well as whites of higher status avoiding whites of lower status.

4. For some empirical evidence on this point, see Richard Lemon, *The Troubled Americans* (New York: Simon and Schuster, 1969), pp. 196-201.

5. See Litwak and Meyer, *Relationship Between School-Community Coordinating Procedures and Reading Achievement*, pp. 110-21, 139-54, 398-409.

These examples show that a community can have a broad set of criteria by which to judge a school as good or bad. In general, the same propositions about linkages hold for variations of family attitudes toward the school as they do for value commitment. Where the attitude toward the school leads to avoidance of contact (avoiding low-status people), the school must use high initiative and high-intensity linkages to close distance. If the attitude toward the school is a condemnation of its teaching philosophy, the school might utilize high-intensity linkages to change the attitude. It is not clear that it needs high initiative. In fact, it might need some linkages to keep the community members out of the school. Each set of attitudes and each situation requires its own diagnosis and prescription of linking mechanisms.

We have assumed thus far that schools will decrease distance by using linkages that have effects on the community groups. However, as pointed out in chapter 3, the school can often reach the outer community by changing its own structure, personnel, or curriculum. An adequate analysis must take both school and community into account.

## Knowledge and Linking Mechanisms

Related to but different from basic values and attitudes are questions of knowledge about the educational process. Distinguishing knowledge from values and attitudes highlights the need to provide focused expertise, as distinguished from initiative and intensity. Thus, an indigenous nonprofessional worker might be as good as, or better than, a professional teacher or social worker as change-agent when it comes to altering attitudes or values of a family. Often the nonprofessional may know more, have greater contact with, and be more trusted by the family when it comes to handling everyday activities.[6] In

6. For a discussion of some of the problems of this general type of linkage, see Gertrude Goldberg, "Nonprofessional Helpers: The Visiting Home Makers," in G. A. Brager and F. P. Purcell (eds.), *Community Action against Poverty* (New Haven: College and University Press, 1967), pp. 133-40.

contrast, the trained professional would be much better when questions of technical knowledge arise. Thus, to inform parents about the "new math" a trained teacher is generally needed.

Recognition of the difference between the dimensions of knowledge and of values helps to clarify the need for school initiative. Generally, when a family has a negative attitude toward education, the school must use high-initiative linkages to reach that family. However, when a family lacks knowledge of education, the school may or may not have to use high-initiative linkages. A family with a positive attitude toward school and low knowledge could probably be reached by low-initiative linkages.

In short, we suggest that school-community agents try to distinguish between knowledge and value-attitude aspects of family orientation. This will aid them in determining the relative needs for initiative, intensity, and expertise in their linkage procedures.

To clarify the diagnostic problem and to make the above abstract presentation more concrete, we present brief illustrations of types of families with respect to knowledge.

*Knowledge of curriculum content.* Some families know more about the content of the school curriculum than others. This knowledge allows parents to supplement the child's knowledge by tutoring, which in turn contributes to academic success. Parents who have gone to college can usually provide direct assistance if questions arise about homework. The less educated the parents, the more the school must seek to reach them by mechanisms that provide expertise. Teaching parents how to read better (or to read at all) relates directly to the child's rate of learning in school. This is recognized by many parents and is one of the reasons some of them give for going to evening school.[7]

*Knowledge of educational processes.* In addition to knowledge of curriculum, families vary also in knowledge about the educational process and the school bureaucracy. A knowledgeable parent can evaluate the quality of education the school is providing (that is, whether reading levels are above or below the national level). If

7. Reported in a study of adult education by Roberta Kean, December 1970, for Professor Donald I. Warren at The University of Michigan.

the child intends to go to college, the knowledgeable parent will try to assure that the school is preparing him for college entrance exams. The parent who is less knowledgeable may assume that the child is being well educated. In addition, knowledgeable parents will know better the education required for different kinds of jobs. They will be more apt to understand the relationship between studying and grades. They are also more likely to appreciate the limitations of their knowledge.

Knowledge of this sort comes to most middle-class parents from their own education, experience, and acquaintance with a range of occupations. By contrast, the less-educated family may have limited contacts with requirements of various occupations and little personal experience with the upper levels of the educational system. For these reasons, schools should offer to less-educated parents some technical information so that they can cooperate with and use the educational system.

*Knowledge indirectly related to education.* As investigators examine the processes of education, they discover environmental, health, and social factors, not directly educational, which influence the education of the child. Children can not be effectively educated if they have deficient diets, inadequate rest, insufficient clothing. Furthermore, their learning is apt to be impeded if their parents are involved in emotional strife.

For assistance with such problems, families must often know about community services. They should know what resources are available to help poor people purchase clothing and food, obtain proper medical attention, deal with emotional problems. Whether the school should offer these services or try to link the families to agencies is not a settled issue. It is clear that the school must be sensitive to knowledge issues such as these and should see that they are handled so as to support the major task of educating the child. Since most of these areas require specialized sources or expertise, the school should use the delegated function approach to handle these knowledge issues.

*Nonexpert knowledge.* Sometimes it is uncertain whether technical knowledge or everyday experience in socialization is needed. In such cases use might be made of linkages that provide high-intensity and moderate or selected kinds of knowledge. The schools might train and utilize indigenous community members, or employ a professional person as a detached worker with special experience in the community. Disciplining a child requires mixed knowledge. Classroom misbehavior may be attributable to parents' failure to socialize their child for proper school behavior. How does one teach parents the complex practices of child rearing? The expert can trace out for the parent the generalized strategy of child rearing currently considered best, for example, use more or less physical discipline, more or less verbal discipline, be more or less consistent. However, no expert can tell parents how to handle the everyday details that constitute the bulk of socialization activities. To teach such everyday activities the expert would have to go into the home and demonstrate them. Alternatively, if a neighbor or relative who has been successful in handling her own child is available, this indigenous person might be used to teach through demonstration. "Homemakers" offer good illustration of the use of indigenous workers as teachers.[8] Disciplining a child is a case of mixed knowledge because part of what needs to be known is learned through everyday socialization and part may be the result of expert knowledge. How to teach adults requires another kind of knowledge.

The central point here is that the type and degree of knowledge families possess or need must be diagnosed so that the school-community agent may decide if linkages require technical expertise and in what form.

*Family Resources and Structures*

Sociologists and practitioners often point out that values, knowledge, and other aspects of the family are secondary considerations for making a family diagnosis. The key factor is often the level of family resources—family income. The socioeconomic status of the family seems most clearly related to educational achievement. Some educators have argued that the single greatest

8. Gertrude Goldberg, "Nonprofessional Helpers: The Visiting Home Makers," in Brager and Purcell.

stimulus to improving educational achievement in our society would be to secure jobs and adequate incomes for all families with children.

The schools increasingly find themselves at the vortex of larger social forces. As a consequence of racial problems, schools have had to adjust their teaching to deal with bussing, with demands for hiring of minority members on teaching staffs, for decentralization. School staff should be increasingly aware that these educationally "remote" social issues have very concrete implications for their immediate tasks of teaching. Therefore, it may be valuable to give attention to the larger problem of income maintenance. School-community programs should seriously consider economic and social reform as part of their legitimate educational goals. If the schools are held responsible for dealing with educational consequences of inadequate income distribution, ignoring the issues of income maintenance, unemployment, and racial discrimination can cost education dearly.

The school must concern itself with additional problems associated with family resources. There are two kinds of poor families in our society. One may have started out with adequate resources and through mismanagement or misfortune fallen into circumstances from which it can not emerge by simply having more money. The business executive who becomes an alcoholic, loses his job, and leads his family to poverty will not be helped by money alone. He needs such services as those of Alcoholics Anonymous. The working man who loses an arm in an industrial accident needs, in addition to money, specialized occupational training and psychological support for carrying out his ordinary life activities. The mother of young children who loses a husband through death, desertion, or divorce needs not only money and perhaps counseling but also day care for her children if she must work. Thus, one part of the poor needs not just money but services as well.

A second—and probably more numerous—kind of poor family is one not brought to that position because of personal inadequacies, lack of knowledge, or lack of services. Its poverty is a consequence of malfunctioning of the larger social system—

racism that prevents black people from job opportunities that would guarantee economic security; technological innovation that disemploys large numbers of people; inadequate education; and other impersonal forces that result in insufficient income.

For this substantial part of the poor, providing jobs and adequate income might end their patterns of poverty, including perhaps the inability of their children to stay in the educational system. There is no assurance that society will pay heed to their plight. If the poor are going to get the money and opportunities they need, they must somehow gain the political and economic power to affect the larger society.

If this analysis is correct, one function that can be provided by such organizations as schools is to serve as a triggering device by providing noneconomic supplements to the limited resources of poor families. With such aid, families with marginal incomes might better understand how to undertake social actions on their own behalves. Thus, contrary to the views of Daniel P. Moynihan and others, critics have pointed out (rightly or wrongly) that the family structure of the poor is actually a vital and viable force protecting the poor in face of the inadequacies of the larger society.[9] These structures, if distinctive, are at best self-defense mechanisms. They do not often provide the basis for positive efforts to change the social system, to move from self defense to effective modification of bureaucratic organizations on their behalf. The schools can, if they will, play an important role in the first stages of community organization.

Lacks in family structures of the poor are not viewed as faults of the families involved, and they can for the most part be corrected by adequate funds. But to insure that there is pressure on the larger system to provide funds it is necessary that large organizations, such as the school system, supplement and support the families as they can.

9. Hylan Lewis "A. Agenda Paper No. V: The Family: Resources for Change—Planning Session for the White House Conference *To Fulfill These Rights*, November 16-18, 1965," in Lee Rainwater and William L. Yancey, *The Moynihan Report and the Politics of Controversy* (Cambridge, Mass.: The MIT Press, 1967), pp. 314-43; Elizabeth Herzog, "Is There a Breakdown of the Negro Family?" *Social Work* (January 1966), pp. 78-184.

Some of the ways in which limited resources manifest themselves in low-income families are noted below:

1. Lack of money might make it impossible for a mother to take advantage of labor-saving devices and hence require exhausting work in handling such everyday household chores as washing clothes. Lack of time and energy means that mothers may not be able to devote the amount of time that middle-class mothers spend in supervising their children's education (for example, attending teacher conferences and reading to the child).

2. Lack of money might mean that parents are unable to provide the child with adequate food and clothing and other prerequisites to the child's energy and capacity to do his schoolwork.

3. Lack of money might increase competition between parents, among other family members, and among neighbors over limited resources. This could lead to hostility among them and lack of cooperation with the school. Perhaps a good index of the latter is the pressure on children to leave school and earn money.

4. Lack of money often means that the man is unemployed. In our society this often leads to a loss of personal self esteem and increasing apathy on the part of the man, hostility and a sense of her husband's inadequacy on the part of the woman, and marital conflict generated from role reversals in which the woman can get a job and the man cannot. As a consequence, there is a strong association of divorce, family breakup, and marital discord with low income. Such tensions between parents are not likely to provide the proper support for children's educational success. Alternatively when one parent leaves the family resources may often become insufficient for supervision of the children.

5. Illness often contributes to poverty and is one of its consequences as well. A family with an adult member crippled by illness can supervise its children even less.

6. The fewer adults there are per child, the more the family resources are limited at a given income level. Thus, a family with only one adult is less able to supervise children than a family with two adults. A family with two adults and two children is better able to supervise a child than a family with two adults and five

children. Assuming the number of adults in the family is the same, the family which can count on aid from relatives will have more resources than a family which cannot.

7. Families that recognize the complementary functions of bureaucracies and kinship systems will have more resources than others. By this we mean that the family recognizes the importance of bureaucratic organizations and utilizes them. On the other hand, the family sees that it does not have unlimited responsibility to relatives. In our study we found some southern white families who mistrusted all governmental agencies. When unemployed they would borrow money from impoverished relatives or encourage their children to drop out of school and become self-supporting rather than have anything to do with agencies designed to help them. Their values and behavior were characteristic of that which social scientists have identified with the "extended family."[10] This contrasts with the "modified extended family," whose members take help from both relatives and bureaucracies.[11]

Illustrations of factors making for weak family structure

10. The classical extended family is one in which married children live with their parents, the household members involved in the same economic endeavor, with one person controlling the finances and occupational career of all others, and where there is a strong view that family relations supersede all other considerations. Family members are expected to hire their relatives in preference to all others, no matter what their competencies may be. Although it is hard to find pure cases of such a family type, except in preindustrial agricultural societies, there are some families in modern society that have many of the essential characteristics we loosely describe as those of the classical extended family. For descriptions of family types and their relationship to modern industrial society see William J. Goode, *World Revolution and Family Patterns* (New York: The Free Press of Glencoe, 1963), pp. 6-18, 296-300; Marvin B. Sussman, "Relationships of Adult Children with their Parents in the United States," in Ethel Shanas and Gordon F. Streib (eds.), *Social Structure and the Family: Generational Relations* (Englewood Cliffs, N. J.: Prentice-Hall, 1965), pp. 62-93; Eugene Litwak, "Extended Kin Relations in an Industrial Democratic Society," in *ibid.*

11. In the modified extended family, kin have semiautonomous relationships to each other. Relatives exchange services in certain nonuniform areas of life, while in others they recognize the autonomy of the nuclear family (husband, wife, and minor children) as well as the need for larger bureaucratic organizations to handle the uniform tasks. For instance, kin are expected to help when a relative is seriously sick. However, doctors and hospitals are expected to handle the major medical treatment problems and nuclear family members are expected to provide the major source of emotional support to the ill family member. Relatives are supposed to provide only the support of helping out with shopping and giving supplemental emotional support. See Eugene Litwak, "Extended Kin Relations in an Industrial Democratic Society," in Shanas and Streib (eds.).

indicate that there is no single principle by which to judge whether defects in structure will require linkages by the bureaucracies
using high or low initiative, high or low intensity, high or low
expertise. In a single-parent home with small children highly
disposed toward education, the parent might be brought into the
school simply by providing babysitting services. On the other
hand, if the resources of the family are very low, and the woman
is ill and unable to cope with managing everyday family affairs,
the way to get her cooperation may be for the bureaucracy to send
someone into the home to provide medical attention or proper
homekeeping. This would require mechanisms with high initiative. If there were a medical problem, high expertise would be
needed, whereas a homemaker with relatively low expertise might
be adequate in a management problem. Breakdown of family
structure is rarely a direct result of education. As a consequence,
the school must either undertake new services not directly educational but seriously affecting education or develop processes for
working through other organizations (delegated function). It is
important that the school-community agent be sensitive to structural problems of families so as to choose linkages best adapted to
the problem in light of the need for balancing distance. There is
no simple set of rules that will automatically provide answers.

There are many substantive areas with which our theory of
linkages does not deal. Our analysis alerts the school to the need
for linkages with low or high initiative, low or high primary group
intensity, low or high expertise. It does not tell the schools within
which substantive areas of life they must be prepared to work. It
does not say that services must be directly educational, medical,
large-scale social reform, marital counseling, or in other areas.

*Family Typology*

Using the three variables previously discussed—values,
knowledge, and structure-resources—we suggest a simplified
scheme for classifying families. These variables can be associated
with certain underlying dimensions of linking mechanisms, such
as focused expertise with family knowledge, primary group inten-

sity with family values, and family resources with both. Moreover, these basic dimensions of the family are not necessarily correlated so that at least three independent assessments need to be made before it is reasonable to state the extent of social distance between the family and the school, and consequently what forms of linkages are preferable.

On this basis, the conceptual table that follows indicates all possible family types derived from combining these variables, assuming each variable to be dichotomous. This is merely a simplifying assumption, and the reader can fit any particular empirical case between the extremes suggested in Table 7.

If we consider the various combinations, it becomes clear that the families closest to the schools are those that have the supportive values ("acceptors"), have the requisite knowledge ("informed"), and have ample resources ("well-off"). Family Type 1 might be represented by parents who feel that education is important and who agree with the school's current educational policy, who have an intact parental family with kin they can draw on if necessary, and who have had sufficient education themselves to be aware of what is necessary to help their children succeed in school. Of all the types, this one also runs the greatest risk of becoming "too close" to the school or over-involved in the educational bureaucracy.

The most difficult family type the school might face, and a type distant from the school, is one with values that are negative toward the school and a structure and knowledge base to support these values (Family Type 8). It is the intact family that is willing and able to use other large organizations as allies against the school. A "modified extended family" recognizes the legitimate division between the nuclear family and bureaucratic organizations. This family type is generally for education but may be very much against the particular philosophy or practice of education in a given school in its neighborhood. It may be against sex education, the pupil centered approach, or the ban on prayers in schools.

Another type of family that may be almost as severe an opponent of the school may be more distant than this type. It

## Table 7   Family Types

| Description of Family Types | Support for Educational Values | Knowledge of Educational Processes | Resource-structure for Implementing Goals |
|---|---|---|---|
| 1. Well-off, informed, acceptors. Educated, intact, well-off family with kin support, and positive toward school policy. | high | high | high |
| 2. Poor, informed, acceptors. Educated, broken and poor family, without kin support and positive toward school policy. | high | high | low |
| 3. Well-off, uninformed, acceptors. Poorly educated, intact, well-off family, with kin support, and positive toward school policy. | high | low | high |
| 4. Poor, uninformed, acceptors. Poorly educated, broken family, poor without kin support, and positive toward school policy. | high | low | low |
| 5. Poor, uninformed, rejectors. Poorly educated, broken family, poor without kin support, and negative toward school policy. | low | low | low |
| 6. Poor, informed, rejectors. Educated, broken family, poor without kin support, and negative toward school policy. | low | high | low |
| 7. Well-off, uninformed, rejectors. Poorly educated family, intact, well-off with kin support, and negative toward school policy. | low | low | high |
| 8. Well-off, informed, rejectors. Educated, intact, well-off with kin support, and negative toward school policy. | low | high | high |

holds values opposed to the school and probably toward education generally, and has a viable structure to support its values. It is likely to be working-class in background and of limited educational level. (Family Type 7 most nearly approximates this family.) Some southern white families that migrate from the Appalachian area but intend to return often have a strong family structure whose aspiration is that the children hold the same occupational level as the father, that of unskilled labor or subsistence farming. The school system is often viewed as an outside and biased bureaucracy, an enemy of the family. The central value is to keep the family intact and to protect its autonomy from all other institutions. This approximates the "classical extended family." This type of family is not easily won over by the school because it is well able to defend the individual's resistance to the school.

On first glance at the typology contained in the paradigm of Table 7, one might think of Type 5 as the most distant from the school. It has negative educational values, limited knowledge about education, and is low in resources and structural capabilities. With these characteristics, families on welfare are often negatively sterotyped: the father absent from the home, the mother burdened by children that she cannot properly supervise, no educational, social, or moral values that can be appealed to. This family situation is most difficult to deal with, but less so than the two types previously discussed. A favorable attitude of some sort toward "education" is so pervasive in American society that this type of family has rarely been encountered in our experience. It is definitely not typical of the families on public welfare we have studied.

Family Type 4 was most often seen among welfare families or very poor families where the parents had received little education yet realized that their children's chances of success depended on education. However, their lack of knowledge and resources prevented them from properly supervising their children. To reach this type of family the school would have to provide linkages with both expertise and primary group intensity. The chances are also very great that there must be a modest degree of initiative since a family without knowledge or resources is difficult to reach even if they have the "proper" values. They most likely cannot attend after-school classes. If they have the motivation they do not have the money. After-school classrooms for parents which provide baby sitting, transportation, and other needed items might illustrate the kind of linkage that may be necessary to reach this type of family. It would probably be necessary for school staff to recruit such families.

Between the extremes lie many other family types, and a brief discussion of some of them might illustrate how the diagnostic problem can be approached and how this leads to specific design of linkages.

Family Type 2 is prevalent in one study of inner city families, generally black, with moderately well-educated parents working at semiskilled or unskilled jobs. They had positive educational values and a good grasp of what it takes to make one's way. But both parents had to work to earn sufficient income for the family. The analogous situation was often found among single women with children on welfare. The mother might be educated and motivated to do something for her child, but had limited resources. In such cases almost any income maintenance scheme which put money into the household could achieve dramatic results educationally. Lacking this, any services the schools can provide to aid in the supervision of the child should be beneficial: baby sitting, after-school supervised recreation, nursery schools for small children, homemakers to help with household work— freeing the mother for supervision of the child. In terms of linkages, these efforts require moderate initiative, high primary-group intensity, and low-focused expertise. These linkages are typified by the use of indigenous workers.

There is yet another group of families that fit Type 3 and have much in common with Type 2. Type 3 families might be fathered by skilled workmen who are earning a good living, who value education, and want their children to "get ahead." However, the parents might both be of less than grade school education. Some rural migrant families from the South fit this description, but most of the inner city families interviewed displayed more education than expected. Type 3 was probably more typical twenty years ago than today. For such families the stress must be on providing a knowledge base. In the case of immigrant families in the 1920s, this meant actually holding language classes. The linkage here can again be fairly passive, with low primary-group intensity and high expertise. Thus, after-school classes in various subject matters—addressed to the parents—would be a major form of appropriate linkage. One reason parents take educational courses is to become more literate so they can help their children in their school work.

Family Type 6 is often associated with downwardly mobile families in our society. This type of family might, as a consequence, also be poor and have only one parent present. The parents may have had considerable education but be alcoholic, addicted to drugs, or mentally ill. A disability makes it difficult for them to stress educational goals. It generally requires linkages with great initiative as well as primary-group intensity. The community agent must be involved in basic value changes as well as provide structural support. Thus, procedures which are equivalent to aggressive casework or detached street work with delinquent gangs should be developed for such families. These families differ from Family Type 8 in that there is no need to intervene with an educational expert. This type of family might do best when put into close contact with other families who are willing to help.

## Neighborhood Forms and School Linkages

The concept of neighborhood has not been well developed in the social sciences because many students of modern societies have argued that neighborhoods are not viable under industrialized, urban conditions. It is said that the neighborhood provides too small a manpower base for sustaining the specialization that modern industrial society requires. It has too much member mobility to maintain primary group ties, and it is subject to external forces of socialization (for example, large school systems and mass media) that destroy the possibility of developing a distinctive living style or identity. Thus, the neighborhood has neither an important function to perform for the larger society nor the means to do it.[12]

We think, to the contrary, that neighborhoods, like other primary groups, must handle the innumerable nonuniform tasks that continue to confront modern societies. Furthermore, we feel that among the possible primary groups only the neighborhood can perform some of these "nonuniform tasks."[13] Two important activities that neighbors are uniquely able to perform are nonuniform tasks which involve time emergencies, or those tasks based technologically on territory.[14] To put the matter in the most common-sense terms, only a neighbor is in a regular position to tell a mother that her small child has wandered into the street; only a neighbor shares common interest with a mother about having a traffic light put on the corner so small children can cross safely; only neighbors have a common interest in having the garbage collection on the street improved; only local residents are strongly concerned about having the local school building well maintained and well staffed. Only children in the neighborhood can provide the immediate everyday socialization that young children receive in their spontaneous play after school. A family must face up to the fact that, very likely, if the neighbor's children are not educationally well prepared, their own children will receive a lower standard of education in the local school. These kinds of nonuniform tasks can not be handled by the larger kin unit because they are unlikely to live in the same neighborhood; they can not be handled by the nuclear family because it does not have sufficient primary group resources.

To handle these essential nonuniform functions, the neighborhood, unlike the nuclear family, has to deal with the problem

12. Roland Warren, *The Community in America* (Chicago: Rand McNally, 1963), pp. 53-94. The trends that Warren points out are destructive to the local neighborhood but not to the local community.

13. Eugene Litwak and Ivan Szelenyi, "Primary Group Structures and Their Functions: Kin, Neighbors, and Friends," *American Sociological Review*, 34 (August, 1969), pp. 465-81.

14. Litwak and Szelenyi, *ibid;* Eugene Litwak and Josefina Figueira, "Technological Innovation and Theoretical Functions of Primary Groups and Bureaucratic Structures," *American Journal of Sociology*, 73 (January 1968), pp. 468-81.

of high mobility among its members, as well as with problems of intergroup conflict. We must therefore analyze ways in which neighborhoods in contemporary society deal with rapid changes in membership and with conflict and still retain cohesiveness.[15]

In addition, it would be foolish for school officials to ignore the immediate realities of the neighborhood. A school in a neighborhood where parents are hostile, where children are not adequately prepared, where families barely maintain minimum living standards, will present a very different teaching problem than one in a community with the opposite characteristics.

We seek to develop a preliminary typology of neighborhoods so that the school-community agent may diagnose the type of neighborhood he is dealing with and the possible implications for linkage policies. Again, we are limited to fairly general descriptions, but hope that an understanding of general principles will enable school personnel to interpret the specific details of their unique situations.

In developing a typology of neighborhoods we will discuss some of the same factors we discussed in our family typology, that is, values and organizational resources. In addition something will be said about the way neighborhoods are organized (organized to handle change, to deal with subgroup conflict or with homogeneous stable situations).

In the following discussion, we refer to several different overlapping geographical areas when talking about neighborhoods. These are "next door neighbors," "people on the block," and "people within a ten-minute walk."[16] There are important differences between these territorial groupings but only the features they have in common will be considered.[17] Our discussion

15. Phillip Fellin and Eugene Litwak, "Neighborhood Cohesion Under Conditions of Mobility," *American Sociological Review,* 28(June 1963), pp. 364-76.

16. Shimon Spiro, "Definitions of Neighborhood." Paper prepared for Seminar on Community Cohesion, University of Michigan School of Social Work, 1966 (Mimeographed). *See also* Richard Dewey, "The Neighborhood, Urban Ecology, and City Planning," in Paul K. Hatt and Albert J. Reiss, Jr. (eds.), *Cities and Society: The Revised Reader in Urban Sociology* (New York: Free Press of Glencoe, 1957), pp. 783-90.

17. The smaller, intimate neighborhoods can handle problems that require only a small increment of resources over those of the nuclear family and at the same time are related to "time emergencies." The larger neighborhoods provide the manpower base for

can be applied with some caution to the high school and junior high communities, even though they generally consist of several neighborhoods. Moreover, a somewhat different analysis would have to be made of school communities where the children are bussed to school from different neighborhoods.

*Neighborhood Norms or Values*

Neighborhoods, like families, can evince positive or negative attitudes toward education or the school system. Studies have suggested that various neighborhoods tend to stress value orientations that are hostile to the larger society's views on good citizenship which the school system usually endorses.[18]

How do these neighborhood considerations differ from those discussed for families? First, in dealing with a neighborhood we have to consider such problems of scope as the number of families to be reached. For instance, attempts to change values generally require a linkage with high intensity. Considering the same problem in a neighborhood context, we must ask how many of the families in the neighborhood the school must reach. If they are considerable in number, the linkage mechanism must be wide in scope. Perhaps there should be a combination of a limited detached worker for recruitment purposes and a settlement house (an after-school activity) which stresses an intensive resocialization program involving T-groups, role-playing groups, behavior modification procedures, and the like, all designed to change attitudes and values. On the other hand, if there are only a few families to be reached, a detached-worker program might suffice, with no need for a large after-school program.

---

developing voluntary associations and political protest movements. They can not handle the intimate neighborhood exchanges that require people to know each other well and be immediately available. They cannot warn a mother that her child has wandered into the street.

18. Solomon Kobrin, "The Conflict of Values in Delinquency Areas," in Herman D. Stein and Richard A. Cloward (eds.), *Social Perspectives on Behavior* (New York: Free Press of Glencoe, 1958), pp. 498-505; Albert J. Reiss, Jr., and Albert L. Rhodes, "The Distribution of Juvenile Delinquency," *Journal of Social Issues,* 14 (July 1958), pp. 38-51.

*Multiple Groups*

The second consideration raised by the analysis of neighborhoods is recognition that the school might simultaneously have to deal with two or more different groups. For instance, it is possible in a low income neighborhood to find that although the majority of the people do not have values conducive to education a small minority do. The school has to decide whether it should try to reach both parts of the community. In the case of the small minority who favor the school, the staff might find that passive, low scope, moderate to low-intensity mechanisms might suffice to attract the families. In our study of inner city schools in 1962, we found several instances where parent-teacher associations were dominated by a small clique of parents who systematically excluded all others. They were generally better educated and more active women who did not want to associate with the rest of their neighbors. What the P.T.A. did for these families was to reinforce their positive attitudes toward school, thereby providing a useful educational function for a limited number of families. However, the use of this passive, low-scope linkage also meant that the majority of the neighborhood whom the school most needed to reach was being ignored. It was clear that trying to reach the two groups by using the same linkage mechanisms would be very difficult. Schools should perhaps use the passive low-scope mechanism for the minority and a high-initiative, high-scope, high-intensity mechanism for the majority. At some later date the two groups might be brought together. Alternatively, the school might decide that its resources were too few to deal with more than one group. Without trying to work through all the alternatives, we stress the central point that where there is more than one group it may be necessary to use different modes of linkage or, at least, make an explicit decision as to which group one will try to reach. Otherwise, the school will attract only those families favorably disposed toward education.

The multiple-group neighborhood has further implications for linkage theories, depending on whether the majority does or does not support the school. Where the neighborhood majority does not support the school, it is often wise for the school to utilize low-scope methods initially in order to reach the minority without alerting the majority. To illustrate, if the school wants to introduce sex education, and the majority of the community is opposed, then the community might contact its supporters with a low-scope method such as sending out detached workers to talk privately to parents who favor the program. Otherwise, if the school's intention becomes too quickly known, the majority may quickly mobilize to act and quash the program before it has a chance to develop.[19]

On the other hand, where the majority supports the school, the school staff can frequently make use of wide-scope methods as well as indigenous workers and opinion leaders to handle the problem of changing deviant values among the minority. This generally works where the school is interested in changing some attitudes or values and where the minority and majority members agree on most other things. For instance, if a family is heavily involved in the neighborhood but is deviant on educational values, the school might do best by asking an opinion leader or an indigenous worker who knows this family well to deal with the problem of change.

Where the minority group is rejected by the majority (for example, low-income families who have just moved into a high-income area), the majority can not be used as a channel of influence because they will refuse to associate with the minority. Similarly, where the residents in a minority refuse to associate with the majority, (a small group of upwardly mobile families in low-income areas), it may be difficult to use the indigenous majority to influence the minority. In such circum-

19. Illustrative of times when limited publicity is important are the fluoridation disputes. There is evidence that when city officials consider a law on the use of fluoridation they are more likely to pass it if they handle it with a minimum of publicity. They are more likely to lose the vote on the law if they maximize publicity by public referendum. Robert Crain, Elihu Katz, and Donald Rosenthal, *Politics of Community Conflict: The Fluoridation Decision* (New York: Bobbs-Merrill, 1968); William Gamson "Community Issues and Their Outcome: How to Lose a Fluoridation Referendum," in A. Gouldner and S. M. Miller (eds.), *Applied Sociology: Principles and Problems* (Glencoe, Ill: Free Press, 1965).

stances, it will be necessary to use a mechanism such as the detached-worker approach to reach the minority.

Thus far in our discussion of neighborhood subunits we have spoken about subgroups that have conforming or nonconforming attitudes toward education. However, some of the major problems arise in multigroup neighborhoods because of ethnic, economic, or racial status conflicts between groups. Thus, there might be neighborhood conflicts between blacks and whites, Italian and Irish, working-class and upper-class people. Even when these conflicts do not take place over educational matters, the very fact of conflict may seriously impede the educational process. The conflict often carries over into the school building and makes teaching difficult.

Traditionally schools have adopted a passive attitude toward such conflicts, implicitly supporting homogeneous neighborhood groupings. For instance, when a new group moved into a city neighborhood and the old group fought to keep them out, the school usually kept silent. If the old group, often wealthier and more educationally oriented, moved to a new neighborhood some members of the school staff would move with them. The more experienced teachers would move to the new neighborhood and the less experienced teachers would continue to be assigned to the old one.

The school desegregation decision of the Supreme Court makes this implicit philosophy of supporting homogeniety less possible. The Supreme Court decision in principle decreed that schools would have to live continously with mixed neighborhoods. Various social science studies have suggested that such mixed-class neighborhoods might be particularly advantageous for children who come from families with fewer resources.[20]

20. There is evidence that poor children who live in wealthier neighborhoods perform better in school than poor children who live in homogeneously poor neighborhoods. See Alan B. Wilson, "Social Stratification and Academic Achievement," in A. Harry Passow (ed.), *Education in Depressed Areas* (New York: Bureau of Publications, Teachers College, Columbia University, 1963); James Coleman *et al., Equality of Educational Opportunity* (Washington, D. C., U. S. Department of Health, Education, and Welfare, U. S. Government Printing Office, 1966); William H. Sewell and J. Michael Armer, "Neighborhood Context and College Plans," *American Sociological Review,* 31 (April 1963), pp. 34-40.

If heterogeneous neighborhoods with potential status or ethnic conflicts are to be typical, the school staff might have to build into its community linkages some adjudication procedures, such as mediation, arbitration, and the like, to settle disputes between community groups. Such procedures would generally seek to avoid open conflicts that might shut down a school, instead encouraging symbolic debates that would permit the school to stay open. To use an analogy, most disagreements in the early days of union-management relations would end up in strikes or work stoppages. As union and management became more sophisticated, they developed a whole system of mediation and arbitration of grievances that meant that the majority of disputes could be settled without a strike. The strike was reserved for major contract negotiation. We do not yet have a good idea of the form that neighborhood adjudication processes might take. We can only say that the school should encourage linkages that have this capacity if they are to have in one school building groups that are hostile to one another. Perhaps a look at the system of grievance procedures developed in the union-management field might serve as a starting point.

*Neighborhood Mobility*

Another set of issues to which the school should give attention concerns variations in responses to neighborhood mobility. Some neighborhoods legitimate the movement of old residents and welcome newcomers while others bitterly resist any efforts to change them.[21] Failure to give attention to ways of handling population change can be serious because an industrial society is a mobile one. Families might be forced to move to find a new job, or because the family has increased or decreased in size. Sometimes they are forced to move because the larger society finds different use for their location, such as for new expressways. At other times they are lured into moving in order to advance their careers and they can afford better housing. Finally, housing, like

21. Fellin and Litwak, "Neighborhood Cohesion Under Conditions of Mobility," *American Sociological Review*.

many other products in an industrial society, is being continuously improved and people sometimes move to get a "better product." Whatever the reason, there is an enormous amount of turnover in the neighborhoods of large cities. It is important to recognize that such movement is not based on personal whim but built into the fiber of an industrial society. Efforts to maintain neighborhoods with stable populations are antithetical to the needs of such a society and are only successful at great sacrifices to the neighborhood inhabitants.

What may be called the "traditional neighborhood" was organized on the principle of membership stability. In general, newcomers were not welcomed and those who moved out were considered deviant. Those who did move often felt obliged to justify themselves by invidious statements about those who remained, describing them as poorly educated, lacking culture, providing a poor school experience for children, and the like. Both mover and stayer were defensive because both accepted the view that the neighborhood was, in ideal terms, permanent. Perhaps classic in this orientation were the immigrant groups whose neighborhood and ethnic identities closely overlapped.[22] Such neighborhood groups resisted the introduction of newcomers. The demands of the larger society for mobility and of the "traditional neighborhood" for stability have produced the conflicts and clashes between ethnic, racial, and socioeconomic groups so characteristic of American urban history. In earlier days when a substantial part of the population had only brief contact with the educational system, schools could afford to ignore the educational consequences of neighborhood changes and disruption. However, as more and more of the population has entered the educational system for longer and longer times, and as the larger society has made greater and greater demands on the educational system to educate every child, the school can no longer avoid dealing with the problem of residential turnover in neighborhoods and the accommodations to meet the problem.

22. See William Foote Whyte, *Street Corner Society* (Chicago: University of Chicago Press, 1955). People who went to college and left the neighborhood were often considered snobs.

One development of importance to the school is the emergence of what we may call "mobility neighborhoods." These are neighborhoods where there is substantial membership turnover but little conflict. A number of studies have suggested that it is possible to have neighborhoods where families move in and out but both mover and stayer have positive feelings about each other.[23] To aid in understanding the principles upon which they operate, we describe some of the distinguishing features of the "mobility neighborhood."

There are two major differences between the "traditional" and the "mobility" neighborhood. Residents in mobility neighborhoods see a complementary relation between large bureaucratic organizations and neighborhood groups. In additions, residents in mobility neighborhoods have a series of techniques designed to speed up the integration of newcomers into the neighborhood. By contrast the residents of "traditional" neighborhoods are inclined to see large bureaucratic organizations as threating to the local neighborhood and to stress techniques to keep newcomers out.[24]

One way by which residents of mobile neighborhoods speed up integration of newcomers is by cultivating a "steppingstone reference group orientation." This means that they do not necessarily view their current neighborhood as a permanent place of residence but as a rung on a ladder. To move up this ladder, it is necessary for all neighbors to help each other. As a consequence, newcomers to the neighborhood are greeted as potential allies and residents who are leaving are helped along as possible future allies.[25] The mobility neighborhood legitimates mobility while legitimating integration into the current neighborhood. To facil-

23. Leon Festinger, Stanley Schacter, and Kurt Back, *Social Pressures in Informal Groups* (Palo Alto, Calif: Stanford University Press, 1967), pp. 33-59; William H. Whyte, Jr., *The Organization Man,* (New York: Simon and Schuster, 1956); Fellin and Litwak, "Neighborhood Cohesion Under Conditions of Mobility."

24. For a classic formulation of the idea that personal orientations can be distinguished by identification with a local group or with the wider society, see Robert K. Merton, "Local and Cosmopolitan Influentials," in Roland L. Warren (ed.), *Perspectives on the American Community* (Chicago: Rand McNally 1966), pp. 251-65.

25. William H. Whyte, Jr., *The Organization Man,*; Fellin and Litwak "Neighborhood Cohesion Under Condition of Mobility."

itate smooth transitions in neighborhood membership, it is necessary to help residents develop something like a "steppingstone
reference orientation."

Residents of mobility neighborhoods also tend to see abilities as determined largely by a person's experience rather than his
biological inheritance. They are therefore inclined to accept advice from others about personal and family relations. There is a
rationale for interaction with neighbors, even newcomers, about
personal and family problems. By contrast, in traditional neighborhoods personal and family problems are seldom discussed or
discussed only with trusted long-time friends. The relative freedom of interaction in the mobility neighborhood encourages the
rapid integration of newcomers. Encouraging the development of
a neighborhood norm that accepts newcomers into more intimate
areas of life is one way to promote the development from a traditional to a mobility neighborhood.

In addition to these cultural norms, mobility neighborhoods often have organizational devices for speeding up the integration of newcomers. For instance, they may have specific organizations set up to welcome newcomers, such as welcome wagons
and PTA mothers who are asked to speak to new parents. These
neighborhoods also often have local voluntary associations consist-
ing of neighbors and dealing with local neighborhood problems
which encourage rapid formation of friendships. Through them,
newcomers can legitimately take the initiative in contacting
neighbors and learn in semipublic ways the particular neighborhood norms. The mobility neighborhood also encourages contact
with newcomers in areas such as schools where there is likely to
be some common value agreement. Furthermore, they tend to
mute possible areas of conflict, for example, by local ecumenical
movements with all faiths meeting in the same building or by
councils of ministers, priests, and rabbis who explicitly cooperate.
They might have a local race relations committee to handle potentially divisive problems related to ethnicity.

Our analysis suggests that many of the mechanisms for
rapid integration in neighborhoods evolve from occupational experiences in large bureaucratic organizations where persons at

management levels frequently have to go through a process of mobility and cooperation. Extended experiences, particularly in higher education, tend to cultivate a long term perspective of orderly change. Some of the procedures used also depend on a knowledge base of residents that equips them to run local organizations, as well as on the availability of adequate resources.[26]

What can be done by schools in poorer and less-educated communities is not clear. Many such neighborhoods lack the necessary occupational experiences, educational level, and resources. We have no direct suggestions for these circumstances but suspect that the experience of immigration to the United States may provide some answers, since various immigrant groups with few resources had to solve similar problems. What is important is being sensitive to this problem when a school-community program is developed.

We suggest that changes in neighborhood values might be encouraged through linkages with high primary-group intensity, such as the detached worker or opinion leader. Some expertise might also be required to assess the direction the changes should take, and to work with "key" leaders. Once local persons are persuaded, they may be the best agents for altering neighborhood norms.

To help develop neighborhood structures for rapid integration of newcomers, a moderate amount of technical knowledge may be required. Hence some stress might be put on focused expertise. If the community is friendly, workshops or adult groups could be offered. If the community is unfriendly, a two-stage process will almost surely be needed, the first for recruitment and initial training by detached workers and, second, a more extensive educational procedure. The lower the educational and occupational level of the neighborhood, the more the use of focused expertise in the linking mechanism will be necessary.

26. The establishment of a local voluntary association might initially require technical skills of a community organizer. However, once set up, local associations can often be taken over and run by the local people themselves. See Richard A. Cloward and Richard M. Elman, "The Storefront on Stanton Street, Advocacy in the Ghetto," in George A. Brager and Francis P. Purcell (eds.), *Community Action Against Poverty* (New Haven: College and University Press, 1967), esp. pp. 272-79.

Most neighborhoods in large urban communities are subject to pressures to change, and the conceptual scheme presented here should alert the school staff to potential problems before they actually emerge. Traditional neighborhoods often seem quite stable until they are invaded by a new population. If the school is alerted ahead of time, it might begin preparatory community programs before the traditional neighborhood is under the pressure and tension of change. The school staff must take care not to precipitate panic.

*Neighborhood Resources*

In the market economy of the United States, income is a generalized means to an end. A low-income neighborhood is by definition a neighborhood with low resources. Family breakup, lack of parental supervision, the fact that children learn to settle disputes with their fists rather than verbally are all in part the response of families to low income.[27] The negative consequences for education of low family income are compounded when the family is also in a low-income neighborhood. Even if a particular family has adequate income and the mother has time and energy for her child, there may still be great counteracting pressures from the neighborhood. The classroom analogy of this situation is when a teacher is unable to help the few well-prepared children because the majority of her class is unprepared. Neighborhood pressure is subtle, but nevertheless evident in situations where a mother encourages her child not to fight but the child's peers settle arguments that way. Under such circumstances the child must learn to fight if only to defend himself. In some low-income neighborhoods adults often resort to "private justice" because police protection is insufficient or not trusted.

The important point here is that if a family lives in a low-income neighborhood it is often forced into behavior that is antithetical to success in the educational system—the use of physical force rather than verbal dialogue. In such situations the

27. See Eugene Litwak and Henry J. Meyer, *Relationship Between School-Community Coordinating Procedures and Reading Achievement*, pp. 208-46.

school-community program must carefully encourage change in patterns of receptive families without changing or neutralizing the larger neighborhood context. A failure to recognize the role of the larger neighborhood could result in serious damage to a particular family living in it.

This raises again the point made in regard to family resources. The school system is often asked to deal with problems whose fundamental source is unequal distribution of income or job opportunities rather than education. The larger society will hold the school responsible for failures in education even when the causes are clearly external. For instance the social evil of racial inequity has recently been attacked primarily through the educational system. School bussing is proposed as a major solution to racial inequality, even though racial inequality has its main roots in the political, economic, and social spheres of our society. Segregated housing and lack of occupational opportunities seem less emphasized than school segregation. Why this is so is unclear. What should be clear to educators is that they can not escape from dealing with the larger issues of society by claiming them to be tangential to problems of education. In American society the public has, like it or not, held educators responsible. Integration of schools to achieve racial equality may take precedence over educational goals if both cannot be achieved.

To deal with such social problems as low income, large-scale resources far beyond the current capacities of the school are needed. As a consequence, a school system serving primarily communities of low-income families can at best follow limited strategies. They can pick neighborhoods which have resources that are nearly adequate and use the limited school resources to raise them to adequate levels. In a few special cases, schools may be able to put substantial resources into one or two poor neighborhoods to show that changes can be produced if income is raised. Usually this can be done only where special project funds are available, and these are seldom of the magnitude needed in most poor neighborhoods for sustained programs.

Another possibility is for the schools to promote the organization of community groups so that they can apply political pressure for better income distribution. Such activity is risky. The larger public takes a dim view of political activity by schools or the use of school funds to encourage political movements. Schools involved in such activities would have to use approaches of exceedingly low scope and quickly "leave the field" as soon as the community groups were launched. Recognizing that education is closely tied to problems of income distribution, a final possiblity is that school personnel might lobby for legislation affecting income distribution, for example, negative income tax, statewide financing, and the like. At the least, the school should make it clear to the larger society that families who are very poor often do not have sufficient resources to perform the functions necessary to support the education of their children.

Thus, it can be seen that attacking the problem of low resources for total neighborhoods requires either large-scale programs that encompass all linkages (Model Cities programs), the use of low-scope primary group linkages to promote the organization of a political movement, or formal linkages addressed to political organizations (teachers' lobbies). Each of these strategies might work under somewhat different circumstances. The first might serve where the population needing resources was very limited. The second might succeed where the population needing aid was large, the economy expanding, and the opposition weak. The third might be appropriate where groups in power saw it to their advantage to help the poor, such as in an expanding economy where an expanded skilled labor force was needed.

*Typology of Neighborhoods*

It is useful to incorporate some of the preceding discussion into a more systematic typology of neighborhoods. In social science literature there are few attempts to develop conceptual types of neighborhoods. One effort was based on family life style and social-economic class of the population.[28] There are data to show

28. Eshref Shevkey and Wendell Bell, *Social Area Analysis* (Stanford: Stanford University Press, 1955); Wendell Bell, "Social Areas: Typology of Neighborhood," in M. B. Sussman (ed.), *Community Structure and Analysis* (New York: Thomas Y. Crowell, 1959), pp.

that living patterns differ in each of the types of neighborhoods so distinguished. Another attempt at classification relates individual identification with the neighborhood, the degree of social exchanges within the neighborhood, and the extent to which the neighborhood is explicitly related to the larger community.[29] This latter classification is close to what we suggest and is not inconsistent with the first. Our typology of neighborhoods, although similar also to our classification of families, differs in the definition of organizational forms. Neighborhoods may be distinguished with respect to organization as follows: those organized for change; those organized for stability; those disorganized because of subunit conflict; and those with minimal organization. For each organizational situation, we designate the extent to which norms are consistent with or nonsupportive of the educational purposes or values of the school. A third dimension distinguishes neighborhoods by the level or extent of their resources, primarily economic resources. The classification is summarized in Table 8.

Complex as this classification is, it does not include all the dimensions discussed. It is intended to give the reader an idea of the kind of diagnosis the school-community agent might undertake when considering problems of linkage. The use of additional dimensions (for example, the amount of knowledge, the stage in family life cycle typical in the area, the degree and type of connection with the larger community, ethnicity, a more refined classification of resources including those of educational level and occupational competence, and others) would permit a much finer analysis on which to base choice of linkage procedures. However, the basic idea can be conveyed with less complexity for illustrative purposes. If the general principles of neighborhood diagnosis are grasped, they may be applied and adapted to the unique features of each actual situation.

---

61-92.

29. Donald Warren, "Neighborhood Structure and Riot Behavior in Detroit: Some Explanatory Findings," *Social Problems,* 16 (Spring 1969) pp. 464-84; Phillip Fellin and Eugene Litwak, "Neighborhood in Urban American Society," *Social Work,* 13 (July 1968) pp. 72-80.

142

## Table 8  Neighborhood Types

| Descriptions of Neighborhood Types | Organizational Capacity of Neighborhood | Neighborhood Support for School Values | Resource Level of Neighborhood |
|---|---|---|---|
| *Mobility neighborhoods* | | | |
| 1. Change-accepting, school-supporting middle-class neighborhood | for change | high | high |
| 2. Change-accepting, school-supporting working-class neighborhood | for change | high | low |
| 3. Change-accepting, middle-class neighborhood opposed to school | for change | low | high |
| 4. Change-accepting, working-class neighborhood opposed to school | for change | low | low |
| *Traditional neighborhoods* | | | |
| 5. Traditional, school-supporting middle-class neighborhood | for stability | high | high |
| 6. Traditional, school-supporting working-class neighborhood | for stability | high | low |
| 7. Traditional, middle-class neighborhood opposed to school | for stability | low | high |
| 8. Traditional, working-class neighborhood opposed to school | for stability | low | low |
| *Volatile neighborhoods* | | | |
| 9. Heterogeneous, middle-class neighborhood in conflict over school | split by conflicting subgroups | both support and opposition | high |
| 10. Heterogeneous, working-class neighborhood in conflict over school | split by conflicting subgroups | both support and opposition | low |

**Table 8** (*continued*)

| Descriptions of Neighborhood Types | Organizational Capacity of Neighborhood | Neighborhood Support for School Values | Resource Level of Neighborhood |
|---|---|---|---|
| *Mass neighborhoods* | | | |
| 11. Residence area of middle-class, school supportive families, e.g., well-off apartment hotel dwellers | lacks organi-zation | most families support school | high |
| 12. Residence area of working-class, school supportive families, e.g., areas of new rural migrants | lacks organi-zation | most families support school | low |
| 13. Residence area of middle-class families mostly non-supportive of schools, e.g., retired business families | lacks organi-zation | most families against or indifferent to school | high |
| 14. Residence area of working-class families mostly non-supportive of schools, e.g., transient, roominghouse areas | lacks organi-zation | most families against or indifferent to school | low |

In Table 8 we distinguished four basic neighborhood types: the "Mobility neighborhood," the "Traditional neighborhood," the "Volatile neighborhood," and the "Mass neighborhood". Each of these types has been further divided into those where the neighborhood values are supportive of the schools or mostly opposed to them. Neighborhoods are also differentiated by level of resources.

We have treated the dimensions of this typology as though each was a simple dichotomy or limited set of categories when, in fact, they are continuous variables. Thus, from the viewpoint of a person on welfare an employed factory worker has great resources, whereas from the factory worker's viewpoint his own resources are low compared to the business man's, and so on. Furthermore, whether the population can be said to have high or low resources will depend on the specific change the community or school is concerned with, such as support for a new building or for sports equipment. For such purposes as gaining support for curriculum change resource level may be of minor relevance except when it accompahies opposition values. In fact, the interaction of the various dimensions that may be involved cannot be adequately represented. Table 8 must be viewed as a highly simplified scheme.

An additional consideration should be mentioned before discussion of major neighborhood types. Sometimes the objectives of the school focus on the neighborhood itself, as when an effort is made to gain support for a school bond issue. Often, the school's objective will be a change in some school families for whom the neighborhood will be context rather than prime target. If the linkage is designed to affect the neighborhood itself, it may need different characteristics from those required if the linkage is designed to affect certain families by changing the context surrounding them. Thus, the extent to which school families are typical of or different from most families in the neighborhood is an important diagnostic item for the school-community agent to consider.

The import of the warning that our typology is greatly simplified is that a school-community program should tailor its linkages to each situation in recognition that both family types and neighborhood types must be considered. Beyond this, it should be noted that peer groups, particularly of older school children, are a further feature of the primary group structure to be considered. We offer no typology of peer groups, nor of ethnic groups, that also in some ways partake of primary group characteristics. But it is necessary to call attention to the interrelations and the relevance of all three of these major primary group forms—families, neighborhoods, and peer groups—for deciding on appropriate linkage procedures for particular objectives in a school-community program.

With all these reservations in mind, each major neighborhood type will be discussed primarily from the viewpoint of the neighborhood itself as the target of school-community mechanisms of influence.

*Mobility Neighborhoods*

As previously pointed out, the mobility neighborhood is

structurally well suited to meet the demands of a modern industrial society. It permits people to be mobile and at the same time
encourages cohesion. This seeming paradox is accomplished by
mechanisms that introduce strangers rapidly into the neighborhood group. People in such neighborhoods generally understand
the separation of bureaucracies from primary groups and the need
to use each when the occasion requires. This should predispose
mobility neighborhoods to support education, but we have noted
the possibilities of opposition as well.

A good description of one positive mobility neighborhood,
Park Forest, Illinois, can be found in W. H. Whyte's *The Organization Man.* This type of neighborhood fits Type 1 in Table 8 and
is favorable to school purposes. However, it is important to realize
that in some situations the school and the mobility neighborhood
can be at odds. For instance, parents might prefer traditional
teaching approaches, whereas the teaching staff wants to use pupil-centered teaching, with each child using different books and
materials. This situation illustrates Type 3 of Table 8. Recognizing the power and resources of the typical mobility neighborhood, the school will probably have to confront two problems
simultaneously. This type of neighborhood can readily marshal
such primary group support as protests, pressure campaigns, and
the like as well as utilize formal bureaucracies. It can use newspapers, legal actions, set up alternative schools, and run campaigns
to elect a new school board and change undesired staff. To deal
with both these aspects of resistance or attack from the community, the school will need two types of linkage mechanism as well
as formal bureaucratic procedures to counter those advanced by
the community. In addition, it must somehow seek to change the
attitudes of community members toward teaching methods. This
will probably require some type of detached worker approach. In
a highly educated neighborhood with great resources, the detached worker can often be effective by emphasing expertise rather than primary-group intensity. This population can be swayed
by "scientific" evidence showing one method as better than another.

Mobility neighborhoods where middle-class parents are in

agreement with the school (Type 1) constitute a different threat than mobility neighborhoods which are hostile (Type 3). The danger to the school from those who agree with its policies is that the parents will become too involved and as a consequence put too much pressure on their children for achievement or too much pressure on the school to show progress whether the children make it or not. The linkage strategy is to keep the family at a fixed distance from the school. The stress is on passive, wide-scope, formal linkages such as mass media and formal Parent Teacher Associations.

In contrast would be mobility neighborhoods which have low resources (Types 2 and 4 in Table 8). One illustration of a low-resource mobility neighborhood would be that described by Festinger, Schacter, and Back of married students living in university housing at M.I.T.[30] It is true that these couples were poor only in a temporary sense; many of them had families who could help them and all of them were highly educated. This group is hardly a classic example from which school-community agents can understand low-resource mobility neighborhoods. However, it is one of the few cases where a group with relatively low income exhibited some of the manifestations of a mobility neighborhood. It might be difficult to find such neighborhoods among the poor because, as already mentioned, the mechanisms for quickly socializing people into the group are often learned in the managerial occupational world and in higher education. Another possible prototype might be found in ethnic groups that rose more quickly than the average when they emigrated to the United States. For instance, Jewish groups that came in large numbers in the early 1900s had, despite their low resources, some of the characteristics of the mobility neighborhoods. They were often able to move to strange communities and quickly be accepted by their fellow ethnic members in the new community; they were very positive toward education; they recognized the need to be mobile in order to deal with the problems of an urban industrial society. Still another possible example would be occupational groups where

30. Festinger, Schacter, and Back, *Social Pressures in Informal Groups.*

mobility is a way of life, such as regular army families, steel workers who migrate with large construction projects, and similar groups.

Low-resource mobility neighborhoods that adhere to school policy present the same threat, in principle, to school-community imbalance as high-resource neighborhoods. However, schools would find them easier to deal with because parents would have fewer resources and the school could keep them at a distance with less powerful types of formal linkages. For instance, in a high-resource mobility neighborhood the school might require parents to make appointments to see teachers, teachers might be discouraged from socializing with parents outside school hours, parent-teacher contacts might be encouraged only in such formal contexts as home room mother's groups, parent teacher associations, and the like. The parents in such neighborhoods have the resources and time to socialize and to visit the school. In neighborhoods where parents do not have such resources, they might be encouraged but not required to make appointments, the teacher might be discouraged from socializing with parents, but again this need not be by rule. A similar analysis would hold for the low-resource mobility neighborhood in which the people disagree with the school. The school could follow the lines suggested for dealing with the high-resource opposition mobility neighborhood but employ more moderate forms of linkage. For both the supportive and nonsupportive low-resource neighborhoods, the school would need to concentrate on linkages that help to raise resources.

As a general comment on the mobility neighborhood, we would say that the central problem for educators is how to help poor and working-class neighborhoods to assume this type of structure, since this is the one most likely to give the community power to defend its rights and support the educational needs of its children. More specifically, the problem facing community organizers is to find functional alternatives to occupational and university training that will permit individuals in low-resource neighborhoods to develop quick modes of socialization and sophistication in the differential use of primary group and bureaucratic resources.

*Traditional Neighborhoods*

As already pointed out, the traditional neighborhood consists of a relatively homogeneous status group that considers the neighborhood its permanent home. It does not take kindly to people who want to leave and it is very slow to accept newcomers. Warner, in his description of the upper class in a small community in New England, catches some of the major elements of these neighborhoods.[31] The traditional neighborhood with high resources contains persons with entreprenurial occupations or professionals whose occupational success rests on the local community, such as physicians whose practice consists of patients from the local community. For these persons there are no occupational imperatives to leave the neighborhood. In the language of sociologists, they are "locals" rather than "cosmopolitans."[32]

People from a traditional entreprenurial type of neighborhood are usually supporters of education. However, it is our impression that they are more likely than people from high-resource mobility neighborhoods to be at odds with the school over teaching philosophy. Persons in such neighborhoods are less likely to accept change than mobile persons. Pressures for change are especially strong on schools because they are subject to the impact of new ideas and scientific knowledge. We would hypothesize that the traditional neighborhood will be more at odds than the mobility neighborhood with school staffs over changes in teaching philosophy and course content, for example, sex education courses, ethnic study courses, and the like.

With this in mind, we can ask what linkage strategies the school should use with the traditional neighborhood structures. It is important to remember that traditional neighborhoods can be expected to be supportive of education only in the short run. In the long run they will be affected by industrial forces that cause neighborhoods to shift radically in population. Not being organ-

31. W. Lloyd Warner and Paul S. Lunt, *The Social Life of a Modern Community* (New Haven, Yale University Press, 1941), pp. 98-99.
32. Robert Merton, "Local and Cosmopolitan Influentials," in Warren.

ized to handle change, the traditional neighborhood can turn into a heterogeneous volatile neighborhood, with consequent conflict and violence. Linkage theory suggests that the school must guard against overcommitment from the traditional-conformist neighborhood. Formal meetings of parents and teachers should be stressed, informal socializing discouraged. The strategy is not different from that for the supporting-mobility neighborhood. However, in the long run the school staff must encourage basic value and knowledge reformation. Linkages are needed that can change attitudes toward newcomers and provide technical expertise on how to set up neighborhood structures to speed processes of integration. Given a friendly orientation of the families and their high level of resources, it would seem that the school staff could use a sequence of detached workers followed by use of local opinion leaders backed up by after-school programs and voluntary associations. Some kind of settlement house approach with focus on expertise could be used to give leadership training as well as experience in handling newcomers.

When the traditional high-resource neighborhood does not support the school, the staff has two options. They can follow the same tack they would take against nonsupportive mobility neighborhoods. A difference might be that the traditional neighborhood would not be able to muster as wide a range of bureaucratic agencies as the mobility neighborhood. On the other hand, the traditional neighborhood might have better connections with local bureaucracies. The second strategy the school staff might follow is simply to wait patiently. Since the traditional entreprenurial neighborhood is vulnerable to such forces of change as changes in the family life cycle, new styles of living, job pressures to move, and the like, the school has only to wait for the consequent disorganization. At that point, the traditional neighborhood will not present such powerful opposition. However, the school will encounter other problems created by this very disorganization. These will be discussed below.

The working-class traditional neighborhood (Type 6) is best typified by residential areas of ethnic groups—Irish, Italian,

Polish, Hungarian, and others. Gans has described one such neighborhood in his *The Urban Villagers*.[33] Historically, these groups have tended to be deferential to school officials and staff.[34] Though most of these neighborhoods value education highly, their limited resources often prevent them from giving education the same priority as wealthier neighborhoods do. We suggest that the school will need to use linkages with higher intensity than in middle-class neighborhoods in order to encourage stronger support of education. The families in the neighborhood will also need the benefit of expert knowledge. With the neighborhood basically sympathetic to the schools, a weak form of detached worker can be used to recruit opinion leaders, who can in turn carry much of the burden of communication. After-school classes might provide technical information and leadership training, supply knowledge about community resources, and at the same time increase resources (for example, by providing baby-sitting services). To help this group toward a "mobility neighborhood" the school would have to draw on more school resources to compensate for the lower resource levels of the neighborhood.

The traditional working-class neighborhood with low support for school values (Type 8) can express itself in various ways. The "middle American" revolt against school bonding issues or the black parents' revolt against "racist" policies of the schools might both be expressions of the traditional working-class neighborhood's hostility toward a given school system. Insofar as the school believes the community viewpoint to be wrong, it will need to use linkages of the sort suggested for the hostile middle-class neighborhood—formalistic procedures to counter those the community might use combined with detached workers to try to change attitudes. Since the working-class neighborhood has fewer

33. Herbert K. Gans, *The Urban Villagers: Group and Class in the Life of Italian-Americans* (New York: Free Press of Glencoe, 1962).

34. This attitude seems to persist, and is reflected in some unstructured interviewing recently undertaken with blue-collar workers in ethnic neighborhoods around Detroit. The deference may not extend, however, to all aspects of the school. Some parents expressed criticism of schools on the subject of dealing with blacks, feeling that black pupils were given preferential treatment, e.g., less severe dicipline for infractions of rules. Another criticism expressed was that teachers tended to be too lenient toward the children by not providing enough dicipline.

resources than the middle-class neighborhood, the school should have an easier time fending off thrusts from the community.

*Heterogeneous-Volatile Neighborhoods*

Perhaps the neighborhood receiving most attention today is what we call the heterogeneous-volatile neighborhood (Types 9 and 10). This is a traditional neighborhood where the status of the area is changing, often from an influx of new residents. A German neighborhood may be invaded by Italians, or Jewish families may move into an Irish neighborhood; black families may be replacing white families, or a middle-class neighborhood may be becoming working class. In the 1960s the most conspicuous intergroup conflict was between blacks and whites. However, earlier in American history similar conflicts took place between many different ethnic groups. There are few instances when volatile neighborhoods were found to give much support to education. Conflict between neighbors soon involves the school and complicates teaching.

In earlier discussion we pointed out that different linkage strategies should be used when the target was a minority or a majority of a neighborhood, depending on the extent of their opposition to school policies and their magnitude of conflict. It is quite possible that where the conflicting groups have high resources much of the conflict may take place through formal organizations with a minimum of physical violence. For example, one group might send its children to private schools and thus eliminate the basis for conflict within the school. In a low-resource neighborhood, however, the community members, lacking the means to use bureaucratic weapons, might exhibit more direct types of primary group conflict. This may involve physical violence and be a major source of instability in the school.

*Mass Neighborhoods*

The mass neighborhood is the type that social commentators often cite as representative of modern urban society. Erich Fromm, C. Wright Mills, and Herbert Marcuse, among others, express the common theme that modern society consists of individuals isolated from each other and manipulated by the mass media and other large bureaucracies.[35] However, when a close look has been taken at any group said to express mass society, observers have found a strong set of interactive bonds between peers, neighbors, and family members. To find a pure example of the mass neighborhood, one would have to look at the residents of a large overnight hotel.

The concept of mass neighborhood becomes less an interpretative metaphor and more descriptive if we think of it in relative terms. In most large cities it is possible to identify transient areas of the wealthy as well as of the poor. These may be areas where people are on the move and where much of their lives are lived outside the neighborhood. If they have school-age children and high resources, they often send their children to private schools. If they are young couples without children, or older couples whose children have left home, they often have little interest in education and the needs of the school. As a consequence, they may oppose efforts on the part of local schools to acquire more resources from the community, they might complain about schoolchildren making noise, or object to restricted traffic patterns, and the like.

When we consider low-resource mass neighborhoods (Types 12 and 14), we must not assume there is no neighborhood interaction at all. Often there is much interaction. In an exploratory study of an inner city school district, we found that social workers, nurses, policemen, businessmen, and teachers were able to give little information about the social life of the neighborhood. The police knew where the prostitutes and the criminals lived, the social workers knew about the people on their case load, the visiting nurses knew the people they saw—and no one knew whether their clients had any neighborhood social life. There is

35. A number of authors have asserted that primary groups in industrial societies have disintegrated and been replaced by large-scale bureaucratic organizations. See C. Wright Mills, *The Power Elite* (New York: Oxford University Press, 1956), pp. 305-307; Louis Wirth, "Urbanism as a Way of Life," in Paul Hatt and Albert J. Reiss, Jr. (eds.), *Cities and Society*, pp. 594 ff; Herbert Marcuse, *One Dimensional Man* (Boston: Beacon Press, 1968); Erich Fromm, *Escape from Freedom* (New York: Rinehart, 1937).

a tendency to assume that very low status areas constitute mass neighborhoods. What made W. F. Whyte's study, *Street Corner Society,* so important was his revelation that a slum area which everybody thought to be highly disorganized was, in fact, a highly organized society with intricate neighborhood and peer group relations.

If there are mass neighborhoods among the poor who are not educationally oriented, we would think that the transient boarding house or high-crime areas would typify them. If we find mass neighborhoods among the poor who are educationally oriented, they might be the areas of rural migrant workers who have moved to the large city.

With respect to linkage strategies and mass neighborhoods, the central point is that there are no good ways by which people "naturally" communicate with each other. Thus linkage techniques that depend on neighbors knowing each other (for example, the opinion leader and indigenous worker) might have limited applicability. In addition, any linkage that leads people to interact might prove difficult to implement since a low level of interaction is characteristic. Organization of a PTA, of a group to greet newcomers, the use of parent groups to help plan an after-school program for the community—all would mean that neighbors have to interact with each other. About the only thing that the school could do without attempting major modification of the mass neighborhood would be to conduct mass media campaigns on issues the community can vote on. The mass media mechanism does not require neighbors to interact with each other nor the school to meet residents face-to-face. The action demanded can be limited and in many instances—as in elections—need not require interaction with others.

If the residents of the mass neighborhood are favorable to education and the schools (Types 11 and 12), mass media techniques have a reasonable chance of achieving desired effects. Extensive saturation campaigns may be needed, since the networks of information and opinion leaders found in other types of neighborhood are largely undeveloped in the mass neighborhood. If mass neighborhood residents oppose the school or are indifferent and their support is needed (Types 13 and 14), few linkages would seem to be effective. A long-term effort with detached workers and a variety of community programs to promote greater community organization might be necessary. Such neighborhoods are also ineffective opponents of the school, making it unlikely that an investment in a long-term program will be undertaken.

*The Neighborhood as a Basis for Community Linkages into the Schools*

The type of neighborhood also seriously affects the kind of linkages that can be used by the community to influence the school. Generally, any community that seeks to use advocate bureaucracies must build its own or depend on outside sources to provide bureaucratic resources for its cause. Only a neighborhood with sufficient resources, knowledge, and social organization can promote voluntary associations, which can in turn provide the financial base for developing a full-fledged bureaucracy. Neighborhoods with little organization (such as mass neighborhoods), or neighborhoods with inconsistent values or conflicting groups (volatile neighborhoods), or those lacking economic resources, will not be able to build advocate bureaucracies. On the other hand, neighborhoods with weak structures can sometimes use advocate bureaucracies supported by the outer community.

In the literature on community strategies it is often said that any group can be organized if the issues can be made meaningful. Recently, some investigators have suggested that this is not so in very poor neighborhoods.[36] The problem is not ignorance or lack of common grievances but lack of resources. The community is too involved in mere survival to have energy left to build linkages that would require more than minimal efforts. Low-resource neighborhoods are capable of responding to linkages of high-primary-group intensity, but only for short periods of time, such as one-day boycotts, demonstration meetings, or sit-ins.

The hypothesis is that neighborhoods that are organized,

36. Frances Piven, "Resident Participation in Community-Action Programs: An Overview," in George A. Brager and Francis P. Purcell (eds.), *Community Action Against Poverty*, pp. 151-60.

have resources, common knowledge, and common values are capable of using the full range of linkage mechanisms to influence bureaucracies. Middle-class mobility neighborhoods and traditional neighborhoods can do so. Similar neighborhoods with low resources are capable of using those linkages that have primary group intensity on an ad hoc limited basis and are capable of calling on advocate bureaucracies from outside the neighborhood. But volatile and mass neighborhoods are unlikely to be able to mount or sustain programs to influence the school.

## Conclusion

In this chapter we have tried to provide the reader with a diagnostic scheme for classifying families and another one for classifying neighborhoods. For families we have suggested eight types based on the extent to which the family supports educational values, the amount of knowledge, and the resources they have for implementing educational values. For each type of family we have suggested the general linkage strategies which should be followed. We have pointed out that the neighborhood involves somewhat different problems than the family. Thus, in a neighborhood we must be concerned with scope or the number of people who will be reached, the extent to which there are internal subgroups in conflict, and the extent to which the neighborhood is organized to handle the mobility problems of its members. From this analysis we developed a classification scheme of fourteen neighborhood types and speculated as to types of linkage strategies that might best be used with them. We labled the four basic types of neighborhood: the mobility neighborhoods (organized to handle change), the traditional neighborhoods (organized to prevent change), the volatile neighborhoods (having conflicting subgroups), and the mass neighborhoods (where there is little neighborhood organization of any type). For each of these four types we considered if it had many resources or few resources and whether it was favorably disposed or not favorably disposed to education.

Though we view these typologies as too general for any given concrete situation, we think they will provide a basic framework for school personnel to use as an important first step in diagnosing a particular situation.

# Part Two

## Mechanisms for Linking School and Community

# 5 ❧ The Detached Worker

When using the detached-worker approach, the school-community agent works outside the physical confines of the school building. He moves freely throughout a neighborhood and mingles with groups he hopes to influence by going directly to their home base. If it is a family, he goes directly to the house; if a delinquent gang, to its favorite hangouts; if a neighborhood, he works directly with groups of neighbors or block clubs. He tries to influence by gaining personal acceptance and friendship. His working hours are dependent upon the habits of the groups he seeks to reach—morning or evening, weekends or weekdays. Whereas the general purpose of his efforts is often quite clear—for example, steering children away from delinquent behavior or encouraging parents to support the education of their children— the exact procedures he should follow are frequently unspecified. He makes many decisions as he works and plans his program for any given day as situations arise. In short, to use this procedure a person must know the general policies of the school well enough to decide on his own what minute-by-minute course of action to take.

Examples of detached workers include street corner workers among juvenile gangs, county agents of the agricultural extension services, and neighborhood or block club workers associated with settlement houses and many "outreach" programs.

There are varying degrees of detachedness. A street club worker might be assigned to a single group of delinquent youth for months or years. But more limited detached work is also possi-

THE COLLABORATION OF JACK ROTHMAN IN THE PREPARATION OF THIS CHAPTER IS ESPECIALLY ACKNOWLEDGED.

ble. For example, workers in the schools may deal intensively with a given family or block club for a few days in a crisis situation and then have little contact with them after that. Or the worker may form a friendly long-term relationship with a group and consult with it from time to time, without the relationship becoming particularly intense. Or the worker may go out into local stores, restaurants, group meetings, and the like, getting to know people casually and hoping to contact neighborhood opinion leaders. Perhaps the detached worker in the schools can be best designated as an urban extension worker. He is much like his rural counterpart, the agricultural extension worker, who has varying contacts with farm families and groups with the aim of improving their capacities as farmers.

## Primary Group Aspects of the Role

### Primary Group Dimensions

In the general description of the detached worker approach, we suggested that he operates informally and as if he were a friend, a family member, or a trusted neighbor. Another way of saying this is that the detached worker operates as though he were a member of a primary group.[1]

Let us examine dimensions of the primary group and explore ways the detached worker may utilize them.

*Positive feelings between group members.* Positive emotional bonds, such as general good will, affection, and trust, must develop between the school-community agent and the people with whom he works for the detached-worker approach to operate. The intensity of this relationship may range at one extreme from feelings analogous to those between members of a family, and at the other extreme to feelings that exist between a public official and a citizen he sees only once.

When situations are fairly simple, clear, and routine, minimal affectional ties are necessary between a community agent and

1. Charles H. Cooley, *Social Organization* (New York: Scribner, 1909). Also Charles H. Cooley, "Primary Groups," in A. P. Hare, E. F. Borgatta, and R. F. Bales (eds.), *Small Groups: Studies in Social Interaction* (New York: Knopf, 1962), pp. 15-20.

his clients. Ambiguous and uncertain matters, such as how to bring up, discipline, or motivate children, may require closer and more sustained feelings and relationships. Friendly feelings help a change agent enter a primary group and use affectional relationships to foster changes in behavior. Differential affectional ties are necessary for dealing with different types of problems. For example, in the case of an unexpected death in a family, particularly if there are no other relatives in the area, the detached worker may step into the situation for a few days to lend emotional support almost as a family member. Where a family is having an evident problem in child-rearing, the detached worker may try to develop the quality of feeling that characterizes good friends so that he and the parents can search out the source of the trouble. For a mother reluctant to take her child to the hospital, or to allow the worker to take her there, the kind of trust which exists between friendly neighbors may be sufficient. This is similar to the kind of relationship developed by the old-time settlement house worker or a county agricultural extension agent. To illustrate even less intensity, and to encourage a family to come to a meeting, only enough positive feeling may be needed to assure that the family will answer the door and listen to the worker.

*Face-to-face relations.* By definition, the detached worker deals with people primarily in face-to-face situations. This can be supplemented by less personal forms of contact such as telephone calls and correspondence. Face-to-face contact is most necessary in ambiguous, complicated, uncertain situations where many questions may arise, many courses of action be proposed, and some courses of action tried and perhaps discarded. Only in face-to-face exchanges can a professional person in these situations answer questions and deal with the problems as they come up. Routine simple situations, on the other hand, may often be handled by more distant communication.

In an extreme case, such as an unexpected death in the family when there are no relatives to turn to, the detached worker may have almost continual face-to-face contact for a few days. Even here, however, there is the expectation that face-to-face contact will come to an end within a reasonable time period. If more intense face-to-face contact over a longer period is called for, it is best for the school-community worker to refer the family to a social work agency equipped to provide the needed assistance. For example, the amount of face-to-face contact necessary to influence a well-organized deviant teen-age gang can be better provided by a street-corner worker from a social agency than by a school-community agent who must deal with the total school community.

*Diffused relations; group members can discuss many areas of life.* One of the characteristics of a primary group is the large number of areas of life which may legitimately fall within its scope. Thus, it is legitimate for a family to discuss business, family and personal problems, courtship, religion, leisure, politics, and many other things. In contrast, in some work situations the specific aspects of the job may be the only legitimate topics of conversation, although some employees may informally expand beyond these. The range of life areas that are of legitimate concern varies among different primary groups. The family probably can discuss the widest range of topics legitimately. Next come close friends, followed by friendly neighbors. Persons who have only occasional contacts usually have very limited areas of serious legitimate conversation.

How wide or how narrow should the range of life areas be that the detached worker deals with? What are the boundaries of his areas of legitimate concern? Two contrasting strategies may be suggested:

One strategy is to focus on a particular problem and be concerned with other issues only if they are necessary to deal with the core problem. Thus, if the problem concerns the child's educational motivation, the detached worker might decide to go directly to the family and present this as an issue. In dealing with this issue he might get into various areas of child rearing and family living, but the worker would limit his range of attention to those things that are essential in dealing with the problem of educational motivation. This direct approach is probably most useful where the family or group is friendly toward the worker, or at least neutral. In such circumstances it saves time and energy to focus directly on the core problem. Suspicious or hostile groups, or problems involving "sensitive" matters (such as religion, sex, or sometimes money), may not be readily susceptible to the direct approach.

A second strategy is the indirect approach. Here the worker uses his ties with the family to consider many areas of life. In so doing, he builds trust and positive feelings in areas where there is no threat, thus establishing a relationship that allows him to work on the core problems of the family or group that may be very threatening and complex.

The detached worker may also deal with a family or group when there are a number of highly interrelated problems, such as health, unemployment, child behavior, clothing, inability to utilize agency resources, marital adjustment, and other problems which often beset families in extremely low income populations. In such cases, the detached worker might have to deal with problems in almost all areas of family life if he is to be effective.

*Enduring relationships.* We suggested earlier the relative permanency of primary group relationships. How permanent should be the relationship of the detached worker to the people with whom he deals? On the one hand, he would like to foster the sense that he will be available to be relied upon in time of need. On the other hand, he wants the family or group to become independent. We suggest that the amount of permanency the detached worker from the schools may find most useful is similar to the relationship between trusted neighbors—a sustained close relationship but one not expected to last a lifetime.

The pressure on a detached worker by his agency will usually be to limit his involvement because this is an expensive way to use agency resources. Yet, relatively enduring relationships allow greater communication, and thereby encourage trust, affection, face-to-face exchange, and the development of diffuse relations. Thus, permanency facilitates development of the other aspects of primary group relations and is useful when problems are especially complex and ambiguous.

*Degrees of Primary Group*
*Intensity and Associated Roles*

When using a detached worker approach for the achievement of objectives of a school-community program, it is possible for the community agent to play different roles with a
family or other primary group at different times. Roles are
affected by the relationship the worker develops with the primary group. Envisioning different degrees of friendly relationships between the worker and the primary group, we can
illustrate some possibilities.

*Maximum Friendly Face-to-Face Relations*

The detached worker may try to simulate a role usually
performed by a real member of the family and hence act as
a quasi family member. He may play such roles as parent
substitute, aunt or uncle to the children, sibling to parents, and
so forth. He must be sensitive to the limitations that inhere in
playing a role, even under most friendly conditions. Nevertheless, by taking the stance that an acceptable family role provides, the detached worker may have a base for helping the
family or other primary group deal with the problems that
have been deemed pertinent to the objectives of the school-
community program.

When approximating the role of a quasi family member
the strategy might vary considerably, depending on the
particular role. In some situations the choice of roles may be
wide. Often, the circumstances of the group will be determina-
tive. Thus, the role of a youth worker with delinquent gangs
will usually differ considerably from that of a detached worker
with an alienated family. In addition to such factors as age
and sex characteristics of the detached worker, the primary
group's own conceptions will affect what is acceptable behavior
in the adopted role. The development of different role strategies is a subject that needs systematic exploration. We can only
stress here the need for the community agent to be sensitive to

the many dimensions involved and therefore to be deliberate about his strategy.

*Moderate Friendly Face-to-Face Relations*

When friendly relations are moderate, the detached worker may act in roles appropriate to a trusted friend. Such a role may orient to the group as a whole or to its segments (for example, the parents, the children) or to individual members. The worker may merely make himself available or take the initiative. Whether friendship roles can cross age and sex lines, involve general or specific interests, reflect symetrical or asymetrical obligations, and other questions need exploration.

*Some Friendly Face-to-Face Relations*

When relations between the detached worker and the primary group are friendly but tend toward acceptance rather than closeness, the term that best describes the role is friendly professional person. The professional aspects, still within friendly face-to-face relations, are emphasized in this situation. The personally interested counselor, resource person, spokesman for the family to the school and for the school to the family are examples of ways the worker may present himself. Which degree of primary group intensity should be used is dependent on the severity of the problem that the client faces as well as the amount of resources the school has. In general, the greater the severity of the problem the more intense should be the primary group relation.

## Different Primary Group
## Situations and the Detached Worker

We may look at the problem of identifying the kinds of situations when the detached worker approach is useful. In general, we suggest two such circumstances: when the client family or group is resistant to the agency's goals, and when the problem of the client requires treatment in the client's own setting.

If families will themselves take the initiative, a settlement house type of approach can be used with less effort and expense than the detached worker approach. Under what circumstances will families not take the initiative? A rough catalogue of such situations includes: (a) hostility to or ignorance of the goals of the school; (b) handicap or serious illness, physical or mental; (c) demands of other areas of life which compete with concern for education (for example, both parents may work); (d) indifference to education; (e) fear or insecurity when approaching an unknown experience; (f) previous negative experiences with the school.

There may be problems that cannot be diagnosed unless the worker is on the scene and can see what is actually going on. In other circumstances, the client may be unable to absorb the helping experience unless it is demonstrated in the actual situation where the worker can participate.

In chapter 4 we discussed at length some variations of families and neighborhoods in the school's local community that affect the choice of appropriate linking mechanisms. Here we note the client types for whom the detached worker approach seems most useful.

The client types previously discussed can be placed on a rough scale of their distance from the school and its educational objectives, starting with the most distant:

1. Internally organized families or neighborhood groups in opposition to the school's goals.

2. Neighborhoods in organized conflict or exhibiting strained race or ethnic relations.

3. Client primary groups opposed to the school's goals but not organized internally.

4. Clients indifferent to education.

5. Clients with positive interests and educational values but unable to implement them.

6. Clients favoring educational values and capable of implementing them.

The detached worker approach is very useful, perhaps essential, when the school-community program must deal with families not educationally oriented, whether the family is organized or disorganized. The detached worker approach is useful only to a modest degree when dealing with families that are educationally oriented but seem unable to implement their interest because they are not knowledgeable or are disorganized. Likewise, the detached worker mechanism is rarely useful and in fact might be dysfunctional when the community consists mostly of well-organized families who are highly motivated educationally.

*Referring extremely deviant client populations.* A school-community program cannot hope to take over or duplicate the services that are supplied by social work and community welfare agencies. Therefore, the detached worker should not try to provide casework treatment to individuals with severe personal disturbances or to families with extensive problems when long-term work is required. Nor, for example, should the treatment of delinquent gangs be attempted. These are the spheres where the competence of the agencies and social workers trained for this kind of work is required. However, the detached worker should be in a position to recognize and diagnose such extreme cases and be sure that the proper agencies in the community undertake some program of action. Inability to specify the exact point at which a case should be referred to a social work agency and cease to be under school auspices should not detract from the general principle that the detached worker is not a caseworker or therapist.

## Basis for Assigning the Detached Worker to Client Populations

A practical problem of using the detached worker approach is to determine which families and groups in the local community to work with. Experience has offered no clear answer to this problem and theoretical guidance is limited. We can, however, report some bases that have been used in deciding the choice of client groups.

1. *"Bad Apple" Basis.* This approach takes its name from the folk saying, "One bad apple spoils the barrel." This idea is often meaningful to school administrators. They may feel that 95 per cent of their pupils are all right but that the other 5 per cent are

so disruptive as to affect the entire school. With this viewpoint, the principal is apt to assign the worst cases to the detached worker. This seems reasonable if the school or neighborhood does indeed consist primarily of families who are knowledgeable and not fearful, indifferent, or hostile. It permits concentration at points of greatest need or urgency.

2. *"Key Leaders" Basis.* Another approach is to seek out the key leaders in the target groups. If the leaders can be persuaded to support the organization, they may in turn persuade others. Hence, detached workers are assigned to work with such leaders. In general, this approach would seem to be useful in two circumstances: where the assessment is made that the key person can be influenced by intensive work by the detached worker to support the goals of the school, and where the community is so highly organized that it is unrealistic to assign detached workers to all target families. Using the key leader as the target involves some risks. In some situations it may actually work against the goal of the detached worker. Some of these problems are discussed in chapter 6 in relation to the opinion leader mechanism.

3. *The "best chance" basis.* An approach opposite to that of the "bad apple" might be called the "best chance" approach. Viewing energies and resources as limited, the detached worker may be assigned to affect those who are most accessible and cooperative, hoping that they will in turn influence others. The assumption is that positive contagion is more effective than negative contagion. Thus, the few who can gain most dramatically from the worker's efforts are selected. For instance, in some very poor neighborhoods the school might use detached workers to involve upwardly mobile families to contribute to solving current neighborhood problems.

4. *The "cross section of the average" basis.* Here the detached worker aims his efforts at the majority of families. In effect, this approach argues that a school can tolerate some extreme families in its community. The effort should be to keep the number from reaching a critical point. This approach poses the need for the detached worker to support the average family over the need to work with the most seriously deviant or the most accessible families.

*State of the community and stage of the program..* The use of the detached worker approach will need to be varied in relation to the situation of the school's community, especially in initial efforts. In Detroit, there was one area that was largely unorganized but in which a delinquent gang was dominant. The worker in those circumstances saw his priority to be to work with the gang ("bad apple" approach) and to build up grassroots community organization. By contrast, in another area the community agent found a developed system of block clubs and hence chose to work through them.

*Children or adults.* In selecting targets for the detached worker approach, selecting the age level to deal with presents a problem. Should adults in a neighborhood or child peer groups in the school be the focus? Adults, including parents, seem usually to have relatively less influence on the behavior of older children, whereas peer groups have increasing importance. Thus, in a high school a school-community program which did not give attention to the student body, its cliques, and its normative patterns would be likely to have little effect. By contrast, in the elementary school any program which did not include the parents would have limited effect. While the family cannot be ignored by the high school, and the children's peers cannot be ignored by the elementary school, there is need for differential emphasis. It should be kept in mind that a child at every age is a member of both family and peer group and these groups might well be weighed against each other with due regard for complications that may result. Thus, when a child's family provides a poor milieu for education, the detached worker might try to place the child among peers who strongly support the school. By contrast, where the child's peer group takes negative views on education, the detached worker might concentrate on buttressing the family to aid it in providing a compensatory stress.

## The Detached Worker and Forms of Influence

Assuming the detached worker wishes to influence families, neighborhood groups, and children in the direction of educational values, what means of influence are at his disposal?

We may draw from the social science literature a number of concepts which help us describe the way one person can influence another.[2] These concepts include:

Referent power—detached worker as an emotionally significant person.

Expert power—detached worker as an expert.

Power by legitimation—detached worker as a legitimate spokesman for society, for the school or other groups.

Reward and punishment power—detached worker as a source of rewards and punishments.

We will discuss each of these concepts and suggest ways in which they might be relevant to the detached worker.

*Referent power—detached worker as emotionally significant person.* The detached worker may become such a significant figure to a family or group that he develops a following because of the strong emotional attachment to him. The power this gives him to influence is what we mean by referent power.

Referent power is an extremely strong form of influence when it can be used. But it is difficult to know how to go about becoming a positively regarded, emotionally significant person. The worker must have characteristics that the individuals being approached can identify with.

One possibility is to emphasize personal characteristics like those of the group one wants to influence. The group may feel at home with such a detached worker, feel he is one of them, and accept him into the group. It can be argued that a detached worker dealing with a poor black group might gain acceptance more readily if he were poor and black. The alternative argument is that he might gain acceptance more readily if he were white and of a higher economic status. Either of these approaches may be successful, depending on the circumstances. The crucial difference

---

2. J. R. P. French and B. Raven, "The Bases of Social Power," in D. Cartwright (ed.), *Studies in Social Power* (Ann Arbor: Institute for Social Research, University of Michigan, 1959), pp. 155-65.

may lie in the attitude of the group members toward their own group. If they are proud of their group (for example, black civil rights militants) and plan to remain in it, stress on similarities between the detached worker and the group members may be most useful. When group members are not proud of their group membership and plan to leave it, such as the upwardly mobile in a low-income neighborhood, it may be most useful to stress the difference between the group and the detached worker. In brief, the decision to seek similarity or dissimilarity to the group may depend on whether or not the group holds itself in high regard.

The decision about whether to stress similarities or differences (or any other technique) depends partly upon the strategies of change the detached worker determines diagnostically, and in part on his ability to use his own personality in a variety of ways. The mode of analysis suggested here opens a range of possibile strategies and roles. Not all personalities can employ all roles. It is up to the detached worker to select approaches and to discard them as it seems appropriate for himself or the situation. He must be willing to try various approaches.

*Expert power—detached worker as an expert.* This form of influence is based on the fact that the influencer has some form of expertise, usually professional. Expert power is a form of influence many educated people prefer. The views of the professional are given weight because of his technical training. Many detached workers use expert power extensively to influence people. The street corner worker with the juvenile gang is more knowledgeable about community resources than members of the gang. He uses this knowledge to help gang members get what they want lawfully and more consistently. Or a detached worker can provide a parent with information on where his child or the family can get medical treatment, jobs, loans, psychiatric help, and so on. This expert knowledge can appear quite impressive to a family.[3]

It should be stressed that the detached worker does not profess to be an expert in all areas. He operates more as a one-man local information and referral bureau. Sometimes he works with

3. See Alfred J. Kahn *et al., Neighborhood Information Centers: A Study and Some Proposals* (New York: Columbia University Press, 1966).

a highly selected population and his expertise becomes somewhat specialized. Working with ADC mothers, for instance, he may become an expert in the problems of raising children in fatherless households. Sometimes more is needed than passing along facts. A mother who needs to take her child to the hospital may be so fearful of the unknown complicated hospital that the child does not get there. A detached worker might take the mother to the hospital and go through the procedures with her, thus teaching her to handle bureaucratic organizations and to fear them less in the future. Telling her she has nothing to fear may not work, but taking her through the experience once may. The detached worker approach is easily adapted to showing people by example, or accompanying them through an experience.

*Power by legitimation—detached worker as legitimate spokesman for society, the school, or other group.* By legitimation we mean that one person accepts the right of another to make a certain decision because this is in accordance with the commonly accepted rules of the group—a friendship group, a religious group, the nation-state, society, and others. It also means that one person accepts a given goal as his own because this is in accordance with the rules of the group. Legitimation differs from referent power in that it refers to larger group norms while referent power refers to personal attraction between two individuals.

The school-community agent wishes children to accept educational achievement as a legitimate goal. He would like them to reject lawbreaking. He would like to be accepted as a legitimate person to help bring about changes in goals. The question is, how does the detached worker gain legitimation? It is rare that he can do so simply because he is a detached worker, especially if he is working in the area of school-community relations. Expectations for detached workers are not yet defined, so they may find it necessary to borrow the legitimation of other professions. Some agents will be invited into homes and listened to because they are identified as teachers. However, the opposite effect might obtain. It is obviously not a good thing to borrow the legitimation of the teacher if the community does not respect teachers. There may be occasions when he might present himself as a social worker since many school-community agents are social workers by training. However, social workers may have no more legitimation than the teacher, and perhaps less. It is the experience of many workers in the schools that it is generally useful to come into a home under some general school auspices. But it is well to keep in mind that this may not always be the case.

*Reward and punishment power.* Sometimes the detached worker is in a position to stimulate change because he can provide rewards or punishments for the family. In this case, particularly when punishment is involved, he is often using official powers which attach to the formal aspects of his role (for example, calling in the attendance officer). When using these official powers, the detached worker is, in effect, using formal authority. We will present the use of formal authority as a separate linking mechanism at a later point. Rewards may include information about resources, recognition for accomplishments, and material gains such as free tickets to special events. Rewards and punishments may be very risky sources of power.

In any given approach to a family, the detached worker can vary the form of influence he uses, selecting what seems to be appropriate. For example, the detached worker may call on a family where a child is chronically absent from school without obvious reasons. If the worker wants to emphasize his referent power, he might take the role of a friendly sympathetic neighbor vis-a-vis the mother, exploring with her some of the difficulties she is facing and trying to create rapport to be used in the future. The detached worker could also stress his role as an expert, pointing out the necessity of the child attending school if he is to get a good job, and suggesting to the mother specific ways in which she could get her child to school based on practical experience in working with other children. If the worker wished to stress legitimation, he would point out as a school official that the child is required by law to come to school, and that local neighbors expect children to attend school. If he wished to use reward and punishment power, he might offer a special inducement, such as recognition of the child in the Christmas program if his attendance improves. A given situation often provides the detached worker with an opportunity to use one form, several forms, or perhaps a subtle blending of all forms of power.

What is not clear is the proper sequencing of such forms of influence, for example, what should come first and what leads to what. There is no real evidence or theory to help us resolve this issue on the community level. Some detached workers working with gangs start out by showing their expertness and reward power in order to win trust, build referent power, and gain eventual legitimation. After referent power and legitimation are won, they may use punitive influence as well. In the case of one agency where detached workers were put in a position that made any actions seem punitive, they quickly swiched to emphasizing their expertise and from this built toward referent and legitimate power. In light of incomplete knowledge the worker will need to be extremely pragmatic, trying different combinations until he finds what will work best to achieve his purposes.

## Techniques for Establishing Contact and Relationships with Client Groups

There are various ways for detached workers to make initial contacts with families or community groups. The strategies discussed below do not exhaust the list. Workers will need to decide which ways best fit the particular situation of families and neighborhoods.

*1. Living in the neighborhood.* The detached worker can live in the neighborhood in which he works and come to know neighborhood residents in the process of everyday living. This strategy maximizes the opportunity to develop primary group relationships but it also has disadvantages. In a neighborhood where there is conflict, it may be difficult to avoid becoming over-identified with one faction, thus antagonizing other factions. Area residents may be suspicious of the motives of the worker. The worker may also find he has very little privacy. Overdependency on the part of neighborhood people also may develop.

*2. Calling on the family in their home.* The detached worker may take the initiative in contacting the family by visiting at home. There should be a specific reason for the first call. General good will is not often an adequate reason for making a call. Reasons related to the child or an immediate family situation (health, employment, lack of food) which affects the child are good bases for gaining entry and involving the parents.

*3. Following a "hanging around" technique.* The detached worker "hangs around" the neighborhood, talks to people in shops, shoots pool with teen-agers, turns up at meetings and community events. He becomes known, sizes up problems and people, and looks for opportunities to be helpful in order to further relationships.

*4. Using third-party introductions.* The detached worker can be introduced through a third party who is acquainted with the residents—a school social worker, the principal, a teacher, a community opinion leader with close ties to the school, and others.

*5. Taking parents to meetings, appointments, etc.* When a family is friendly but apprehensive, the detached worker may pick them up at their home and take them to a first meeting, may accompany them to hospitals or clinics the first time, and in similar ways encourage trust and confidence.

*6. Seeking only for a limited initial commitment from the client.* In order that the client not feel trapped or overwhelmed, it has proven useful to ask for a limited initial commitment from a family or other primary group. For example, arrange for attendance at only one parent-teacher conference or one PTA meeting.

*7. Helping make practical arrangements so that clients can get involved in desired activities.* Real baby-sitting problems can keep many parents from attending meetings, keeping medical appointments, and the like. If not recognized, such limitations can frustrate much of the detached worker's efforts. "Sitters" may not be included in the family budget, there may be no relatives available, and neighbors may not be accustomed to exchange of sitting services. The detached worker may help neighbors learn to exchange services or he may arrange for child-care services in the community or at the school.

*8. Being sensitive to areas where extra reassurances or assistance may be needed.*

a. *Clothing:* Parents may stay away from events because they do not feel they have the proper clothing. Depending on the worker's sense of the situation, reassurances or even offers of clothing might be made with sensitivity to feelings of pride and rejection of "charity."

b. *Racial tensions:* Racial tensions seem to be constantly at a level of awareness, although there may be variation in how overtly they are expressed. In a situation of racial difference, the worker must be aware of the reactions of others to himself. In one school, where there were white and black community agents, the two conferred and they tried to minimize the strain of racial feelings between the worker and the people contacted. The worker must exercise skill and sensitivity as situations arise. For example, in one school the white agent was especially careful not to put the children of Black Muslim parents in situations where they must interact with her in front of their parents, a very stressful situation.

c. *Money:* In general, this is a topic which is best dealt with on a one-to-one basis, rather than in even a semipublic situation, since it is usually an area of great sensitivity. For example, in one homemaking class for adults, class members were asked to fill out cards with their names, addresses, and the amount of money they spent on groceries in a given period of time. The instructor noted that the amounts given were exaggerated, and deduced that they were concealing the amount actually spent.

d. *Reading and writing ability and the general educational level of clients:* It is best to avoid situations where clients would publicly reveal ignorance or lack of formal education. Clients may be especially sensitive when uninformed on matters closely related to the school. Parents in particular may be embarrassed to be found to have less skill in reading and writing than their children.

## Special Problems of the Detached Worker Approach

There are several special problems associated with the detached worker approach. These may be costs that the agency must be prepared to meet with additional support. One problem involves institutional strain that arises because the detached worker is a link between two very different kinds of organizations (formal organizations and primary groups) which have different atmospheres and place different expectations on the detached worker. The other cost relates to the high degrees of professional training required of the detached worker in order to do a job involving great complexity and independent functioning away from direct support and supervision.

1. *Institutional strain.* The detached worker is always at the vortex of institutional conflict. The school expects him to be objective, confine himself to organizational goals, and proceed on the basis of institutionally familiar methods. The primary group expects him to be broad-gauged in his goals and have an affectional commitment to the group itself. The school has a formal climate and wants to tie all his efforts to explicit educational goals, whereas the family has an informal climate and wants to consult with him on a wide range of problems. For the worker, the feeling of being always in the middle is the personal definition of the institutional dilemma. Without adequate protection it is our view that detached workers will quickly "burn out." Some protective steps are suggested below.

a. Make the detached worker explicitly aware of the institutional strain involved and thus lessen the sense of tension and frustration. Institutional strain should be seen as an intrinsic part of the job situation.

b. Explicitly state to the detached worker and primary group the agency's policy regarding outer limits of primary group behavior acceptable to the worker. For example, the New York City Youth Board overtly requires that workers must report to the police illegal activities, such as possession of weapons. This takes off the worker's shoulders many decisions about what to report or not report.

c. Set up a system of dual authority over the detached worker. That is, make the school-community agent responsible not only to the local school principal but also to a less directly

involved administrative level, such as a school-community relations headquarters within the central Board of Education. In
this way the agent as detached worker will receive organizational support should legitimate interests and desires of neighborhood groups run into opposition from local school administrators and staff with narrower perspectives.

  d. Help the detached worker refer certain problems to
other community agencies when personal involvement means a
clash with local school personnel. In one situation parents believed school personnel were biased. Rather than engage with
parents in attacking the school the agent suggested to the
parents that they place the problem in the hands of the city-
wide Human Relations Commission for investigation and action.

  e. Provide opportunity for frequent meetings among
school-community agents so that they can talk out their problems and obtain mutual support. These meetings should encourage candor and their setting should be nonthreatening (for
example, without superiors present).

  f. Rotate agents in and out of the detached worker assignment. There are limits to the amount of strain a worker
can tolerate over sustained periods of time. Temporarily moving people to different jobs in the system can provide an emotional rest. Other ways to provide rest and relief can also be
sought.

  2. *Training.* Because of the complexity of the detached
worker role, specialized training is usually necessary. Several
aspects of that training are noted below:

  a. The detached worker will be in fairly intimate contact with people regarding a wide variety of problems. In
low-income areas personal problems are not often discussed
with neighbors, nor do many persons use counseling services of
social agencies in contrast to public welfare and social services.
They may expose problems to a knowledgeable detached worker who is friendly, sympathetic, and trusted. The agent should
be trained to understand and counsel appropriately as the
need arises. He should have a well-developed sense of profes-

sional confidentiality. At the same time the detached worker should know how to avoid by effective referral becoming so involved in personal problems that he has no time left for organizational work in the neighborhood and for working on social problems on a broader basis.

b. Since the detached worker is separated from his agency, he is exposed much of the time to the values of neighborhood families and groups. He should be trained to evaluate situations objectively and determine legitimate priorities rather than accept the usual primary group value that group members should be protected before all else. The worker's training in the purposes of the detached worker approach and the nature of the job should be thorough. It will be only through internalizing professional values that he will maintain standards of merit in his job performance.

c. The detached worker should have knowledge and understanding of different cultures. He should be given techniques and special encouragement to cross class lines and immerse himself in the lives and needs of the client class. He should understand cultural differences not only in order to accept people but to work with them effectively. For instance, serious diagnostic errors can be made if the worker assumes that those who see no importance in schooling are unintelligent or that people who are loud and boisterous are emotionally unstable. The worker may be dealing with people who were brought up differently rather than people who were brought up "right."[4] The understanding of cultural difference does not necessarily mean accepting the other person's point of view. Thus, cleanliness and educational achievement may be seen as desirable even when the local population does not see their import. But a school teacher, who becomes fixated on dirty fingernails and criticizes the child on this basis may drive the child further away from educational goals. It would be better to accept the dirty fingernails, establish communication and close bonds with the child, and use these to foster both educational motivation and clean fingernails.

d. The detached worker needs substantial training: knowl-

4. Herbert H. Hyman, "The Value Systems of Different Classes: A Social Psychological Contribution to the Analysis of Stratification," in R. Bendix and S. M. Lipset (eds.), *Class, Status and Power* (Glencoe, Ill.: The Free Press (1953)), pp. 426-42.

edge of community resources, personality diagnosis, community structure, family structure, child development, and modes of community organization and action. The training requirements and expertise needed raise questions about current efforts utilizing undertrained-indigenous residents as detached workers.[5]

## The Detached Worker as a Mechanism by which the Community Influences the School

From the viewpoint of the community concerned with influencing the school, the detached worker mechanism may be considered in two ways: the possibilities for families and other community groups to influence the school through detached workers *employed by the school,* and the suitability of the detached worker as a mechanism directly *employed by the community.*

*Community use of the school's detached workers.* The greatest value for a family in having a detached worker from the school is access to a direct channel to the school. The obvious limits to this process are set by the capacity of the detached worker to effect changes in the school and the relatively few families or other groups that have access to detached workers. Nevertheless, if a number of families deliberately utilize the expectations of commitment to community interests and values that the detached worker approach requires as a lever to press its purposes on the school it can sometimes convert the detached worker into its own agent. Indeed, in some instances school-community agents acting as detached workers have, from the viewpoint of the school, over-identified with the community and undertaken community-serving roles (such as organizing pressure groups and campaigns) that

5. For a discussion on the dangers of hiring indigenous workers, see Edgar S. and Jean C. Cohn, "The War on Poverty: A Civilian Perspective," *The Yale Law Journal,* 73 (July 1964). These authors point out the dangers of using indigenous leaders in a neighborhood law firm, e.g., the problem of representing leaders from the same neighborhood who have opposing views. See George Brager, "The Indigenous Worker: A New Approach to the Social Work Technician," *Social Work,* 10 (April 1965), pp. 33-40, for a report on the use of indigenous workers in local community work.

not only increase the institutional strain of the role, previously noted, but also call forth restrictive responses from the school. The agent may be withdrawn by the school or even dismissed for "making trouble." The community may then be faced with considering whether it can effectively sustain such a means from its own resources and at its level of organizational capacity. Co-opting the detached worker may, however, be one way of initiating movement toward community organization capable of utilizing other mechanisms to influence the school.

*Community use of its own detached worker.* To what extent can community primary groups hire their own detached workers to influence the school? A crucial consideration is the matter of economic and organizational resources. It is more likely to be possible where families are relatively wealthy, educated, and experienced in voluntary organizational activity. Economically limited communities—the ones most likely to feel that the school should be changed—may have to depend on outside sources of support and not be able to control the selection or activities of persons employed. If sufficient political power can be developed to obtain public funds and keep control in the hands of the community, this risk can be averted. Occasionally funds are available from established voluntary associations, shifting the problem of control but by no means eliminating it.

In addition to the problem of resources, it is also true that the qualifications required for a community agent to operate as a detached worker in the school are in most ways directly the opposite of those for agents of the school working in the community. To gain access to the bureaucracy on behalf of the community, the community's detached worker needs knowledge of the workings of the bureaucracy and a capacity to reach and influence key persons within it. Persons are likely to have gained such knowledge by working within the system and hence to share, at least in part, the values and perspectives the community seeks to change. Persons do switch allegiance, however. Former teachers or school social workers may be willing to work for community groups and represent their interests. Social workers who understand the welfare system have been effectively used.[6] Lawyers with experience in government have been used by business firms to handle relations with government agencies. In general, the concept of the detached worker serving the community tends toward the professional or experienced person serving as expert advocate.

## Summary of Analysis of the Detached Worker

It is useful to briefly summarize our discussion. The detached worker is one who works outside the confines of an agency building, mingling freely with those he hopes to influence. He fosters informal friendly relationships as a basis for gaining personal acceptance and inducing change.

We have suggested that the role of a friendly neighbor is a useful model for the detached worker to adopt, although there are times when he will choose to act almost as a family member and others when he will choose to emphasize the formal professional aspects of the role. We discussed the pros and cons of several bases for assigning opinion leaders, that is, "bad apple," "key leader," "best chance," and the "average citizen."

There are certain problem situations for which the detached worker approach is most useful. Generally, these are the situations where clients are resistant to agency goals, and where the problem calls for someone to diagnose and correct the situation on the spot.

The detached worker has a variety of forms of influence he can use to bring about change. These include: referent power, the detached worker using the personal liking which a family has for him as a basis for inducing change; expert power, the detached worker using his status as a professional expert to bring about change; power by legitimation, the detached worker using his power as legitimate spokesman for society, for the school, or for some other group to bring about

6. Richard A. Cloward and Richard M. Elman, "The Storefront on Stanton Street: Advocacy in the Ghetto," in George A. Brager and Francis P. Purcell (eds.), *Community Action Against Poverty* (New Haven, Conn.: College & University Press, 1967), Chapter 16.

change; and reward and punishment power, the detached worker using his power to provide rewards and punishments to bring about change.

The major costs of the detached worker approach are twofold. The detached worker is subject to enormous strain because he is institutionally located between the conflicting expectations of the family and the school. And his role requires considerable and costly professional training. Finally the detached worker mechanism presents difficulties of control for the community if it tries to use it against bureaucracies.

# 6 ✦ The Opinion Leader

The opinion leader approach makes use of people who are influential in the local community, indigenous leaders who are in continuous contact with the life of the neighborhood because they reside there or engage in work that calls for such contact. Opinion leaders may occupy formal positions in the neighborhood, such as clergymen, or they may have no formal position (for example, a housewife on the block). Furthermore, different persons may be opinion leaders depending on area of interest or the issue involved. In one study it was pointed out that children were most influential in deciding what breakfast food the family should buy, fathers were decisive in the realm of politics, and women were most influential with respect to style of clothing.[1]

Since opinion leaders are, by definition, influential in the neighborhood, the essence of the opinion leader approach is the selection of those who are most likely to contribute to the goals of the school with respect to the particular problems involved. This will entail careful study of the school's community, with due sensitivity to various age groups and to segments of the population which the school seeks to influence. It will entail the establishment of effective relationships with leaders so as to enhance their understanding and support of the goals to be attained, as well as to utiltize their knowledge of the neighborhood. Generally, the opinion leader approach will be most useful when the clients (families and other community groups) are predisposed toward the values and goals of the school and when the community agent wishes to

THE COLLABORATION OF JACK ROTHMAN IN THE PREPARATION OF THIS CHAPTER IS ESPECIALLY ACKNOWL-EDGED.

1. Elihu Katz and Paul F. Lazarsfeld, *Personal Influence* (Glencoe, Ill.: The Free Press, 1955), pp. 245, 269, 271.

direct or mobilize the neighborhood for a particular objective. It will also be useful to influence a small segment of the community or a few families who are indifferent or negative toward the school when most of the neighborhood is positive. Even in circumstances where there is considerable opposition to school efforts and some indigenous leaders support such opposition, the opinion leader approach may be useful in neutralizing the opposition and in cultivating more positively oriented leadership influences. This will often require the use of other linking procedures coupled with the opinion leader approach.

As noted in chapter 1, the opinion leader approach does not permit great organizational initiative, but it does involve very high intensity of contact with the client groups. It does not provide much focused expertise, but it does possess moderate scope. Compared to the detached worker approach, this approach has less focused expertise and less initiative, but greater intensity and greater scope. A detached worker goes directly from the school to the client group. In contrast, the opinion leader is an intermediary between the school and the client group, volunteering his services because the agency or organization has no direct supervisory control over him. From an organizational point of view, this approach requires a recruitment procedure. However, the opinion leader approach has the advantage of utilizing an existing, and often powerful, network of influence to carry the school's message.

## Primary Group Dimensions
## of the Opinion Leader Approach

Like the detached worker, the opinion leader makes use of primary group relationships. These relationships are usually stronger than those of the detached worker because they are natural rather than established deliberately to deal with a particular problem. Furthermore, there are apt to be many different opinion leaders in any given school neighborhood but usually only a limited number of detached workers from the school.

In our discussion of the detached worker we suggested that

positive feelings between people involved in common or related tasks become increasingly necessary the more uncertain and ambiguous the task may be. In such a situation, there must be trust between the people involved in order to gain cooperation. In this regard the opinion leader, as a respected natural group member, may be able to generate more trust than the detached worker. Consequently, where a problem requires trust for solution, it may be desirable to involve opinion leaders in preference to direct activity with clients. There are two important qualifications. First it is important that the opinion leader be oriented toward the goals of the school. For instance, if a mother who is an opinion leader sees no reason why a quiet place should be provided for home study, it may have negative effects to bring her into contact with families whose practice in this respect the community agent is trying to change. On the other hand, where the opinion leader exhibits or supports forms of child socialization the school seeks to encourage, she may have more influence than a detached worker because modes of child development may be taught best by example or model.

The second qualification is related to the amount of expert knowledge necessary to solve a given problem. For instance, where knowledge of which agency to turn to for help is critical, the detached worker's professionalism may be more important than the opinion leader's greater intensity of positive feeling.

The opinion leader approach, more than any other, is likely to require sustained face-to-face relations with community residents. Such contact is most necessary in ambiguous situations requiring immediate response so as to give support to persons who depend on the opinion leader.

The opinion leader ordinarily has closer contact with families and community groups than does the detached worker. He can be involved in many aspects of living in the course of his usual activities. This depends, however, on whether the opinion leader is engaged in local employment, as is a local storekeeper, or is a local resident. However, while the opinion leader may be involved in many areas of primary group life, the detached worker may more easily discuss with families certain very private areas, such as personality problems or personal philosophy. The opinion leader probably will not have the expertise of the detached worker nor the latter's professional assurance of confidentiality.

The opinion leader can establish permanent relations with community families and groups as a neighbor rather than as a professional person with his clients. In addition, there is pressure on a detached worker from his agency to move on because another problem may seem more pressing. When opinion leaders have been located, and working relationships established they can provide continuing contacts in the neighborhood even when there is a succession of detached workers.

## The Opinion Leader Approach and Forms of Influence

### Referent Influence

With opinion leaders, referent power is likely to be strong and persuasive. The personal influence of the opinion leader or his success in carrying through activities will often inspire imitation or serve as a symbol to his neighbors. It is frequently through his force of personality that the opinion leader influences rather than through his economic status or formal position. Social scientists have observed that people will sometimes imitate each other without even realizing it, and this may be the case with opinion leader influence.[2]

### Legitimation

Unlike the family, where the roles of mother and father have some clearly legitimized forms of influence in our society, neighbors are not vested with official authority over other neighbors, although certain types of opinion leaders, such as clergymen, can draw on their institutional positions for legitimation. This is

2. Ronald Lippitt, Norman Polansky, Fritz Redl, and Sidney Rosen, "The Dynamics of Power: A Field Study of Social Influence in Groups of Children," in Eleanor E. Maccoby, Theodore M. Newcomb, and Eugene L. Hartley (eds.), *Readings in Social Psychology,* 3rd edition (New York: Holt, Rinehart and Winston, 1958), pp. 251-64; *see also* Albert Bandura and Richard H. Walters, *Social Learning and Personality Development* (New York: Holt, Rinehart and Winston, 1963), Chapter 2, "The Role of Imitation," pp. 47-108.

not to say that legitimate power may not be an attribute of some "neighbor" who is an opinion leader. There is no general social mandate to legitimize the influence of a neighbor. Indeed, a balance must be struck between being "nosey" and being "helpful" to sustain the leadership role. One cannot assume that neighbors will accept such leadership. Norms may have to be deliberately encouraged for a given neighborhood. Thus, norms of helping a neighbor in distress, of greeting newcomers and making them feel at home, or of watching out for the property of a neighbor when he is away must be cultivated in some neighborhoods. The processes by which this is done are not clearly understood. However, once such norms have been established, opinion leaders who uphold or symbolize such norms can gain aspects of legitimate power. The opinion leader's legitimate influence, therefore, will probably be directly related to the normative development of the neighborhood.

*Reward and Punishment*

The above considerations generally hold also for reward and punishment as a basis for influence by opinion leaders. Such influence depends on a relatively cohesive neighborhood. The opinion leader's major means for punishment and reward are his withdrawal of neighborhood contact and help and increase in such interpersonal rewards as approval or friendship. In the small rural community and in some ethnic urban neighborhoods, where much of a family's social and economic activity may take place, the effect of local group support can be decisive. The threat of withdrawal of group support, or ostracism, is one of the most severe punishments that can be leveled against an individual.

*Expertise*

As already pointed out, the opinion leader is most effective where everyday practical experience is a sufficient knowledge base. He knows the specific neighborhood and its people intimately, an advantage that may compensate for lack of expertise as a basis of influence.

In summary, the distinguishing characteristics of the opinion leader as contrasted with the detached worker are the extent to which the opinion leader depends on referent power and a fairly cohesive group. An opinion leader approach is not likely to be very useful where local social organization is weak or disorganized. We have not discussed the geographic scope of influence of a given opinion leader—a single home, block, neighborhood, wider district. The scope is probably best determined by the state of social organization. When the school-community agent has such information he can be selective in his choice of opinion leaders and his use of them.

## The Opinion Leader and Group Hostility to Agency Goals

There is a feeling among many practioners that the best way to reach local groups is to find out who the leader is and appeal to the group through him. However, some studies suggest that the leader does not necessarily set group values; he may be a follower and upholder of group values.[3] As such he is frequently the last to give up a position taken by a group. Consequently, when the group's values and practices are contrary to those of the school, the opinion leader may be the least helpful channel of communication. He functions like a lightning rod, attracting messages he considers contrary to group norms and turning them aside before they reach the group. Under such circumstances the group might be reached better by nonleaders or by persons who wish to see the group changed. However, in situations where the group is receptive to the school's purposes, the opinion leader may

3. Several studies have shown that group leaders who are influential find it difficult to resist group norms once they are established. F. Merei, "Group Leadership and Institutionalization," *Human Relations,* 2 (January 1949), pp. 23-39; also in Eleanor E. Maccoby, T. M. Newcomb, and E. L. Hartley (eds.), *Readings in Social Psychology,* 3rd edition (New York: Holt, Rinehart and Winston, 1958), pp. 522-32; R. J. Pellegrin, "The Achievement of High Status and Leadership in the Small Group," *Social Forces,* 32 (October 1953), pp. 10-16; A. Paul Hare, *Handbook of Small Group Research* (Glencoe, Ill.: The Free Press, 1962), Chapter 2, "Norms and Social Control," pp. 23-48.

serve to reinforce the message and make sure it is listened to by group members. As a rule of thumb, the opinion leader approach is not useful when the opinion leaders are negative. Furthermore, it should be noted that it is often difficult to persuade an opinion leader to change his views because to do so would weaken his leadership position. In one school split by racial conflicts, a southern white leader was persuaded to join the after-school program composed predominantly of black mothers. The white woman became an enthusiastic supporter of the after-school program, but her former white friends would no longer speak to her.

Even though a neighborhood might be hostile to parts of a school program, a group seldom has such a unified set of values that some basis of common contact cannot be established between the neighborhood group and the school.[4] Therefore, an opinion leader need not be put in the position of having to choose between leadership in his group and demands of some outside formal organization. Rather, the school should establish bonds with the opinion leader (and through him with the group) on a wide range of issues. When these bonds are strong, the school can move into the more sensitive areas of difference with some hope of producing change. Put more simply, where there is some area of conflict between the school and the primary group, the school should first approach community leaders on the basis of what they have in common. The extent to which the opinion leader can link the school with his group is directly related to the number of common ties he can find outside the area of disagreement. In one case where an agent was trying to set up an inter-racial after-school program in a community where the southern whites bitterly resented black participation, he was able to make some headway by first offering physical facilities for church activities, although the white fundamentalist churches were strongholds of segregationists. In addition, he emphasized the common efforts of school and

4. The point is that groups usually have multiple value systems; thus, there is room for agreement on some issues. M. Tumin, for example, showed that segregationists in the South frequently have a conflict between their segregationist policy and their educational values, or between their segregationist policies and their value of law and order. "Exposure to Mass Media and Readiness for Desegregation," *Public Opinion Quarterly*, 2 (Summer, 1957), pp. 237-51.

church to educate the child. As the number of bonds between the school and the community of white southerners grew, the school could more directly move into the issue of segregation. Eventually, the white ministers went so far as to permit blacks to become members of their churches. This kind of approach assumes that the school and the opinion leader are involved in a diffuse set of relations with each other. This is certainly true of the opinion leader's relationship to his group, and the school can systematically use this to pursue its policy.

## The Location of Opinion Leaders

As noted earlier, the crucial problem with the opinion leader approach pertains to locating neighborhood opinion leaders. The problem is least when the opinion leaders in the area can with confidence be assumed to accurately understand communications about the school's program, have interest in the program, and support it. Where these assumptions can be made, the community agent can usually communicate throughout the area with some form of the mass media, expecting that the message will come to the attention of opinion leaders and be passed along in a favorable manner.[5] In some cases the opinion leader himself may not come into direct contact with the message, but the information may be passed on to him by someone else (who may be called an information leader) who is informed but does not have the social influence of a true opinion leader.[6] In this case, the opinion leader may pick up the facts from the information leader and pass them along, communicating concurrently his interest in favorable action.

When the worker cannot assume knowledge, interest, and support on the part of the opinion leaders in the area, he will have to utilize other means than mass media to reach them if he wants

5. Katz and Lazarsfeld, in *Personal Influence*, point out that mass media primarily reach opinion leaders. We are suggesting that opinion leaders will not pass on messages of the organization that are negatively oriented to the group. When messages are positively oriented to the group, they will be relayed with less distortion.

6. See Katz and Lazarsfeld's discussion, in *Personal Influence*, of the information leader who is not an opinion leader.

to capitalize on the opinion leader approach. There are a number of ways opinion leaders may be located, each tending to select different and sometimes distinct groups of leaders.

Most agents feel that every neighborhood has opinion leaders and that they are especially important in fragmented, disorganized neighborhoods where people put enormous trust in the few sources of advice and counsel they feel are reliable.[7] These opinion leaders may be different from those visible in stable, middle-class neighborhoods. They may be informal and perhaps appear as deviant types. School-community agents have reported that where individual families are cohesive and ties between families few, a family is likely to have its own internal opinion leader and therefore must be approached separately. In neighborhoods where the families themselves may be somewhat disorganized, it may be better to use opinion leaders from outside the family but in daily contact with it. In such situations the local (usually informal) opinion leaders can be of great help to the community worker if he can locate them and form working relationships. Some ways opinion leaders may be located are discussed below.

*Contact organizations working in the area for names of leaders.* The convenience of this source is obvious but the opinion leaders so identified may be selectively biased in a number of ways. If informants in the agencies mention those with whom they have strong working relationships, such persons may be especially positive toward the particular agency and may in general be more favorable toward established organizations—including the school—than the population in general. To guard against this bias the agency might be asked to name both positive and negative opinion leaders. The ways that agencies articulate with the community affect their likelihood of knowing opinion leaders. For example, health agencies, welfare agencies, the police, churches, community centers, and community-action agencies differ in the extent to which they direct their efforts to individual families or broader segments of the community. Opinion leaders identified by clergymen are more likely to be "positive" and those identified by

7. Nicholas Von Hoffman, "Reorganization in the Casbah," *Social Progress* (United Presbyterian Church), Vol. LII, 6 (April 1962).

the police more likely to be "negative". Sensitivity to such differences should guide the community agent to a sampling of organizations as sources of names of opinion leaders who best fit the purposes to be achieved in the school-community program.

Another source of bias reported by some community workers arises from the tendency of agency personnel to suggest persons in the local community who play formal leadership roles or have a formally recognized responsibility (for example, as officers of associations). Such leaders may have formal prestige but the extent to which they actually function as opinion leaders in the local community requires careful examination. If they are, indeed, opinion leaders, they are likely to represent the positive, cooperative end of the range of values within the community toward established organizations, including the school.

The school-community agent must consider the position of his informant within nominating organizations in order to assess the information obtained about opinion leaders. Informants at different levels of the agency hierarchy may identify different kinds of opinion leaders who exercise their influence in different ways and in different areas of life. Administrative personnel may be better acquainted with local leaders in formal roles, whereas agency personnel who deal directly with clients may be better informed about informal grassroots opinion leaders. The same point may be made for organizations themselves. In our own initial observations we found that representatives of professional organizations were less informed about leaders in lower economic areas. At the lowest economic level, welfare workers, police, visiting nurses, local community newspaper officials, and local politicians knew more about the leadership structure of a given school district.

*Visit local places and attend local events to observe interaction.*[8] Many school-community agents believe that it is necessary to go

8. See Alexander H. Leighton's report on a World War II relocation center for Japanese. He describes how evacuee cooperation and assistance were enlisted when government personnel sought to identify leaders among the evacuees. *The Governing of Men* (Princeton, N. J.: Princeton University Press, 1946). pp. 90-98. Also see Gene C. Fusco, *School-Home Partnership in Depressed Urban Neighborhoods* (Washington, D. C.: U.S. Department of Health, Education and Welfare, Office of Education, 1964).

out into the community to locate true grassroots opinion leaders who are operating in the neighborhood. It is useful to look for local opinion leaders in places popular with a cross-section of the local community, such as grocery stores, eating places, drug stores, car washes, laundromats, beauty salons, and barbershops. Frequently, people who own or operate these businesses seem to know about the people they serve. When they serve a cross-section of the community, their potential knowledge of opinion leaders is great. They may be opinion leaders themselves.

Another way to try to locate local opinion leaders is to frequent a range of local places, each of which serves a different segment of the population. Such places could include bars and poolrooms. However, the worker should consider the effect on his image if he is seen going into places considered disreputable.

Another possibility is to attend special events in the area—political rallies, church affairs, school programs—and observe who are active and influential.

In general, when he is observing in the local community, certain issues must be faced by the community agent. In what role should he present himself, his professional role or informally as a friend? How soon can he expect people to give him information and how much information can he expect to get? How can he evaluate the authenticity of information and its source? When appearing in local places, is his presence viewed as threatening or helpful? On what does the agent focus his conversation? In order to make use of local opinion leaders, there must be some kind of informal tie between the worker and the local resident, not necessarily as intimate as friendship, but resting on some basis of mutual knowledge and trust.

We know of two cases where school-community agents learned who the collectors were for the local numbers game, an illegal gambling operation. In one instance, the agent used these persons as a source of information on local life and tried to pass information along through this channel, with undetermined success. In the other case, numbers collectors, who went into almost every home, cooperated in getting out the vote on a school millage issue, with seeming success. Agents involved in this situation regarded these community persons as an excellent future source of influence, but one that needed to be used discreetly. For example, they did not expect block club leaders who seek to influence the local population to confer with the numbers runners in order to pass along information in the neighborhood, a situation that would be mutually embarrassing. The agents felt they could act inconspicuously as go-betweens for the two groups, or possibly in time bring the numbers runners and block club leaders together at school events. But the numbers runners would require some other reason than their unique "business" role in the neighborhood as the basis for such contacts; they could not appear as numbers runners.

*Knock on doors in the neighborhood.* In this basically sociometric approach, a selected person in the household is asked a series of questions intended to ascertain the people with whom he or she has ties of friendship and influence.[9] Survey forms have been designed for this purpose and a network of influence relationships can be determined in this way. There are some drawbacks to this approach. It is time-consuming and if done by professionals would be costly. If attempted by volunteers, it is questionable whether or not local inner city people would feel free to give information. The same fear of retaliation which keeps residents from reporting misdemeanors to the police may keep them from providing names in a sociometric interview.

*Determine who heads various civic organizations in the neighborhood.* Heads of various civic groups and associations in the neighborhood can be identified—political clubs, veterans associations, businessmen's boards, fraternal clubs such as Masons or Elks, lay church groups, and the like. This gives a valid but limited picture

9. Nicholas Von Hoffman, "Finding and Making Leaders," Ann Arbor Economic Research and Action Project (mimeographed), 1964. Nanci Gitlin describes in detail an approach utilized in identifying and organizing tenants in a public housing project. "Public Housing: The Welfare State in Action" (mimeographed), 1965. For information on studying informal structures of communities, see Charles P. Loomis, "Tapping Human Power Lines," *Adult Leadership*, 1 (February 1953), and Roland L. Warren, *Studying your Community* (New York: Russell Sage Foundation, 1955), pp. 352-55. For an example of a sociometric questionaire, see E. Katz and P. F. Lazarsfeld, *Personal Influence*, Appendix B, p. 340.

of leadership associated with the formal workings of community voluntary associations and institutions. It misses informal and subtle leadership processes and is biased in the direction of people with a middle-class status or outlook. Such leaders and their organizations can be helpful on city-wide issues, such as millage elections and general Board of Education policy. Usually the principal of the school can give the agent an initial list of some of these leaders, and through interviewing them a wider circle of similar influential persons can be put together.

This method has the additional limitation arising from the likelihood that city neighborhoods tend to lack formal voluntary associations or institutions from which to draw opinion leaders.

*Draw on past personal experience in the neighborhood.* This ready source of information is subject to bias. Just as the police tend to know the local troublemakers and visiting teachers are likely to know individual families but little about neighborhood variables, the school-community agent is likely to have systematically biased contacts with community members. The temptation is to characterize an entire neighborhood on the basis of limited personal experience. This can lead to errors in judgement about programming or errors of assessment in the effectiveness of one's own activities. The agent needs some objective check to set his experience in perspective. This may be as simple as keeping a record of the demographic characteristics of the people with whom he comes into contact and comparing it with the demographic characteristics of the neighborhood in general. This would reveal whether contacts were grossly nonrepresentative as to race, age, or income level.

*Selective mass recruitment.* This approach assumes that if one publicizes a program via the mass media, the opinion leaders are likely to respond if they have any interest at all in the program. The community agent needs then to develop a means of assessing who the opinion leaders actually are among the people who come to some publicized event or who participate in some program. Some agents have done this by observing the participants in ongoing programs and making common-sense judgments. Some agents believe that persons who first gravitate to positions of leadership in program activities are likely to be local opinion leaders. This can be checked by further observation. The mass-media approach as generally used probably selects opinion leaders who support the school's program. Moreover these opinion leaders may not be typical of the community population and therefore influential only in small segments of the local community.

Some agents have believed that opinion leaders were present in their after-school and evening programs, but that these opinion leaders would not act on behalf of the school or encourage attendance by others because they did not want to share the school program. In areas where symbols of prestige are relatively hard to obtain, participation in school events may come to be regarded as prestigious, and attempts may be made to maintain a closed prestige system.

*Deliberately train for opinion leadership.* In some circumstances an agent may want deliberately to train opinion leaders, such as in neighborhoods where the natural opinion leaders are either negatively oriented or simply not interested in his program; in situations where there is a leadership vacuum, perhaps because opinion leaders in low-income neighborhoods leave when their economic circumstance permits; or in situations where only part of the neighborhood has natural opinion leaders and the agent would like to train leaders to affect the other portion.

Training opinion leaders usually involves several components: (a) organizational information skills in running meetings and planning, committee work, and the like; (b) community information—resources, workings of city government, and the like; (c) human relations and interpersonal skills.

There are some differences between natural opinion leaders and trained opinion leaders. Trained leaders may in fact more nearly approximate the information leader than the opinion leader. School-community agents seem to think that, on the whole, they deal most often with modified opinion leaders, or information leaders, and that such leaders are also likely to be the products of the formal and informal training experiences they obtain in the school.

The training and developing of opinion leaders requires a

long-term effort that is interlocked with other aspects of the school-community program—such as the stimulation of community action and of voluntary associations. Experienced community agents have suggested that the essence of developing opinion leaders is the creation of situations in which leadership can emerge.

## The Use of the Child as an Opinion Leader

It may be possible under certain circumstances for the child to function as an opinion leader in the family. For example, if a school program is attractive to the child but children can attend only if accompanied by their parents, the child may be effective in getting his parents to the school. There may be other circumstances in which the child may influence his parents considerably.[10] Obviously, the child as an opinion leader is narrowly limited, but should not be overlooked.

It may be noted that the school has often without realizing it made use of children as opinion leaders, particularly in such areas as citizenship and healthful living habits. The child in many families has more education, and sometimes wider experiences in community living, than his parents. In such circumstances there is potential for considerable strain for the child and for the family. Therefore, it may be desirable that the process not be made too conscious or explicit. However, the school-community agent should be aware that the child can function as an opinion leader and information bearer for certain objectives in some segments of the community.

## Hiring Opinion Leaders

Persons who are opinion leaders can be hired and made part of the school's community program. This could involve employing people from the neighborhood as classroom aides, nonpro-

10. In some extreme cases, children actually dictate to their parents. See Katz and Lazarsfeld, *Personal Influence*, p. 245.

fessional workers, afternoon program group leaders, and in similar roles. Some of the issues involved in hiring such personnel can be explored more appropriately in chapters on the settlement house and common-messenger approaches. In general it is noted here that hiring persons from the local community allows the school to exercise more control than if the persons were volunteers. This can be a costly venture unless the local person has the requisite skill to perform the job and high motivation to perform well.

It is felt by some agents that the volunteer opinion leader who is involved out of personal commitment is a more reliable and sustained source of help than paid leaders. However, the agent cannot be as directive or as focused in making demands upon the volunteer opinion leader as he can upon one who is employed. It should be kept in mind that opinion leaders, working closely with an organization and in a sense co-opted by it, will influence the organization as well as be influenced by it. The possible consequences of such influence must be counted among the costs of using this approach.[11]

## The Stage in Program Development
## Where Opinion Leaders Are Most Useful

Where opinion leaders support the organization's goals, they can be used to attract members of the community into various programs, especially those of voluntary associations or those operated in the mode of the settlement house approach. Under these circumstances the opinion leader approach can be the first linking mechanism in a sequence.

Under other conditions the opinion leader approach may be used to lend continuing support and publicity to ongoing programs. Settlement house type programs may also prepare class members, either intentionally or as a by-product, to act as opinion or information leaders in the community.

There is often the risk that negative opinion leaders will

11. Philip Selznick, *TVA and the Grass Roots: A Study in the Sociology of Formal Organizations* (Berkeley and Los Angeles: University of California Press, 1949).

become involved in school-community activities. The community worker must assess the consequences of such negative leadership and decide whether he can temporarily overlook it while dealing with such positive leadership as does exist, or whether it is necessary to work with the negative leaders before he can really get any program underway. By helping critical leaders get some of the things they desire or by trying to isolate or neutralize them, the community agent may tip the balance toward the positive, supportive opinion leaders.

## Special Problems and Costs
## of the Opinion Leader Approach

Compared to the detached worker approach, the opinion leader mechanism generally requires far less in terms of training time and economic resources (especially salary). In addition, when it is operative it can reach far more people. There are, however, organizational problems of agency control, problems of knowledge, and training requirements.

*Agency control.* Insofar as the school utilizes the opinion leader, and insofar as the opinion leader influences because of his leadership in the group, it may well be that the interests of the group receive more attention from the opinion leader than the needs of the school. Even if these needs in general overlap, at any given time the priorities that the neighborhood and the school assign to a problem might differ markedly. An opinion leader may have his own timetable, sometimes personal, such as taking a vacation at the time when the school would like to organize a summer activity. Or the neighborhood might be more interested in engaging in a campaign for a better interracial housing policy at the time the school would want energy put into the local after-school program. The more the school depends for its chief source of influence on an opinion leader procedure the more it is likely to lose control over the exact timing, occurrence, or content of a given event.

Not only may there be legitimate competing interests, but

nepotism and nonmerit considerations are liable to enter the picture as well. Because of his strong sense of loyalty to the primary group, the opinion leader may become a special pleader for its narrow interests. Thus, if a group member wishes special classes or arrangements for his child, the opinion leader may push for this out of a sense of personal obligation to the person or because he knows and likes the child. The opinion leader, like the detached worker, is at the nexus of two social forces—the neighborhood group life and the bureaucratic school—which have antithetical atmospheres. However, because of his lack of professional identity and lack of close economic ties to the school, the opinion leader when in doubt will most likely respond to the norms of the family and the community, diminishing agency control over his activities.

*Problems of knowledge.* In utilizing opinion leaders the agency relinquishes to some extent direct application of its knowledge to client groups. The opinion leader, an indigenous neighbor rather than a trained professional, becomes the vehicle of intervention into community group life, which sets the limits on the knowledge available. Therefore, the school-community agent will want to inform himself in advance about the knowledge, capacities, and potential utility of the opinion leader he may seek to use in his program. In general, he will see to it that expert knowledge is made available by some other procedure and hence will couple the opinion leader approach with that of the detached worker, settlement house, or delegated function. In neighborhoods where orientations are positive toward the school and education level is fairly high, the lack of expert knowledge by opinion leaders is less important.

*Training problems.* It is difficult to know what makes one person rather than another an opinion leader. Less than other forms of leadership, it may not be a function of superior status or income but more of interpersonal dynamics. It frequently rests on referent power of a particularly subtle kind; some observers have suggested in other contexts that social contagion or unconscious imitation may play a part. It is difficult to know how to train people to radiate this kind of personal magnetism, but it would seem to be somewhat similar to aspects we have discussed in training detached workers. Rather than train opinion leaders, it is more promising to recruit natural opinion leaders and provide them with kinds of information which will enhance their leadership, for example, knowledge of community resources and of school objectives and programs.

An additional problem is the training of the school-community agent to prepare him to utilize opinion leaders effectively. This involves training in locating opinion leaders as well as in when to use them, as discussed in earlier sections of this chapter. Training should focus on diagnosis of group structure so that one can spot opinion leaders and determine whether they are positive, negative, or mixed. Personnel must also be trained in analysis of the conditions under which opinion leaders can be effective, what their limitations are, and how the opinion leader approach can be used in sequence with and in conjunction with other linking mechanisms.

## The Use of Opinion Leaders by the Community to Influence the School

As a linking mechanism, the use of community opinion leaders by groups in the community seeking to change the school presents difficult problems. If it can be used, it has the advantage of requiring very few additional resources, in contrast, for example, to using an employed advocate. This possibility assumes that the local community is sufficiently cohesive to have opinion leaders who can speak with effective backing. The more fundamental question is, however, how effective a community opinion leader can be as an influence for change in a bureaucratic organization. The qualities of opinion leadership in the neighborhood are quite different from the kind of technical knowledge often required to produce change in a bureaucracy. Community opinion leaders can primarily contribute to change in organizations through their ability to mobilize community groups for pressure and protest. They are not likely to deal very effectively with technical matters, such as details of the school budget and accounting system, or the educational qualities of a textbook in mathematics or chemistry or black history. These require expert specialists. The community's opinion leaders may, however, press for the school to accept independent expert advocates.

Another conception of community use of the opinion leader is that the community can try to reach opinion leaders *within* the bureaucracy, among the school staff. Aside from acquiring the resources and the means of penetrating the school organization sufficiently to identify opinion leaders, such leaders are likely to be in formal positions within the organization. For instance, the principal is often the most influential person in a building or the superintendent in a school system. The usual authority structure of the school bureaucracy is intended, partly, to make this so. Very often, therefore, such persons are targets for community change efforts rather than being accessible as agents of change on behalf of the community. Furthermore, administrative officials in schools are generally drawn from middle and upper-middle socioeconomic levels and are likely to reflect viewpoints of these levels rather that those of lower socioeconomic segments of the community. Their notions of what "the people in our community think" will be biased, unless special efforts are made to see that this is not so.

Other opinion leaders within the school may be sought, such as teachers or social workers or school community agents known for their influence in the informal organization of the school. If they are in contact with community interests, they may serve as communication channels. This is especially useful when the primary need of the community is to correct impressions about community situations, such as a misperception about family responsibility or about support for educational programs. When values and choices are at issue, such persons as links from the community will face dilemmas of loyalty in which they may have to choose whether to become advocates for community objectives or to support the school. If the former, they lose influence within the school as opinion leaders; if the latter they no longer serve community purposes by their influence.

In summary, we would suggest that the opinion leader

mechanism is of limited usefulness to the community for its own purposes. In technical matters community opinion leaders are seriously handicapped. Opinion leaders inside the school are often either class-biased in perspective or likely to lose effectiveness from the community's viewpoint whenever issues between the school and the community involve more than transmission of information.

# 7 ❧ The Settlement House

The objective of the settlement house approach, like that of the detached worker, is to provide attractive services whose proximity will induce families to participate in them. What differentiates it from the detached worker is the provision of physical facilities and the fact that the worker does not go to the home of the client group. Programs carried on regularly may induce intense face-to-face encounters, as when therapy sessions are offered. If the objectives of a particular effort require either special equipment or an accessible meeting place, the settlement house procedure may be ideal. The purpose of the settlement house approach is to bring people together. They meet in a location "central" to the community under professional staff guidance. Probably the best-known school program of the settlement house type is the "lighted" school.[1] In many cities school buildings remain open after school hours to allow the adult community to use the facilities.

Bringing parents and other community residents into the school building is an obvious and widely adopted practice once a school has decided to develop a local school-community program. However, it should be regarded as an approach with rather specific qualities, and school-community agents are cautioned against relying on it too exclusively. It permits a range of intensive contacts between professional experts and community groups, but has a low degree of organizational initiative, depending as it does on the voluntary cooperation of persons. Its range of scope is variable,

THE COLLABORATION OF JOHN L. ERLICH IN THE PREPARATION OF THIS CHAPTER IS ESPECIALLY ACKNOWL-
EDGED.

1. See the following for a description of the "lighted" school concept: Carl L. Marburger, "Considerations for Educational Planning," in A. Harry Passon (ed.), *Education in Depressed Areas* (New York: Bureau of Publications, Teachers College, Columbia University, 1963), pp. 298-321; and Henry Saltzman, "The Community School in the Urban Setting," pp. 322-31.

determined by both physical (location, transportation, etc.) and such social factors as orientation of the community toward education and the school and neighborhood conflicts.

The considerable experience of community agents with the settlement house approach allows us to present some of their practical conclusions as well as to consider some of the theoretical characteristics of this linking mechanism.

## Forms of Influence

*Expertise.* An opportunity is provided for professional expertise to be focused on the client population. As a rule the staff person has specific long-range change goals for the client group, such as improved self-image, increased academic skills for parent or child, or increased parental ability to motivate the child academically. Client groups are usually small and informal, thus allowing much interaction through which the professional person can bring his skills to bear.

The settlement house approach is limited for the professional "expert" in situations where teaching is best done by example or where the content of learning must arise from on-the-scene examination of the problem. However, where knowledge of how to deal with a problem has become somewhat standardized, the settlement house approach may be a superior vehicle.

*Legitimation.* The settlement house approach makes less use of legitimate power than the voluntary association procedure. The areas of life the worker can legitimately influence are not clear. The worker's role definition is likely to be ambiguous, his role changing as the community changes, or as new information or skills which may be taught to local residents are developed. The job may be extremely diverse, ranging from direct teaching to planning for experts to teach, to supervising the entire program. A strong group with a stable membership may develop norms about appropriate behavior, so the worker can acquire legitimation in this manner. Legitimation on this basis generally will not be as powerful as that available to the detached worker. The settlement house groups may seem artificial in the sense that they are set up for specific and limited purposes, with little contact between group members occurring outside the class situation. Consequently, they do not develop norms as capable of controlling behavior as those of a primary group. However, borrowing legitimation from the school, the worker may reinforce norms that support the school, or he may try to alter those not in support of the school.

*Referent power.* Referent power may be developed by the worker because he is often with his client group long enough to become emotionally significant for the members. His own leadership capacities and status conferred on him because of specialized knowledge may contribute to his referent power.

*Reward and punishment power.* The physical facilities of the settlement house program are set up to provide recreational and educational services to the client population. The use of special equipment and staff services can be withheld as punishment for poor behavior and made available as a reward for cooperative behavior.

## *Types of Families and the Settlement House Approach*

For the well-organized family, this approach offers little except when changes in the school (for example, in curriculum) require extensive and systematic learning by parents. Thus, those who want to learn the new math so as to help the child would benefit from a more intensive expert explanation than can usually be provided by voluntary associations. Even with little organizational initiative, the settlement house approach does not discourage such families. They take the initiative to find out about the program, are able to ask for what they want, and participate largely of their own accord.

By contrast, parents who are indifferent or hostile might never join in the settlement house programs. Unless something like a detached worker approach is used to recruit this type of family, it may not be reached.

Families oriented positively toward the school but that lack basic knowledge or are disorganized can benefit from a settlement house approach. They generally have enough initiative to come on their own to groups. In addition, their problems often require the expertise which the settlement house can provide through its trained leaders.

## Forms of Settlement House

The settlement house and the auxiliary voluntary association approaches may be viewed as forming a continuum, with most actual programs in either approach combining characteristics of both. For example, at one extreme a voluntary association group might be a PTA which meets three or four times a year to deal with general issues. At the other extreme—indistinguishable from the settlement house idea—one can find a PTA which breaks down into parent study groups meeting frequently with professional people to develop ways of motivating and helping their children academically. Most PTA groups actually fall somewhere between these extremes, spending some time on specific educational issues but given little professional assistance in dealing with them.

One type of program which appears to be similar to both voluntary association and the settlement house approach is a separate kind of activity. After-school and evening courses, taught by regular teachers who are paid for their time can be regarded simply as part of the ongoing educational activities of the school, except that the participants act as common messengers with dual membership in the school group and local family or neighborhood unit. Adult education classes may also occur in a blended form, with some characteristics of a voluntary association or settlement house program, rather than being strictly adult education activities.

There is a marked difference between an adult education class and a settlement house class. Adult education courses most often have a classroom atmosphere: formal interpersonal relations, formally planned class content, and a large attendance. Often fees are charged for these classes. A settlement house class tends to have informal interpersonal relations, flexible programming, small numbers in the class, nominal fees or none at all.[2]

2. Studies on group decisions suggest that when members participate in group discussion and decision-making, as opposed to listening to a lecture, there is more effective change in their behavior and attitudes. See K. Lewin "Group Decision and Social Changes," in T. M. Newcomb and E. L. Hartley (eds.), *Readings in Social Psychology* (New York: Holt, Rinehart and Winston, 1947), pp. 330-44. More recent studies have stressed the importance of commitment to engage in activities. J. W. Brehm and A. R. Cohen, *Explorations in Cognitive Dissonance* (New York: Wiley, 1962); see chapters 9 and 10 on "The Participation Hypothesis," in Sidney Verba, *Small Groups and Political Behavior: A Study of*

## Issues in Using the Settlement House Approach

*Recruitment for Settlement House Programs*

Some settlement house activities may already be underway but often a program has to be launched. A combination of techniques may be used—especially mass media, the modified detached worker, and the common messenger approach. Recruitment on a mass media basis tends to attract people who already support the schools. This has the advantage of drawing in friendly cooperative persons who tend to be least upsetting to traditional school personnel. However, if the agent wants to contact the hard-to-reach families, a combined recruitment approach is necessary. Families hostile or indifferent to the schools are unlikely to respond to mass media appeals. One effective sequence has been to establish a firm program for preschool families who are attracted and then, when the program is underway, begin to draw in hard-to-reach families.

Some other recruitment procedures which have been used include: (a.) flyers distributed in local businesses with heavy neighborhood trade—grocery stores, laundromats, beauty salons, etc.; (b.) flyers sent home to parents via the children; (c.) questionaires tapping program interests, filled out by parents at parent-teacher conferences; (d.) formation of a committee of parents active in local churches and block clubs who help plan the program and publicize it in their groups; (e.) recruitment of individuals on a modified detached worker basis, or as they come into the schools for other reasons; (f.) use of word-of-mouth publicity—that is, reliance on the opinion leader approach.

As recruiters, participants are apt to attract people like themselves. This may be particularly relevant in racially mixed areas. White participants generally draw in other white participants, and black participants draw in blacks.

The specialized drawing power of certain kinds of programs

should again be noted. Different types of programs attract different types of people. For example, experience suggests that courses in auto mechanics and classes preparing for navy and post-office exams can be effective in recruiting school dropouts and others especially hard to reach.

Two recruiting sequences which different agents employed to get a settlement house type program underway are given below as examples of different combined recruitment techniques.

1. The agent used a modified detached worker approach to contact parents who were either in support of him or at worst, indifferent. These parents were active in other local organizations, such as churches and neighborhood associations, and were chosen, in part, for this reason. These parents formed a program committee to plan program content which they felt would meet community needs. The committee then did the bulk of the recruitment for the program, using flyers and capitalizing on their membership in other organizations to aid publicity (mass media and common messenger approaches).

2. The agent tried to contact as many parents as possible at parent-teacher conferences. She gave them a questionaire to assess their reactions to the school program. Flyers were sent home with the children with a section to be returned where the parents checked whether or not they were interested in the adult program. Those interested were contacted by mail or phone, and a regular class program was planned, based on this information. The agent publicized the classes widely by distributing flyers in public places and by acting as a semidetached worker, publicizing the program by word of mouth with the owners of neighborhood stores.

*Program Oriented to Child, Adult, or Both?*

Programming for the child assumes that it is most effective to focus attention directly on the person in whom change is ultimately sought. Programming for adults assumes that changes in parental outlook and behavior will have the desired effect on their children. It may be desirable to seek a combined impact on both parents and children, perhaps in a sequence if it is impossible to do both simultaneously. One should consider programming for the family where the child is uninterested, or reverse the order when the family is uninterested. Another principle is to select the most relevant issue, for example, where the child's weakness is poor reading, work with the child or the family on the reading problem.

Programs for children have stressed recreation, socialization, and supplemental education. The goal is to use groups to motivate the child academically so he will be able to take advantage of classroom experiences and other opportunities. It has been demonstrated that participation in informal classes and groups under competent leadership can be a positive experience which contributes to raising children's self-esteem.

When the agent is dealing with hostile, indifferent or low-esteem populations, his major task may be simply to get people into the school building. This is also true for communities where parents have usually been unwelcome at school, or where staff members must be convinced that parents will come into the schools.

*Stress on Intermediate Goals or Long-Range Goals*

A general strategy is to begin with a high-appeal program. This brings people in and lets them know you are there. Some initial assessment of high-appeal courses may be made by using questionaires, involving parents in planning, visiting homes, getting teachers' suggestions, and more. Once a group is developed, new program ideas may flow from the group. At the outset, the goals of the participants and those of the agent may not be the same. The agent hopes that rapport will be established between the parents, himself, and other school personnel so that the parents will stay on and gradually focus more explicitly on the problems of education. Agents suggest that some key problems to guard against in beginning with high-appeal programs are: (a) parents may develop inaccurate expectations about the program, for example, that they will get full job retraining through courses at the school; (b) once very informal programs have been established, it may be difficult to move toward a more structured program, to move a "coffee and conversations" group toward sewing classes, parents' organizations, and so on; (c) a new program may attract people as a novelty, but it may be considerably more difficult to plan a program that will carry well over a period of years.

When it is difficult to attract parents, some agents have succeeded by planning a program attractive to children and making it a condition for participating that they bring a parent with them. Once the parents are there, the group leader has an opportunity to get to know them.

The degree to which the agent focuses upon long-range goals may also reflect the visibility and severity of local educational problems. Where problems are both visible and severe, a very direct intervention to bring about change in academic achievement or other behavior may be most desirable. For example, in schools where the average reading level is extremely low, direct action with the parents aimed at doing something about this may be the best beginning point.[3] Some of the following strategies may be employed:

1. Give the parents something "real" to do in the school that is within the range of their capabilities.

2. Teach parents what the children are being taught so that they can be informed and keep intellectually ahead of the child.

3. Teach parents how to supervise their children's homework so that they can help, even if they are poorly educated themselves.

4. Make a point of stressing the advantages of education and the disadvantages of too little education.

It is helpful for the agent to keep the long-range goals of his program in mind. The pressure of the job on the school-community agent is such that intermediate goals easily displace long-range goals. Many agents warn particularly against get-

---

3. For a brief discussion of such an approach in St. Louis, Missouri, under the leadership of Dr. Samuel Shepard, Assistant School Superintendent, see A. Harry Passow (ed.), *Education in Depressed Areas*, pp. 338-39.

ting caught in the "numbers game," that is, believing they have succeeded when they have been able to attract large numbers by entertainment programs that may not necessarily further the long-range goals.

*Stress on School Families,*
*Neighborhood Families, or Both*

In setting up settlement house programs, should the agent focus primarily on the parents with children currently in school, on neighborhood families in general, or on both, depending on the issue? A rule of thumb which has been developed is to program for parents alone when you are dealing with clear-cut educational issues, but to program for the neighborhood when dealing with broader issues such as community upgrading. This rule may be elaborated as follows:

1. *Reasons for Programming for Parents Alone*

a. It is a quicker, more direct way to focus upon the academic achievement problems of the children.

b. The needs and orientations of the parents, as well as the impact of the program, may be easier to evaluate.

c. Parents may be brought together for a much more specific purpose.

d. The school is the major agency which can legitimately and easily focus upon parents; other agencies may be focusing on other neighborhood groups.

e. It is a good device to control size if numbers are too large and have to be reduced.

2. *Reasons for Programming for Families without School Children*

a. Deal with neighborhood problems which have a negative impact on education, for example, get rid of drug pushers, correct dangerous traffic patterns, etc.

b. Take advantage of lines of communication which nonparents may have with other groups, such as block clubs, church members' organizations, and so on, to help reach school parents and to get extra school resources, for example, school trips, musical instruments, tutoring help, etc.

c. Broad issues, such as legal rights, are proper concerns of the total community. Other issues, such as millage, and school reform, require city-wide support for success.

d. Work with parents of preschool children may better prepare both parents and children for the school experience.

A related issue is whether the program should be open to people who live outside the area served by the school. One basis for making a decision about this may be whether or not the same classes or services are available closer to the participant's home.

*Stress on City-Wide*
*or Local Implications of a Problem*

The emphasis on the city-wide or local implications of a problem tends to reflect the scope of the problem and the scope of the agency providing the solution to the problem. Certain problems—like unemployment, the role of the ADC parent, and millage issues—are of city-wide proportions. When a problem is city-wide, the agent may well become involved with other agencies while searching for a solution. This whole area is explored in the section dealing with the delegated function procedure.

In other cases, the city-wide implications of a problem may be stressed because the agent needs the help of an agency which serves a city-wide clientele, or at least a broader clientele than the local school district.

## Staffing the Settlement House Program

*Content of the Human Relations Specialist*

The ideal leader is the professional who knows the course content and also has human relations skills. It is absolutley necessary that the instructor have real competence in the area in which he is teaching. On the other hand, informal, friendly social relations are a key part of most classes and are sought by many of the participants.

A beginning strategy, when both skills cannot be found in a single person, is to be sure the leader is competent in the content to be taught. Then the agent can attempt to create a better balance between emphasis on the technical and human relations aspects of the job by (a) orienting the teachers to the human relations goals of the job, (b) stressing that from the agent's long-range point of view the technical skills are steps toward broader goals, and (c) suggesting variations in the class program to heighten the informality and sociability of the class (for example, as part of a sewing class, the members might plan a fashion show).

When a teacher displays poor human relations skills and seems unable to improve upon them, the agent can sometimes fill the gap. He may do this by being present when members are gathering before the class begins, by dropping in during the class, and by taking part in coffee breaks or concluding social hours. Agents often enlist the aid of a parent in class who is a natural social leader to deal with some of the human relations needs of the group.

Another approach to the leadership problem is to hold systematic training sessions. This could be done locally ("on-the-job" training) or centrally to provide a corps of special teachers trained to work in areas where skilled leadership is scarce. Generally, agents prefer local training.

What are the pros and cons of using local residents who have special skills as class instructors? Again, limited human relations skills may be a major concern, and when local residents are used as leaders the issue of training may become considerably more important. There is also the question of whether or not local residents will accept one of their peers as a course instructor.

*Paid or volunteer leaders.* Volunteer leadership has proven excellent for one-shot affairs where only limited commitment from the leader is needed. Participation as a leader in a one-shot affair often provides an opportunity for the leader to identify himself with the program, which may lead to future participation.

One problem with volunteer leaders is the strength of their commitment. The volunteer may feel he has made his major contribution in the act of volunteering and take little responsibility for carrying the job through to completion with work of real quality. The agent has limited control over the volunteer leader in the sense that he has no contractual basis for demanding good job performance. If he applies too much pressure, the volunteer may simply quit.

Paid leadership has the advantage of providing the agent with a contractual basis for demanding reliable work of high quality. Where leaders are difficult to recruit, pay may be offered as an inducement. Some leaders have taken the job primarily for money, and shown little interest in the goals of the job or in teaching. It is easier to dismiss paid leaders in this kind of situation.

Generally, agents suggest avoiding paid leadership when an extensive volunteer-based program is anticipated. One serious question that arises is the exploitation of regular teachers as volunteers. Many programs have been launched with volunteer leadership provided by the regular teaching staff. Can this volunteer leadership be expected to continue? A number of schools have compromised the issue by setting up some guiding principles such as: (a) an after-school programs staffed by volunteer leadership while the evening program is run by paid leadership; (b) the after-school and evening programs are both centered around a core of traditional on-going activities based on volunteer leadership, activities above and beyond these being staffed with paid leadership; and (c) using volunteers if possible but paying if necessary. The last involves assessing the rewards that the leader is getting from the job. Is pay necessary to hold him or is the satisfaction of leadership great enough in inself? In the experience of some agents, a hit-and-miss blending of paid and volunteer leadership creates much conflict.

## Cost of the Settlement House Approach

Most of the potential costs of this approach have already been mentioned. A few may require further attention. Fairly extensive physical facilities and provision of competent leadership are needed. The cost of the latter may be in paid salary, in time required to train and supervise leaders, or both. Another problem may be either staff or member over-involvement in the program. After a period of intense over-participation the staff person (or parent) may be "burned out" and drop the program completely.

A further problem which may be counted as a cost of this approach is the potential for conflict when a number of people gather together who have poor self-images and are unknown to one another. Fear and anxiety may be high and the tendency to use the personality problems or personal quirks of others as weapons of self defense may be exaggerated. One way of mediating this potential for conflict, at least initially, is to structure the situation so that friendly interaction is encouraged and expectations are very clear.

## Community Use of the Settlement House to Reach Bureaucracy

Of all the linkage mechanisms, the settlement house is the most difficult for families or community primary groups to initiate on their own. It requires more financial resources and technical knowledge than most primary groups have. Like the detached worker, the settlement house is an approach which often requires the development of strong voluntary associations before it can come into being. Thus, it becomes progressively more difficult for the settlement house type of arrangements to be set up by primary groups with very limited economic resources. Those working among the very poor in the United States have rarely been able to initiate this type of linkage using the resources of the primary group members themselves. Perhaps one of the closest approximations to this was that of the immigrant groups which came to America in the late 1800s through the early 1900s. Such groups often formed strong voluntary associations to help each other, and these in turn sometimes established local settlement-like agencies which hired professionals to help their members.

In general, in the United States the development of settlement house activities was initiated by large-scale bureaucratic organizations at the behest of some more powerfully located community groups in society. The "lighted schools," the social work settlement houses, the programs of the United States agricultural department which accompanied their extension workers, the Salvation Army type of operation for the destitute, the varied local programs which accompanied religious missionary efforts to convert "pagans"—all usually had as their source either a group of very wealthy families or already formed bureaucracies which on their own developed such programs.

From the community point of view, the development of settlement houses is a very important precursor of the development of an advocate bureaucracy to work on its behalf. The detached worker approach, as discussed earlier, was also such a precursor but it differs in that it stressed the expert as an individual. The settlement house by its very existence stresses the beginnings of a large-scale organizational effort. Thus, it not only has one expert but may have several. Furthermore, it stresses the importance of physical facilities and perhaps the beginnings of specialization. Most important, it stresses the need to have large-scale community backing. All of these are important lessons for communities in developing their own bureaucracies to fight recalcitrant or hostile bureaucracies. This suggests that for the very poor or moderately poor the only hope they have for getting settlement house types of services is through wealthy families or through the good offices of existing bureaucracies.

The above analysis leads to a series of paradoxes with respect to social change among the very poor. A bureaucratic agency, in order to solve its own immediate problem, will set up a settlement house type of organization among its poor clients. For instance, in one large city in the early 1950s the housing agency sent community organizers to a local area to set up block clubs with the purpose in mind of getting the people to paint their houses, mow their lawns, and in general salvage what might be a slum if allowed to deteriorate. In another city a large foundation provided money for a local group to hire some full time staff and in cooperation with the school system to experiment in greater local control of the schools. In yet a third case the federal and city governments supported a very substantial social change project which had as one of its major components the provision of local services to the very poor. The sponsors of all these settlement house approaches envisioned changes which would benefit their organizations and surely not oppose them. However, the changes which the organizations initiated quickly went beyond what the sponsors intended and did in fact cause the sponsors to withdraw their support. Thus, in the case of the housing commission, the groups once organized for beautifying their houses then requested better garbage collection, better police protection, better schools for their children, and the like. Such demands required a fundamental reordering of the city budget. The consequences were that the housing commission was requested by various city agencies to withdraw its local organizers, which it did. In the case of the school, the problems moved from reading achievement of the child into the more central problems of hiring and firing school staff. This shift caused the larger school system to withdraw its support. In the final illustration, the large social change project, through its local units, attacked many of the standing organizations in the community such as the schools and the welfare agencies. These in turn put enormous pressure on the sponsoring agencies to withdraw support for the change project. Possibly the last straw occurred when the local settlement house units began to develop their own political groups, thus presenting a direct challenge to the city and federal governments supplying the money. This in turn led to a seizure of control of this change project by the city government and a fundamental alteration in the role of the settlement houses.

One of the major lessons to be learned from these experiences is that it is very difficult for the community to make use of the settlement house facilities of a bureaucracy if in the long run the community will seek to use these as a base from which to attack the bureaucracy or other major bureaucracies in society with which the sponsoring agency is in close relations. This has caused community organizers like Saul Alinsky to lay down as a basic organizational principle that at least half of the financial support for a grassroots program must be raised from the local participants Such a demand probably means, however, that the very poor will not be a suitable base for organization because it is very difficult, if not impossible, for them to provide such resources. At least it cannot be done until an organizer comes in to help set up a voluntary association. Thus, this implicitly suggests that one not start with the most deprived group but with a group with at least some resources and with interests sufficiently close to those who are poorer so that when they are organized they will attract those at the lower economic level. If we look at one case where a group succeeded in building its own advocate bureaucracy, we can find some resemblance to such a strategy. Thus, unions in the United States were built up as advocate bureaucracies for the working man against very strong opposition from business bureaucracies. But it is important to note that they started with the skilled trades where the unions could make use of powerful primary group associations to support strikes or withdrawal of labor.

However, if one pursues the examples given above, there is another theme which emerges. If we follow up the housing case, we find that the block club organization did not fully collapse when the organizer was withdrawn. It held together sufficiently to vote the organizer into political office at the next election. He in turn was able to use his political position to effect some change. In the case of the school system, the local community did not collapse when the school sought to withdraw support. Eventually the school was forced to modify its organizational stance. While the community members might feel that their fight was in vain and that the changes agreed to were not significant, it does seem to the outside observer that they did succeed in bringing the attention of the larger community to the problems of the school organization and did move the school system to make significant changes. At any rate, the potential for change was created. These illustrations suggest that the local community can borrow a settlement house from a friendly bureaucracy, use it to organize its own community, and, once organized, be in a position to do without the support of the initial sponsor. Indeed, they can move in directions which are quite contrary to the initial sponsor. To develop this thinking into a deliberate strategy of change would require some radical rethinking of what professionals in community organizations have advocated as sound policy. For instance, this type of strategy would require that the community worker not communicate fully with the sponsoring organization. Second, it would require holding back from most real organizational action until the local community has sufficient strength to go it alone. Since for many purposes the community worker needs to engage in   organizational action in order to build his influence—that is, to show the client population that something can be done for them—this suggests a delicate programming of tasks. First, one deals with problems which the clients and the sponsoring organizations have in common and then moves on to issues about which the community and the sponsoring agencies diverge.

It can be seen that the problem of the community utilizing the settlement house against the bureaucracy is not an easy one because it often assumes that the community will either have to develop its own bureaucracy (or something very close to it) or it will have to use the settlement house as a base against the very agency which sponsors it.

# 8 ✦ The Auxiliary Voluntary Association and the Voluntary Association

## Description of the Auxiliary Voluntary Association

Auxiliary voluntary associations are attached to formal organizations, sponsored by them, and have a quasi-legal status in the organization to which they are related. In the schools the parent-teacher associations or the "home room" mothers' clubs have this character. In hospitals "gray ladies" and in churches lay groups serve this function. Alumni associations of universities, volunteer groups to aid in fund-raising for community chest drives, and officer associations closely related to the military are also auxiliary voluntary associations. The milieu of the voluntary association, as a form of organization, falls somewhere between that of the primary group and the bureaucratic organization and combines attributes of both. Therefore, it can provide a meeting place for members of both social forms and is unlikely to produce the kind of conflict that their antithetical atmospheres might ordinarily entail. Thus, the teacher and the parent may come together in a situation sufficiently removed from the classroom that the teacher does not think that parents are interfering in technical matters of teaching which should not concern them. On the other hand, it is sufficiently outside the milieu of the family so that family members do not feel the teacher is intervening in family affairs. This allows

THE COLLABORATION OF JACK ROTHMAN AND JOHN L. ERLICH IN THE PREPARATION OF THIS CHAPTER IS ESPECIALLY ACKNOWLEDGED.

each person to maintain his own role identity —he teacher to feel still a teacher and the parent to feel still a parent — without threatening each other.

The moderate or low degree of intensity is frequently reflected in the lack of spontaneity. Meetings are scheduled with a formal agenda and are handled in a relatively formal way with a chairman and rules of order. The informal interchange of the primary group is lacking. Because of its low intensity, this mechanism cannot be used readily to change basic values or to provide complex information for which firsthand demonstration is necessary.

The auxiliary voluntary association is a form of organization that permits little organizational initiative. The parents come to meetings or join of their own volition. It is possible for a school to recruit parents for voluntary associations, but this requires other linking procedures, such as mass media, common messenger (sending a note via the child), or formal authority. It is not an effective procedure for closing social distance or dealing with families hostile to the school, being most useful in neighborhoods where families already support the school's goals.

The auxiliary voluntary association provides a moderate amount of focused expertise. It is true that teachers are present, but they are not expected to instruct parents on the details of a new curriculum or other technical subjects. It is legitimate on occasion for the teacher to undertake the role of the expert. However, if the voluntary association were to take on the character of a regular teaching situation, it would require much more regular attendance than is customary in voluntary associations. In addition, this would alter the relations between teacher and parent from that of equals to teacher-student. This means the character would shift either toward a settlement house milieu or a formal bureaucratic organization, depending on how much intensity the teachers generated. Therefore, the auxiliary voluntary association can provide only sporadic focused expertise, for example, a speaker is invited to discuss a special topic. The moderate degree of focused expertise provided by the auxiliary voluntary association is suitable for a family that is well organized and has positive orientations toward the school, but requires information about a change in the education situation, such as the introduction of a new course or a new grading procedure. It is not suited to the deviant family in need of intense work over an extended period of time.

The voluntary association has relatively wide scope. Parent-teacher meetings can be quite large — as large as school facilities can contain. In some elementary schools as many as 500 parents can attend meetings. In scope, this procedure falls between that of the mass media or common messenger and the detached worker. On an over-all basis it is a procedure ideally suited for maintaining communication at a moderate distance with families who are positively oriented toward the school. It is not a very good procedure for closing distance between the school and indifferent or hostile families.

## The Auxiliary Voluntary Association and Forms of Influence

The auxiliary voluntary association can be assessed in terms of the modes of influence it makes available.

*Legitimation.* The major avenue of influence used by the auxiliary voluntary association is the one of legitimation. The coming together of teachers and parents in a semiformal atmosphere provides each with an opportunity to evaluate the other and to make inquiries about some features of the school and the home. The parent can see if the teachers are reasonable, if the curriculum of the school seems appropriate, and if what is taught has some rationale behind it. At its best, it offers the parent a visual experience that reinforces the norms which legitimate the teacher's function as a teacher. For the teacher it permits a casual survey of the family, a means of communication, and permits explanation of any gross or obvious misunderstandings.

*Referent power.* In general the meetings are too infrequent and the contact too brief for the teachers to have much referent power vis-a-vis the parent. However, they might supplement referent power that has already been established.

*Expertise.* The auxiliary voluntary association experience is too limited for teachers to demonstrate their expertise. However, it is possible to transmit knowledge that can be handled quickly, such as explaining a rather simple procedure for handling a limited reading problem, or providing factual information on how the children are doing compared to a national norm, and the like.

*Reward and punishment power.* Generally there is very little coercion that can be used on parents through the auxiliary voluntary association. This is inherent in the very meaning of a voluntary group. The school has many other ways of utilizing coercive or reward power, and it is unlikely that the voluntary association would be used for this purpose.

The auxiliary voluntary association may be a source of reward to some families through the prestige of offices held, public recognition, and similar rewards.

## Dimensions of Auxiliary Voluntary Associations

1. *Formality versus informality.* Auxiliary voluntary associations vary from informal and intimate to highly formal. An inclusive organization in which all parents are automatically members, meeting seldom or never, and conducting its business by mail is obviously quite formal. At the other extreme might be an informal PTA executive committee made up of parents who meet every other week in the school. What degree of formality is most likely to attract populations characterized by low self-esteem? A great degree of formality, especially unfamiliar procedures such as parliamentry rules, may scare people off. On the other hand, too great a degree of intimacy may be intimidating to people who have little self-confidence in interpersonal situations. A middle ground, where there is some structure but of a kind familiar to group members, might be least threatening. This might involve running PTA meetings that are planned but informal, in contrast to strict use of parliamentary procedure. Experience has shown

that parents of low socioeconomic status have a lower tolerance for formal rules and procedures than do middle class parents. Actually, membership and participation in voluntary associations is greatly affected by social class factors.[1]

2. *Size: small versus large.* Although size and degree of intimacy may frequently co-vary — small size correlating with intimacy — these dimensions need not necessarily be correlated. We must ask again whether a small group or a large group is more effective in attracting a population of low self-esteem? Small groups offer high visibility to the individual, with the opportunity of gaining prestige for individual performance. On the other hand, visibility may be threatening. Persons with low self-esteem may be more comfortable in large groups where they can maintain their anonymity. Some agents have formed groups of moderate size, structured so that the individual chooses the degree of anonymity he desires. Among some populations an event is not considered successful if only a few people participate. The community agent should be sensitive to the minimum size a group will consider "successful." Large groups may be especially useful for "one shot" events or a short series of meetings.[2]

3. *Limited membership versus unlimited membership.* Membership may be influenced by the interest of the group or the problem it deals with, and by formal and informal barriers to membership. A room-mothers' group for sixth-grade parents has more limited scope than a PTA. Theoretically, all parents of children in a given school can belong to a group such as the PTA; however, in some instances only a small number actually belong. In some cases this comes about because membership is closed informally by a small

1. Several studies have shown that membership in voluntary associations is a function of socioeconomic status. There is no evidence, however, to suggest that high socioeconomic status groups are more interested in education. Charles R. Wright and Herbert H. Hyman, "Voluntary Association Memberships of American Adults: Evidence From National Sample Surveys." *American Sociological Review,* 23 (June 1958), pp. 284-94; Morris Axelrod, "Urban Structure and Social Participation," *American Sociological Review,* 21 (February 1956), pp. 13-18; Scott Greer, "Urbanism Reconsidered: A Comparative Study of Local Areas in a Metropolis," *ibid.,* pp. 19-25.

2. For a summary of the literature on the effects of group size on interaction, see E. J. Thomas and C. F. Fink, "Group Size," *Psychological Bulletin,* 60 (June 1963), pp. 371-84.

group which has captured the leadership of the organization and admits only friends as members. This may happen especially in inner city areas where prestige and status symbols are hard to come by. Being an officer in an organization, such as PTA President, is prestigeful. The incumbent may be reluctant to give up this status symbol and seeks protection by keeping membership in the organization small and composed of friends, assuming that these friends will challenge the leadership only at the price of friendship. We referred before to the group of mothers who organized themselves for a protest trip to the state capitol but would not publicize the trip generally, inviting only a few people of higher prestige than themselves. They regarded the entire undertaking as a sign of status, and wanted to keep a closed group.

To counteract these tendencies the school-community agent might consider several approaches to broadening membership and participation: (a) encourage present leaders to see expansion as a sign of success; (b) change the structure so as to encourage rotation of leadership; (c) give explicit instruction in leadership skills and other kinds of modifications or inputs.

4. *Local (neighborhood) versus nonlocal organizations.* The idea of scope suggests the geographical area from which the auxiliary voluntary association draws. Some groups, such as school alumni associations, may draw from a nation-wide area. However, such groups as room-mothers' clubs or PTAs often share a very small common geographical territory within which there are common school-related problems. Some problems impinging upon education have their basis in the larger community; in these situations it may be useful to draw from an area outside the geographical neighborhood to form a group to tackle the problem, or the problem could be referred to another organization, such as a community council, which already draws from a wider geographical base.

5. *Focused and not focused on the task of the formal organization.* Auxiliary voluntary associations may vary in the degree to which they are focused on the task of the formal organization to which they are tied. Gray ladies have a focused active interest in the major task of the hospital — caring for the sick; an alumni group may have a more general and less active interest in the major task of the college

or university — the development of knowledge and the education of students.

Among auxiliary voluntary associations tied to the school, there may be variations in how directly they are focused on the problems of education. The PTA can vary from being primarily a social club to being a focused learning group dealing explicitly with the problems of education.

Populations which have a hostile or fearful view of the schools may not attend programs which are focused explicitly on the problems of education. In such situations it may be necessary to draw them into adult-education groups while they become acquainted with the school, with each other, and with school personnel. School-community agents have reported that one of the best programs for getting people into the building is training in job skills, often including instruction in reading, writing, and arithmetic as well as typing and shorthand. This suggests that activities developed in a settlement-house approach may facilitate the use of the auxiliary voluntary association as a linking mechanism.

6. *Frequency of meeting.* Frequency of meeting may vary considerably for voluntary associations. It is not clear what frequency is most desirable for what tasks. Gray ladies may be on duty every day; on the other hand they may seldom meet together as a group. An alumni group meets at intervals of years, if ever, and members may act primarily by making financial contributions and casting occasional ballots. In the schools, a volunteer service group of parents may be active almost every school day to help teachers with classroom clerical tasks but may seldom meet as a group; the PTA may meet as a group several times a year but be relatively inactive between meetings.

7. *Relationship to the formal organization: semiofficial or unofficial?* The relationships of the auxiliary voluntary association and the formal organization may vary. Certain retired officers groups in the armed forces may act as semiofficial spokesmen for the military. Parent volunteer assistants in the schools may have little official standing in the school organization; however under some circumstances a PTA might act as semiofficial spokesman for the

school. Under what circumstances is it most useful to have a voluntary association in a more rather than less official relationship to the school? This may be related to the question of expertise. Possibly, the greater the expertise of the group members in an area of concern to the organization, the more desirable it may be to have an official relationship between the voluntary association and the organization.

8. *Limited financial resources versus greater resources.* Some groups have limited financial resources, such as a room-mothers' group. However, this is secondary to the fact that the parents are in a position to exercise direct influence on the child. In other cases financial resources become crucial, as in setting up a clinic in an elementary school. If a group has limited financial resources this will certainly place limits on the kinds of activities it can undertake. The formal organization can exercise a degree of control over the auxiliary voluntary association through the amount of funds allocated and stipulations placed upon them.

## Autonomous Neighborhood Voluntary Associations

In addition to auxiliary voluntary associations, the school may find it useful to link with or influence autonomous neighborhood voluntary associations which are part of the school's external environment.

Grassroots voluntary associations are often close in structure to primary groups and, as a consequence, can perform some of their functions. Whereas the school can at best shore up weak families or help broken families deal with the world, it is frequently in the position to help in the creation of grassroots voluntary associations. In such a way it may provide the child with additional primary group-type support.

A variety of services might be carried on by local grassroots organizations outside the boundaries of the school, but which are related directly or indirectly to school activities. For instance, in some neighborhoods mothers have set up cooperative nurseries where one mother looks after the children while the others work. In other neighborhoods they have organized so that one mother takes over the job of watching the children on the block for a given day, reporting suspicious strangers, settling disputes, and the like. There are, of course, the traditional block clubs which provide aid in time of illness, greet and introduce newcomers to the neighborhood, or try to develop strong social ties between neighbors.[3] Voluntary associations also perform the function of locating and bringing out leadership within a given population.[4]

There are local social action, civic, and protest groups designed to avoid rent exploitation, insure adequate city services, or obtain other resources, services, or facilities for the neighborhood. Somewhat more formal in character is the development of local services by volunteers who may or may not come from the neighborhood. For instance, there are reading tutorial groups to give children extra help, located right in the neighborhood and manned by volunteers who may or may not come from the neighborhood. Similarly, there might be local library services operating out of storefronts and manned by volunteers. In principle, there is no reason why most functions cannot be carried on at this level, for example, housekeeping information, shopping information, cooking information, and child-rearing advice. The development of locally based services combined with volunteerism is something which many people are now seriously advocating. It should be clear that some of the problems and advantages of this approach are very different from those discussed for such auxiliary voluntary associations as PTAs.

In general, the functions of autonomous voluntary associations include the following: (a) civic and political action to obtain

3. E. Litwak, "Voluntary Associations and Neighborhood Cohesion," *American Sociological Review*, 26 (April 1961), pp. 258-66.

4. Earlier studies of leadership, both social-psychological and political, concentrated on the traits of leaders. See R. M. Stogdill, "Personal Factors Associated with Leadership: A Survey of the Literature," *Journal of Psychology*, 25 (1948), pp. 37-71; and C. A. Gibb, "The Principles and Traits of Leadership," *Journal of Abnormal and Social Psychology*, 42 (1947); also in A. P. Hare, E. F. Borgatta, R. F. Bales (eds.), *Small Groups: Studies in Social Interaction* (New York: Knopf, 1953), pp. 87-94.

More recently, leadership has been viewed as a functional relationship within groups. See T. M. Newcomb, R. H. Turner, and P. E. Converse, *Social Psychology: The Study of Human Interaction* (New York: Holt, Rinehart and Winston, Inc., 1965), pp. 473-86; also D. Cartwright and A. Zander (eds.), *Group Dynamics* (Evanston and White Plains: Row, Peterson, 1953), pp.535-47.

needed services and resources and to deal with concrete local social problems; (b) integrating and socializing functions, enhancing local community cohesion, strengthening primary group life, and aiding in the socialization of children and new comers; (c) mutual-aid self-help functions that organize residents to meet some of their own needs; (d) recreational-social functions that support specialized hobby and cultural interests and provide outlets for leisure time activities.

Autonomous voluntary associations, unlike auxiliary associations, are not limited by direct ties to a formal organization which restrict membership, activities, and methods. The development of voluntary associations outside the boundaries of the school offers advantages such as trying new ideas and considering a range of goals that may be unacceptable to the professional bureaucracy, the possibility of much closer involvement in the primary group life of the neighborhood without introducing favoritism into the school, and, finally, the possibility of drawing on a wide range of primary group resources.

To point out these advantages is not to deny the possible disadvantages, the foremost of which is the lack of durability of groups based on volunteers. Without the continuity provided by regular paid staff, many volunteer groups falter and collapse. The enthusiasm generated in the excitement of creation is often not sufficient to support the organization on a continuing basis. What can hold the volunteer service organization together, especially when the administrative problems of maintaining the organization become very burdensome? In effect, the voluntary organization has to compete for the time and attention of members against their obligations to much stronger forms of organization — those of job and family. If a mother is a tutor in a voluntary program and her child becomes ill, she might halt her voluntary service. By contrast, a working mother may arrange for a baby sitter or visiting nurse to attend to an ill child. The parent is often willing to make financial sacrifices (and considering the nature of money in our society, sacrifices of most other values as well) when confronted by cross-pressures from family and work. Will volunteers act likewise when faced with cross-pressure from family and vol-

untary associations? We would assume that for short periods of
time they may do so. For short periods of time ideological commitment can be a powerful force. But in the long run the ideological
commitment itself is not likely to withstand both the value placed
on work and family situations and the social interactions that are
involved.

Voluntary associations, accordingly, should be structured
so as to minimize competition with family and work. (Don't
schedule meetings at a time a working man is on the job if you
want him to attend!) The voluntary association should be geared
toward meeting real and compelling local needs and this should
be made plain to local residents.

Autonomous voluntary associations risk separation from
sources of expert knowledge and information. For instance, it is
a disadvantage not to have available the expert knowledge of the
school on how to teach reading or comparative information about
reading abilities of children in the community. It is sometimes
possible to get a professional person to join a volunteer movement.
But the social pressures of occupations are such that people rarely
donate what they are professionally paid for. Professionals might
contribute time on a short-term basis to volunteer movements, or
a few ideologically committed professionals might sustain interest,
but long-term or widespread availability of professionals is unlikely. The school may provide some professional assistance to neighborhood voluntary associations, especially when they are dealing
with matters that have a discernible connection to education.

While voluntary movements are often unstable and tenu-
ous, they may still have tremendous impact. Thus, many political
organizations depend on volunteers. The political machinery is
moribund for most of the year, but when election time comes the
volunteer organization is mobilized. Its activities in this short
period may have important long-run consequences, such as election of a candidate for a six-year term. In addition, volunteer
organizations sometimes grow into permanent, established organizations. A movement that brings mothers into situations where
they tutor children may lead them to become semiprofessional-
ized. They may raise money to hire someone who can take over

the problem of scheduling, substituting, and arranging for new members when old ones move out. Once staffed, though no longer a strictly grassroots voluntary association, the organization may have significant impact on the education of children.

## Pragmatic Issues in Using
## the Voluntary Association Approach

1. *The location of significant voluntary associations.* Use of autonomous neighborhood voluntary associations is affected by the existing situation, expecially the presence of established associations or their absence and hence the necessity to organize them. In the latter circumstances, the worker will have to adopt a strategy based on his diagnosis of the neighborhood. He may employ the detached worker approach or recruit directly for voluntary association programs focused on problems of education or on other interests.

In some cases the school may offer physical facilities, even though the groups are tied to other organizations. This may provide a basis for starting groups or forming cooperative relationships with existing groups. Usually schools are reluctant to offer facilities to religious, political, or controversial groups.

2. *The question of control.* Theoretically an auxiliary voluntary association provides a common ground where organization personnel and members of the lay community can meet and share control for common purposes. However, the component constituencies usually maintain identities, and it is quite possible for one or the other to take control. For example, there are PTAs where the school principal has insisted on controlling the organization and using it primarily for public relations purposes. In other situations, parents have dominated the PTA and organized it against current policies and practices in the school, sometimes by-passing the principal to gain support in the hierarchy of the school system. There is much less possibility of school personnel taking control of external autonomous voluntary associations.

3. *Dealing with hostile and friendly voluntary associations.* A volun-

tary association may become hostile to the formal organization which is related to it, as cited above. The community worker may want to stay out of the situation in order to avoid becoming identified with one side and hence rejected by the other. On the other hand, there are instances where the agent has supported the voluntary association in opposition to school officials. In one case a parents' organization was protesting school policy concerning homework. The principal left it up to the individual teacher to assign homework or not. The parents wanted homework routinely assigned. They took the matter to the principal, who would not change his policy. At this point the agent intervened, and after talking the matter over with the principal went to the central administration of the school-community program, which settled the problem from its position. The policy concerning homework was eventually changed.

There are various courses of action the worker can adopt in a situation involving a hostile voluntary association. He can stay out of the situation, expecially if his rapport with either of the contending parties is poor. He can arrange an open forum where the issues can be publicly discussed, or appeal to outside authority, such as the central school administration or to another superior office, to handle the situation. He can act as mediator between the parties, especially when his rapport with both is good. Finally, he can take the part of one or another of the hostile parties and hope for the best. There are limits to how actively the worker can support a voluntary association which is attacking the school without jeopardizing his position, but apparently he can be somewhat involved.

4. *Voluntary associations for which types of family.* In general, the auxiliary voluntary association seems to be an excellent device for reaching families that are highly identified with the school, who are well organized, and for whom one wants to pass on relatively complex information, for example, a new testing program. The approach is also good in high-mobility neighborhoods. It generally serves to maintain contact while preventing the highly motivated family from coming too close to the school. The same point holds concerning external voluntary associations.

It may be possible for the school to reach some families opposed to educational goals and organized in autonomous voluntary associations. If the school can enter such associations through a detached worker approach, there may be a possibility through provision of information (expert power) or good will (referent power) to effect a change in attitudes.

## Costs of the Voluntary Association Approach

The voluntary association approach brings parents together to deal with school and community matters. So long as the parents and the school see eye to eye on most issues there is no problem. However, voluntary associations provide the parents with an organizational base from which to coordinate their behavior. This can make them more effective in opposition as well as in support of school objectives. Therefore, one of the real risks of the voluntary association approach is the amount of potential power it puts into the hands of the parents vis-a-vis the school. This should, of course, be a problem only when the parents seek to impinge on spheres reserved for professional judgment.

Because this approach has relatively low initiative, it is likely to encompass largely those people who are highly motivated. As a consequence there is a real danger that only the "better" people will be connected to the school and those most in need of help might systematically be overlooked. Within the auxiliary voluntary association (such as a PTA), where holding an office is associated with status, lower class people might be excluded from positions of influence.

If the auxiliary voluntary association is to be more than a gesture toward school-community relations, it will require commitment of time and interest from school staff. A potential cost of the approach may be the added strain on the social structure of the school that such demands entail.

## Community Use of Voluntary Associations

When neighborhood residents, or residents of a local community, are concerned with schools they find unresponsive or
hostile to their viewpoints, the voluntary association is often a
crucial mechanism to be used. It is crucial, first, because the
voluntary association allows interested persons to structure and
focus their activities while maintaining, at least for an initial
period, the qualities of flexibility and response characteristic of
primary groups. The block club, the neighborhood association,
the citizen's group — all loosely organized voluntary membership
associations — acquire a collective voice without pre-empting the
voices of separate families or individuals. A second reason why the
voluntary association may be crucial is that it provides a location
for the pooling of resources, particularly funds, but the working
hours of individuals as well. This in turn potentially lays the base
for acquiring kinds of expertise beyond the capacity of most families or other groups. Since community concerns with the school
frequently involve technical questions, the expertise of the school
must be met with that used on behalf of the community. Only
experts may be able to have an effect on uniform tasks for which
the bureaucratic organization is especially equipped.

The voluntary association is, as already pointed out, intermediate between separate primary groups and the bureaucratic
organization. Little knowledge and few resources beyond those of
most families or neighborhoods are needed to establish voluntary
associations. Outside assistance may sometimes be helpful but
usually is not necessary. Almost at once after formation, the voluntary association can become a base for political pressure and the
development of economic resources. Persistence, growth, and considerably increased resources, together with organizational capacity to employ personnel, allow the voluntary association to move
toward becoming an organization capable of using experts as the
community's own advocate bureaucracy. If it does so, some of the
primary group features that give strength to the voluntary association will disappear, but may be replaced by the formation of new

voluntary associations. Community gain from having an advocate bureaucracy available offsets the losses.

There are requirements to be met, however, for successful formation of voluntary associations. Primary group members must have sufficient time and interest to participate. A minimum level of skill in interpersonal relations is necessary to initiate the organization and allow it to survive. Persistent interpersonal conflicts or incapacity to recognize wider interests than those of the immediate family or some other narrow group will block or break the voluntary association. Some tolerance for persons of different status groups is necessary. Such requirements as these can usually be met in most local communities, but some community organizers feel that many low-income communities have great difficulty developing voluntary associations, even with external help.

It should not be assumed that families in poor neighborhoods will readily join voluntary associations because they have many interests in common, such as poor housing, poor public services, and the like. In fact, factors limiting formation of voluntary associations often outweigh common problems. All the time and energy of the very poor are needed to survive. They do not have means (such as money to pay for baby sitters, or energy after taking care of the family or engaging in heavy physical labor) to permit activities outside the family. Scarce resources in poor neighborhoods often make neighbors suspicious of each other rather than leading them to develop cooperative attitudes. Families motivated by rewards of the larger society move away from poor nieghborhoods when they can. The status system of our society encourages families to separate themselves from those who are poorer than they. Furthermore, poor neighborhoods often contain an extraordinary mix of families, in contrast to more homogeneous middle-class neighborhoods.[5] We found that intact families where the father worked, the mother was homemaker, and there were fewer than five children constituted more than 50 per cent of middle-class school neighborhoods. In the very poor

5. E. Litwak and H. J. Meyer, *Relationship Between School-Community Coordinating Procedures and Reading Achievement.* Final Report Project No. 5-0355, Contract OE-3-10-033, Office of Education, Bureau of Research, HEW, December 1966), pp.168-70.

neighborhoods studied, no definable type constituted more than 20 per cent of all families. Heterogeneity was characteristic even in areas where the majority of families were on welfare and lived in public housing projects. The homogeneity of social "pathology" of low-income urban neighborhoods — broken families, many children, unemployment, and the like — just did not appear. More typical was variety of family situations among the poor and similarity of family situations among the middle class. The consequences are that families in poor neighborhoods have many immediate family problems which they do not share in common with their neighbors. This heterogenity of interests is often overlooked by organizers who see only the common problems or the poor — bad housing, bad transportation, bad garbage collection, and so on.

The community can sometimes "capture" an auxiliary voluntary association, such as a PTA, and use it for its own purposes. We have noted earlier some difficulties this procedure faces, and some reasons why the school is likely to resist such efforts sucessfully. It is more likely that the local community will need to form its own autonomous voluntary association if it is to have the benefit of this most useful linking procedure through which to influence the school.

We note, in conclusion, that many features of the voluntary association as a tool for the community depend on particular circumstances. Analysis of this approach is incomplete without recognizing wide variations in form and operation.

# 9 ✤ Mass Media

The use of instruments of communication—newspapers, mailings, posters and leaflets, radio, television, sound trucks—to convey messages from an organization to the general public or to selected publics is a familiar feature of modern society. In the form of advertising and public relations, it constitutes a huge industry employing many technical and semiprofessional personnel. For a school-community relations program, the use of mass media is unlikely to be overlooked. Indeed, it may be relied on beyond its utility, and therefore the school-community agent must be especially sensitive to the limitations as well as the advantages of mass media as a procedure for linking school and the local school community.

The major advantages of the mass media approach as a linking mechanism are its relatively low cost, the great extent to which it is under control of the school (and hence requires little external cooperation), and the wide scope of its potential coverage among those to whom it is directed. Its chief limitations arise from the low level of effective initiative it can carry from the organization (since it is difficult to be sure that the intended targets will be reached), its low intensity (since it involves no face-to-face contact with the client groups), and its low capacity to bring focused expertise into flexible interaction with client groups.

## Social Science Studies of Mass Media

Social scientists have devoted much effort to studying the

237

238   *School-Community Linking Mechanisms*

nature and effectiveness of mass media.[1] Some of that work concerned the limitations previously mentioned, since these stand in the way of influencing resistant or indifferent populations, whether the objective is to sell a product, promote a viewpoint, or convey information for educational purposes. Hence, studies have sought to test various techniques for increasing the qualities of initiative, intensity, and accepted expertness of messages communicated through mass media. A few examples may be instructive.[2]

Social scientists have sought to find out whether the extent to which people listen to a message can be increased by having high status persons deliver the message[3] or by having the message contain, in addition to its basic content, something known to be of great interest to the population. Similar techniques have been tried to increase the primary group tone—intensity—of messages. To assess attempts to increase focused expertise, students of mass media have asked whether it is better to present both sides or one side of the message,[4] and whether it is better for the message to have an emotional or a rational tone.[5] The question of the lan-

1. Carl I. Hovland, "Effects of the Mass Media of Communication," in Gardner Lindzey (ed.), *Handbook of Social Psychology*, Vol. 2 (Cambridge, Mass; Addison-Wesley, 1954) pp. 1063-1103; Daniel Katz, Darwin Cartwright, Samuel Eldersveld, and Alfred M. Lee (eds.), *Public Opinion and Propaganda* (New York: Dryden Press, 1954); Wilbur Schramm, *The Process and Effects of Mass Communications* (Urbana, Ill.: University of Illinois Press, 1955); Herbert I. Abelson, *Persuasion: How Opinions and Attitudes Are Changed* (New York: Springer, 1959).

2. The following discussion is based on Eugene Litwak, "Some Policy Implications in Communications Theory with Emphasis on Group Factors," *Education for Social Work*, Proceedings of Seventh Annual Program Meeting (New York: Council on Social Work Education, 1959), pp. 96-109.

3. Carl I. Hovland and W. Weiss, "The Influence of Source Credibility on Communication Effectiveness," in Daniel Katz *et al.* (eds.), *Public Opinion and Propaganda,*pp. 337-47; H. Wilensky, *Intellectuals in Labor Unions: Organizational Pressures on Professional Roles* (Glencoe, Ill.: Free Press, 1956).

4. A. A. Lumsdaine and I. L. Janis, "Resistance to 'Counter-propaganda' Produced by a One-sided versus Two-sided 'Propaganda' Presentation," *Public Opinion Quarterly*, 17 (1953), pp. 311-18.

5. There are inconsistent outcomes on the superiority of an emotional versus a rational argument. Studies show positive results for both appeals. Hovland suggests that these two kinds of arguments are not exclusive alternatives. Rather, the use of either appeal depends upon the issue to be discussed and the composition of the group. This same author implicitly suggests that the rational appeal is probably more effective for an educated group because of the great emphasis placed by educators on the "virtues" of the rational

guage level best understood by the population has been raised.[6] The placement of the major point in the message has been studied to see whether it is more effective for instance, in terms of retention of the message, to have the main point presented first or last.[7]

The evidence is not conclusive, but it does indicate that it is probable that in dealing with an indifferent or hostile audience it is better to have a person who has high status with the target public as the source of the message. It is probably best to start the message with something the audience strongly approves of. If the group is well educated, it is probably better to present both sides of the issues; if the audience is less educated, but known to be resistant, it is also wise to present both sides. But if the target population is already favorable it is probably best to reinforce only its side. When using mass media, it is important to recognize that language level varies by social class and to tailor the language to that of the population one wants to reach. It is wiser to use the language most likely to be used by the population than the language that meets some concept of "good English." With regard to the question of presenting first a rational or an emotional argument, there is some suggestion that for lower-educated groups the emotional argument might be the first step, whereas for the more educated it doesn't matter. Finally, research has suggested no real basis for saying where the crucial part of the message should be located — at the beinning or at the end.

and the deprecation of the emotional. Carl I. Hovland, "Effects of the Mass Media of Communication," pp. 1075-76.

6. Leonard Schatman and Anselm Strauss, "Social Class and Modes of Communication," *American Journal of Sociology,* 60 (January 1955), pp. 329-33.

7. There are contradictory findings on effectiveness as to whether the opening or the closing parts of the message should contain the more important material. H. Sponberg's data support the idea that the most important issues be given first position. "A Study of the Relative Effectiveness of Climax and Anti-Climax Order in an Argumentative Speech," *Speech Monograph,* 13 (1946), pp. 35-44. Cited in C. I. Hovland, I. L. Janis and H. H. Kelley, *Communication and Persuasion* (New Haven and London: Yale University Press, 1953), pp. 112-14. H. Cronwell's findings support the weak to strong order of presentation. "The Relative Effect on Audience Attitude of the First Versus the Second Argumentative Speech of a Series," *Speech Monograph,* 21 (1954), pp. 280-84. Cited in Hovland, Janis, and Kelley, *Communication and Persuasion,* pp. 113-14.

## The Limited Power of Mass Media
## Compared to Other Linking Mechanisms

On examining the mass media we become aware that manipulations such as those mentioned above are almost trivial in their capacity to provide organizational initiative when dealing with hostile audiences as compared to a detached worker or formal authority approach. Furthermore, the mass media approach is much weaker in intensity with hostile audiences than the opinion leader and the settlement house approaches, and it has far less capacity to develop focused expertise than the detached worker, formal authority, or settlement house approaches.

Selective listening is the basic weakness of mass media as a mechanism. Those most likely to "get the message" will be persons already predisposed to accept it. The people least likely to get the message are those most hostile to the organization sending the message. Likewise, communications through mass media are least likely to convert people, even when they are reached, because these communications are not capable of generating much primary group intensity with a hostile group. This is likely to be so even if one recognizes that messages may be channeled through opinion leaders since opinion leaders of hostile groups are themselves unlikely to cooperate.[8] The mass media approach is possibly limited even with friendly groups if the information to be communicated is complex because it does not facilitate feedback of questions and answers necessary in dealing with complex messages. Even where the media are capable of producing changes in knowledge they might not be able to produce changes in attitudes or behavior because of the low level of intensity.

The reader may well wonder whether there is any point in considering so weak a linking mechanism. There is. This will sometimes be the only procedure acceptable in the early stages of

8. Katz and Lazarsfeld discuss the "two-step flow of communications" principle, i.e., the combination of mass media and opinion leader. Unfortunately, these authors do not systematically consider the consequences of negative and positive opinion leaders. *See Personal Influence* (Glencoe, Ill.; The Free Press, 1955), pp. 3-4; 44-45; 116-17.

a program. Mass media may also serve to supplement and bolster other approaches. It is the mechanism of choice when it is useful to mobilize large numbers of people who are already favorably disposed toward the school. There is some potential, discussed later, for the mass media procedure, even when the client groups are hostile or indifferent.

## The Mass Media Approach and Forms of Influence

The mass media approach differs from those of the detached worker, opinion leader, and settlement house in the ways in which it can exercise influence on the population. Unlike these approaches, it provides no face-to-face contact and hence cannot directly use primary group forms of influence. It is, by comparison, a mass approach that must deal with problems that are sufficiently standardized for a large body of people to recognize as meaningful. Furthermore, use of the approach requires continuous attention because the communication it provides must be determined and procedures set in motion. The more elaborate forms of mass media may require specialists with prior training. In contrast to the detached worker approach, the mass media approach cannot effectively deal with the unexpected or idiosyncratic event.

*Reward and punishment power.* Mass media can be used to affect a person's reputation, and hence damage or enhance his situation at times. Fear of adverse public notice might deter some actions unfavorable to a school-community program. However, the unfavorable act must be viewed by some significant public in that light. Otherwise, publicizing an action may have quite unintended and contrary consequences, as sometimes happens when gang fighting or robberies are publicized. Under similar principles, favorable actions may be encouraged by use of mass media. But for the most part, reward and punishment cannot be directly manipulated by mass media.

*Legitimation.* With regard to the power of legitimation, the same reservations hold. The newspapers and other media can bolster norms that have widespread recognition and are accepted as important by significant groups in the public. For example, newspaper publicity can help build and support the belief that at least a high school education is a vital need in our society and that those who do not have it are not living up to social expectations. This normative pressure can in turn be a significant force, encouraging some people to finish high school who might not otherwise do so. However, such appeal to legitimate norms is not possible when norms are varied or uncrystallized, or in areas where knowledge is uncertain. The community agent might try to establish a general norm of reading to younger children in the family. Who reads, when, and how much may differ widely among families, and the inflexibility of mass media makes it unsuitable to confirm a wide range of family practices as legitimate.

*Referent power.* Similarly, the mass media can use referent power only around issues that are widely understood by the public. The use of the popular hero, the athlete, or movie star to endorse programs are examples of the mass media's attempt to use referent power. Effectiveness of testimonials rests on the qualities of the hero that are widely attractive for a large number of people. The highly personal and idiosyncratic characteristics that generate reference influence by opinion leaders or particular friends cannot be communicated through the mass media but require immediate interaction to be felt.

*Expertness.* The influence of the expert through mass media is often attempted but with uncertain effect. Toothpaste ads seek endorsement of dental societies; psychologists write columns on child rearing. The school- community agent might have the reading specialist describe new methods in the school newspaper. The effect depends in part on the educational level of the population, which limits the complexity of the message that can be understood. It depends also on acceptance by the population that the message is indeed from an expert. Dentists may be so recognized but reading specialists may not. It is sometimes possible to "build up" an expert—that is, to encourage wide acceptance of someone as an expert. This usually involves both a planned information campaign and use of means other than mass media to substantiate the expertness of the person involved, such as provision of situations where following the expert's advice has been beneficial. In complex areas—such as educational philosophy and practices or socialization procedures—demonstration of the superiority of the expert opinion is difficult. This is not to say that so-called experts are not giving advice through mass media and having it accepted, but this is often because they are viewed as legitimate authorities or have popular (referent) appeal.

## The Use of Mass Media Approach with Friendly and Resistant Populations

As already noted, the mass media approach reaches those people in the school community who are already better motivated to support educational goals or who already have an interest in the particular topic with which the message deals. This is due to selective inattention, that is, people simply do not pay attention to messages they are not interested in.

1. *Friendly populations.* The wide scope of the mass media makes it especially useful to draw friendly populations into program activities. There are a number of reasons why reaching such a population benefits a school-community program.

The better motivated people, if drawn together by messages from the school, have a chance to meet and support one another in their favorable values. This may be particularly helpful to highly motivated people who live in areas where a large part of the population is not particularly concerned with the problems of education. Meeting people with similar positive attitudes toward education may give them the sense of not being alone in their struggle.

It is possible—but only assumed—that the better-motivated people will eventually come into contact with others and will influence them favorably. The motivated person who participates in program activities may possibly act as an opinion leader, or information leader, among others not so well motivated. Under some circumstances this may be a reasonable assumption; for example, when the unmotivated population is apathetic or simply not aware of the relevance of school activities for achieving some things they value. Under other circumstances the assumption may be unwarranted, as when unmotivated people have negative attitudes toward the school and are responsive to leaders hostile to it.

The population, though friendly, may nevertheless lack important skills or kinds of information that can be provided by mass media or in program activities to which the people have been attracted through the mass media approach. High motivation may not be enough to help these people achieve their educational goals for their children. For example, a parent may want very much to have his child graduate from high school but have little understanding of the importance of regular homework to achieve this goal, or little understanding of conditions the child needs in order to do his homework—a place to work, at least a minimum of quiet. Such a parent may profit greatly by attending a meeting or discussion group with other parents dealing with ways in which parents can help their children in their school work. Drawing in the highly motivated person may be an excellent opportunity for improving the skill, knowledge, and understanding of that person.

Drawing in a number of highly motivated people may be useful to the school-community agent in helping him influence teacher attitudes. The attraction of a number of parents, highly visible and active in programs at the school, may give teachers impetus to revise notions that "parents aren't interested in the school," "parents will never come to school." It provides tangible evidence of community interest in education and gives teachers some sense that there is parental support for their activities.

In some instances, the mass media may be used to draw in populations which are not particularly motivated concerning educational issues but who can be involved through other interests and brought around to educational matters. This may be done by publicizing activities of high interest to certain populations. In one instance the fathers and mothers of school dropouts who would attend no other school events all participated in courses to improve job skills. The problem, of course, is to keep these people coming once they have been drawn in on the basis of the initial specialized program.

2. *Resistant populations.* There are some things which can be accomplished by the mass media approach even with hostile audiences. It can be used as a "triggering device," a procedure to get people into a program, such as a settlement house, where other more intensive approaches can then be used. This assumes that there are some common areas of interest between the hostile group and the school. Thus, some schools have advertised free food and entertainment at social events. This inducement in low-income areas has been successful in bringing people into the school. However, the job of changing their attitudes toward education will require a different procedure once contact has been made. The mass media cannot do this.

This recruiting potential can be quite useful also with a class of parents particularly frustrating to many agents: those with positive attitudes but who lack both motivation and knowledge to do the right things. Once such people are brought into face-to-face contact, areas of common interests can be quickly established. By use of focused expertise, meaningful changes can be encouraged.

A triggering procedure may be very useful where a single and largely irreversible action is required of the respondent. On this basis, personal smear tactics sometimes work just before an election. By the time the information is proven false, it is too late, the vote has been cast. The same principle has application in some commerical advertising when false claims are made for a product, which is then purchased before the claims are found to be erroneous. Some developments in the dissonance theory of psychology suggest that people cajoled or tricked into taking a given course of action by the mass media might eventually decide that their action was correct—that is, they will change their point of view because of their misguided action.[9] Examples where irreversibility is involved need not always be negative, a trick played on the unsuspecting. For example, appeals to pass school bonds in a local election can involve the same principle. There are obvious diffi-

9. Jack W. Brehm and Arthur R. Cohen, *Explorations in Cognitive Dissonance* (New York and London: Wiley, 1962), pp. 50-60.

culties when using mass media as triggering devices, difficulties of making the influence effective and of the subsequent situation. In general, follow-up efforts are required to accomplish more than the immediate purpose, and almost all school-community program objectives contemplate long-range goals.

The use of mass media even as a triggering device probably has little effect with strongly hostile populations. It may play an important part in affecting an indifferent population. Thus, if a school begins a new school-community program for which there is no precedent and where there has been no neighborhood opinion organized, pro or con, and which involves some nonreversible action, such as giving funds for the purchase of new equipment or bringing in after-school teachers, the mass media might play an important role in setting the community's views.

## Some Practical Considerations
## in Using the Mass Media Approach

The mass media approach makes use of familiar media—newspapers, radio, television—as well as such borderline media as rallies and announcements at large meetings. Because of its broad scope, and because it can often be used at low cost, this linking mechanism is widely used. For example, a school can easily and cheaply distribute flyers announcing a special PTA meeting with a high potential for reaching the majority of the parents. As previously noted, these advantages are counterbalanced by low initiative, intensity, and expertise. As an example, even if parents receive flyers announcing a special PTA meeting, there is no guarantee they will read them or, if they do read them, be influenced to attend. Some techniques of saturation advertising may improve the chances of the message actually reaching its target but they are expensive, require expert management, and still leave the possibility that the message will be misunderstood or considered unimportant by the target person.

Communicating with a low-income population has been particularly problematical for people working in the schools.

Time and again, when they thought the message had gotten through, they found it had been distorted or lost completely.


## Types of Mass Media Available

We need only catalogue some familiar forms of mass media used by workers in the schools, with brief comments on less familiar forms.

*Traditional Forms of Mass Media*

1. Radio, television, and the metropolitan newspapers.
2. Neighborhood newspapers.[10] Neighborhood newspapers are an effective way of reaching the local nonparent population, for giving neighborhood-wide public recognition to particular individuals or groups.
3. School newspapers. Tailored to the needs of the specific population of the school, school newspapers can also be used to confer status on individuals or groups. Perhaps a greater use is to convey the impression of an active school with an ongoing program for children and adults.
4. Pamphlets and flyers. Small pamphlets and flyers have the advantages of being cheap, adaptable, and can be produced by the school's own facilities. They possess great flexibility for being adapted to the school's unique needs. Only a limited amount of information can be passed along by pamphlets and flyers.
5. Announcements in church bulletins, community council newsletters, and the like.
6. Posters. Posters are expensive and time-consuming to make.

10. Morris Janowitz, *The Community Press in Urban Setting* (Glencoe, Ill.: The Free Press, 1952). Also "The Imagery of the Urban Community Press," in Paul K. Hatt and Albert J. Reiss, Jr. (eds.), *Cities and Society: The Revised Reader in Urban Sociology* (Glencoe, Ill.; the Free Press, 1957), pp. 597-606.

*Borderline Forms of Mass Media*

Letters and telephone calls as forms of mass media are less personal and intimate than face-to-face contact, but more so than the traditional mass media. Their use depends in part on how routine or complicated the message is. Routine messages are probably most efficiently transmitted by traditional mass media. Those same messages can be transmitted by letter when it is essential that the message get to the target person. When the message is moderately complicated a phone call may be more effective, since it allows for feedback and restatement. An extremely nonroutine and complex message requires face-to-face contact, such as through a detached worker. Announcements may be made at public meetings or large social events, such as dances. This can be especially useful when the school has no formal tie to the special population. For example, a grade school may send someone to a youth center meeting to publicize the need for summer school recreation volunteers.

Parades, sound trucks, and public spectacles have the advantage of high psychological impact, but it is counterbalanced by a high cost in time to organize their use.

## When to Use the Mass Media Approach

From the experience of school-community agents who have used the mass media in their programs, the following guidelines are suggested. Others will be developed by those who use this approach extensively.

1. Use the mass media to convey simple information, such as the time, date, and place of a meeting.

2. Use the mass media to convey messages of wide relevance. Where the message is relevant to a small segment of the population employ a modified or blended medium, such as direct mailings or announcements at meetings where this population is gathered.

3. Use the mass media to announce and publicize spe-

cial events which come up unexpectedly but have mass appeal.

4. Use the mass media to publicize events of high interest.

## Special Dangers of the Mass Media Approach

Not because the mass media approach is useless, but because its use is likely to be so appealing and attractive, we summarize some dangers the school-community agent should recognize when he considers this approach.

1. Developing a publicity campaign can be an escape, perhaps unconsciously, for the middle-class professional from the awkwardness and hard work of making personal contact with possibly hostile persons of lower social class. He should examine his reasons for spending time and money on mass media procedures to assure that the assumptions justifying their use on behalf of the school-community program are reasonably met. He must be sure he is not simply taking the easier way.

2. It is easy to misjudge the impact and the success of the program when using the mass media approach. Two kinds of mistakes should be avoided: the error of believing that great effort sending out messages means that they are received or have any impact; and the error of believing that the number of persons attracted to some well-publicized event indicates successful promotion of the school's program. Those already interested are most likely to respond and others who attend may have interests limited to the particular event.

3. Without careful assessment of impact and modification of communications, it is quite possible through mass media to mispublicize or overpublicize. The community agent should be careful not to build "paper images" of the school that cannot be lived up to in fact and will only serve to confirm negative attitudes and to disillusion friendly persons. It is easy to "promise too much" in publicity releases.

4. The community agent should remember that there are special skills required for effective use of mass media. He should

not assume that anyone who can run a mimeograph machine or type a letter can turn out effective messages. He will need some training and practice himself in these essentially journalistic and public relations skills, and he will need to give more time than may at first be apparent in the technical aspects of mass communication. In particular, the assessment of impact is essential, requiring both technical and analytical sophistication.[11]

## The Use of Mass Media by the Community to Influence the School

Resources of money, time, and technical skill required for an extensive use of mass media campaigns to influence the school are generally beyond the capacity of local community groups unless they are already organized into voluntary associations or there are exceptionally wealthy families willing to support them.

However, community groups can take advantage of the democratic tradition of an "open" and "free" press, and hence make use of the mass media on an occasional, but deliberate, basis. Newspapers and other mass media often pay special attention to more sensational events and "human interest" stories. A mother who dramatizes a situation may be able to get publicity. In a democratic society, large bureaucracies—particularly public-interest (for example, utilities) and governmental bureaucracies—need public support. A dramatic suggestion that the school is not doing a good job or is possibly violating the law is likely to be reported. And adverse publicity is likely to be attended to in some way by the school. How the school reacts is not always predictable, and the outcome can be unfavorable or favorable, depending on factors not necessarily known to the community group or family stimulating the publicity. Furthermore, how the event and the problem will be presented is not much under the control of the

11. H. H. Hyman and P. B. Sheatsley, "Some Reasons Why Information Campaigns Fail," *Public Opinion Quarterly*, 11 (Fall 1947), pp. 413-23; also reprinted in G. E. Swanson, T. M. Newcomb, and E. L. Hartley (eds.), *Readings in Social Psychology* (New York: Holt, 1952), pp. 86-95.

community group. The understanding and support of the media staff are necessary, and these are often uncertain. Moreover, such publicity is usually short-term, with very limited follow-through unless there is continuing effort to keep the problem and the desired change "newsworthy." This, in turn, requires more than community groups can do unless they can work through a fairly strong voluntary association to carry out the publicity campaign.

Techniques community groups can use to bring their problems to public attention cover a wide range—picketing, marches, boycotts, and an array of ingenious counterparts. However, without organizational support efforts along these lines can only be sporadic and their effects uncertain. Publicity and the means of generating it may be most effective when they accompany other types of efforts to influence the school, such as the use of an advocate organization or expert, or an attempt to promote a favored candidate for the school board through political organization.

Finally, we would note that mass media techniques can be used best, within the limits previously discussed, to influence target bureaucracies if the larger community is sympathetic to the objectives or, at least, if the staff of news media are sympathetic. Unless community groups develop their own associations, or obtain access to existing advocate organizations, the mass media approach is likely to be very limited or to reflect viewpoints of members of the community with the resources to support it. Thus, it risks a bias toward middle-class perspectives which may be unrepresentative of wider community interests in some local communities.

# 10 ✤ The Common Messenger Approach

The common messenger approach makes use of individuals who are simultaneously members of a formal organization and of the local community, with common membership in both groups. The most obvious example in the school setting is the child, who is both a member of the school and a member of the family and neighborhood play group or teen-age "crowd" or "gang." The schools have increasingly included adults who are in a position to serve as common messengers, for example, parents who work in the schools and teachers who live in the neighborhood. Parents have been brought into regular school operations, on a paid or a volunteer basis, as teacher aides, tutors, lunchroom attendants, and school crossing guards.[1] In New York City, membership on the local school boards established by the Board of Education also represents a position that comes close to that of the common messenger.

The common messenger approach takes advantage of the fact that persons in such dual locations can serve as channels of communication in the interests of a school-community relations program. Their positions inherently link school and local primary groups and constitute means by which each social form obtains information about the other. The child, for example, cannot help but bring school experiences into the home and home experiences into the school. The nature and extent of the communication may vary widely among different children and is not usually symmetrical. The school-commu-

1. A. Harry Passow (ed.), *Education in Depressed Areas* (New York: Teachers College, Columbia University, 1963); also Gene C. Fusco, *School-Home Partnership in Depressed Urban Neighborhoods*, U.S. Office of Education, Bulletin, 1964.

nity agent can deliberately seek to affect the primary groups through communications carried by the common messenger.

To some extent, the type of linkage represented by the common messenger is also a by-product of some other linking procedures. For example, when a voluntary association approach develops an active PTA, parent-officers may come to feel themselves part of both school and community. Homeroom mothers' groups may feel the same way when they assist teachers by taking children on field trips. Parents who are involved in after-school activities developed with a settlement house approach may be similarly affected, especially if their participation entails some responsibilities for program activities, such as leading discussion groups or helping in the instruction of sewing or cooking classes. The community agent should be aware of this secondary feature of these approaches so as to recognize its effects even if he does not make positive use of it.

## Advantages and Risks of
## the Common Messenger Approach

The advantages of the common messenger approach arise chiefly from the fact that it is anchored directly in the primary groups—families, peer groups, neighborhood groups—that the school-community program wants to affect. The common messenger has no problem of access and acceptance, of continuity of interaction and inclusiveness of areas of appropriate interest of the primary group. His other anchorage in the school means that the common messenger also is readily available to the community agent.

The most obvious difficulties in using this approach are related to the limitations imposed on the common messenger by role membership in both school and primary group, and the extent to which the purposes of the school can be given priority. The common messenger, even more than the detached worker or the opinion leader, is potentially at the point of conflicting expectations, especially in those very situations where the school is most likely to want to produce change, that is, those families whose values and attitudes differ from those the school wants to promote. The conflict is potentially so intense that it is not surprising that much of the usual communication that takes place by means of the common messenger tends to be formal rather than intimate and personal. For example, teachers are more likely to send a meeting notice home by the child than to try to get the child to influence some family practice.

It will increase our understanding of the common messenger approach to analyze briefly some ways to minimize conflict for persons in the role of common messenger. From a sociological viewpoint, this is an analysis of mechanisms that prevent the primary group and the formal organization from impinging adversely on one another.

### Analysis of Safeguards on the Common Messenger Approach

As noted in chapter 1, sociologists studying the family have asked why the characteristic social patterns of the formal organizations where so much time is spent—the work place, the school, voluntary associations, and so forth—do not overwhelm the primary group patterns of the family. Given common membership, what keeps the two forms from damaging interferences? We may suggest the following:

*Role segregation.*[2] One way to keep the conflicting norms of the family and the organization from contaminating one another is to maintain a clear distinctiveness of roles for the person who is in the two settings. He keeps the roles separate as much as possible and it is clear to him when he should shift roles. For example, in his business a man may properly be expected to compete aggressively, but this is clearly not the expectation in relationships with his wife and children.

We can see role segregation operating in the case of the detached worker and the opinion leader. Although he works in a primary group atmosphere, the detached worker is a highly

2. See Part VIII in Bruce J. Biddle and Edwin J. Thomas (eds.), *Role Theory: Concepts and Research* (New York: Wiley, 1966), pp. 273-310.

trained professional. As such he is unlikely to lose sight of the distinction between his work role for the school and his role in the client groups. Similarly, although the opinion leader is in touch with the organization, he is clearly not a member of the organization. As such, he is separated from the internal working of the organization and is unlikely, even if he wished, to be able to introduce the personalized norms of his community network into the organization. In contrast, the common messenger does not have such a clear role separation. He is a legitimate member of both the family and other primary groups and of the formal organization. When he should act as a family member and when he should act as an organization member may not always be clear to him. Consequently, it is easy for him to introduce norms of his primary groups into the organization or organizational norms into primary groups. Such a blending of norms might lead a neighborhood mother working in the school to deal with children on the basis of how she feels about their parents or her personal relationship with them. It might also lead her to evaluate her own child at home according to the performance standards that are used at school.

Because the problem of providing role segregation is difficult for the common messenger, the community agent should be sensitive to further confounding of roles when he uses persons in the common messenger procedure to advance his school-community program.

*Fewest possible links.* Another device that keeps the family and the organization appropriately separate is a limitation on the number of links between the two groups.[3] The more links there are the more difficult it becomes to keep the norms of the two groups separate. Thus, it has been argued that it is functional for only one parent in a family to hold a regular job—the husband or the wife, but not both—since this reduces the chance that occupational norms will intrude on family life. In a similar manner it can be argued that either the child or the parent, but not both, should be used as a common messenger between the school and the family.

*Low-powered people as links.* In the school situation there is an additional safeguard. The child used as a chief connecting link be-

3. T. Parsons, "The Social Structure of the Family," in *The Family: Its Function and Destiny,* in Ruth Anshen (ed.) (New York: Harper, 1949), pp. 260-63.

tween the two systems is usually a low-powered figure in each system.
As a consequence the child is in a weak position to introduce
family norms in the school situation or organizational norms in
the home situation. The situation can be quite the opposite where
an adult becomes a member of both systems. Thus, a parent who
works in the school can exert considerable informal pressure on
teachers to take special care of her child, or a teacher who lives
in the community can easily be caught between the extreme cross-
pressures of her duties as a teacher and her personal life.

The common messenger approach requires safeguards such
as those mentioned for keeping the norms of family and organization from contaminating one another. Great care is therefore
required when adult common messengers are used to establish
contact with the local community. Their use may close distance
between school and community but the risk of damage may outweigh the advantages. However, where the school and community
are physically separated, reducing to some extent the immediacy
of contact, there may be distinct advantages and fewer risks.

The hiring of school parents seems to be a popular way to
tie school and local community together. Three reasons are often
given in support of hiring parents: (a) to give parents better means
of communication to the school and teachers better means of
communication to the community; (b) to add needed manpower
for school tasks that would otherwise require the more costly time
of professional teachers; and (c) to provide some income, often
sorely needed, in low income areas. If these reasons are important,
alternatives to hiring parents may reduce some of the undesirable
risks mentioned above. First, to promote closer feelings of parents
for the school and educational values, or of teachers to the community and its life-styles, a settlement house or a very active
auxiliary voluntary association approach may be tried. Persons
with similar backgrounds but not parents of children in the school
may be employed. Second, manpower for the school may be obtained and income for local residents provided by employing not
parents but persons of similar background whose children are in
different schools. In the use of indigenous workers—parents or
nonparents—there should be a clear-cut statement of duties and

limits of responsibilities in the school. It should be made especially clear that persons are employed to perform tasks not simply because they are school parents. Such tasks, in general, should be those of a nonuniform, nonexpert character. Even if the parent employed has some expertise that the school can use, it may be undesirable to use him or her in that capacity since it adds to the strain of role conflict.

If duties are clear and the risk of conflicting pressures understood when parents are employed, potential problems can be reduced. The type of situation to avoid is illustrated by an incident that took place at one school where parents were working on the school staff. Role confusion became so great that the regular staff did not know what to do when they needed to discuss family problems of neighborhood residents which affected a child's school behavior. The staff felt they could not discuss these matters in front of the employed parents without the discussion getting back to the community and possibly being misunderstood. But they also felt that the parent-employees would be offended if excluded from the discussions. Such situations can be avoided if it is clearly understood in advance that there are private staff considerations that are not the responsibility of parent-employees. Alternatively, but with limitations still evident, parent-employees can be given some training to develop standards of confidentiality.

Our conclusion is that the community agent should use adult common messengers with care. The child can be used with fewer risks since his is a relatively low-powered position in both systems.[4] But when using the child as a common messenger, the community agent should keep in mind that the low position and younger age status make him vulnerable to potential crossfire from school and home. Therefore, he should not be expected to carry messages that will antagonize the

---

4. The use of low-powered people as links between the school and family is the opposite of the opinion leader approach, which uses high-powered people. See the discussion of status differentiations in groups in T. M. Newcomb, R. H. Turner, and P. E. Converse, *Social Psychology: The Study of Human Interaction* (New York: Holt, Rinehart and Winston, 1965), pp. 336-46.

parents. In fact, using the child as a common messenger may be most appropriate as a way to maintain a given distance between school and home by making it clear that values and attitudes are similar or congruent.

## The Common Messenger Approach and Forms of Influence

We refer here to the child or the clearly circumscribed adult. Given the relatively low power of the child and of such an adult in both systems, the common messenger may in general be said to possess relatively low levels of influence. This is in keeping with the separation maintained generally in our society between family life and school or work life.

The child may have considerable referent power in some situations and little in others.[5] His emotional appeal in the family is likely to be limited by his subordinate position, his influence greatest when it concerns things directly affecting him rather than the family as a whole. He may well be able to influence the family on some concern of the school—such as that a special children's publication be subscribed to—but this influence is not likely to be strong enough to alter economic priorities in a family of limited means.

The limited referent power which an adult common messenger may use on behalf of the school arises from limitations imposed on his role in the school. Nevertheless, the adult common messenger may be able to convey a general orientation, such as good will or genuine interest, which the school wishes to indicate in the community. He may also serve well to convey more specific information, such as plans for meetings and new programs, more or less in the fashion of an opinion leader and subject to limitations of that approach.

The limitations affecting referent power apply also to legiti-

5. E. Katz and P. F. Lazarsfeld's data on children's influence in the purchase of family breakfast cereal suggest that in some areas of family life the child has high influence. *Personal Influence* (Glencoe, Ill.: The Free Press, 1955), p. 245.

macy as a form of influence exercised by the common messenger or his manipulation of rewards and punishments. Whatever his influence in his primary group roles, he is not likely to be able to wield it on behalf of the school except in the most general way without endangering the separation of roles we have discussed. For example, if he claims legitimate right to speak in the family or neighborhood on behalf of the school, he alters his position in each system. Similarly, if viewed as capable of meting out rewards or punishment because of his position in the school, his position in the primary groups will change.

What the child or adult as common messenger may provide is some degree of expertise. His influence may be enhanced because he is in a position to know more about a particular aspect of the school and its program than others. Since his role in the school under the circumscribed conditions assumed here is necessarily of relatively low status, his expertise cannot become as great as that of professionals involved in a detached worker or settlement house approach. With respect to three types of knowledge, however, he may achieve considerable expertise and thereby come to possess considerable power: (a) factual information, such as that about school-community programs, when they occur, and simple but essential information that needs to be communicated accurately and with certainty to parents and others; (b) knowledge of the general values and norms supported by the school, such as the importance of education, respect for the child as a person, and consistency in discipline; and (c) knowledge of the extent and quality of interest that the school and its personnel have in the local community. Because he is regularly a part of the school organization, the adult or child common messenger (in different ways and to different degrees) may readily be seen by the community groups as knowledgeable in matters that do not require specialized training. The school-community agent should try to see that the influence of the common messenger is used positively for the school's purposes. He should be sure to provide the common messengers with accurate and timely information of the sort that they can best transmit.

## Specific Considerations When Using
## the Common Messenger Approach

1. *Level of competence of the common messenger.* The competency of the common messenger may vary considerably—for example, the younger the child the less he can be trusted to deliver complicated messages reliably; or, the less well-educated the adult the less he can be expected to transmit technical messages reliably. An assessment should be made of the competence of the messenger to deliver the message. Where the message seems too complicated for the messenger to transmit verbally, it may be carried in written form, such as printed notices sent home with children. Generally not a trained expert, the common messenger cannot be expected to deliver messages that require professional understanding, such as new curriculum content or teaching techniques.

2. *Reliability of the common messenger.* If the messenger is competent to deliver the message, can he be relied upon to do so? Will children in fact deliver messages to their parents? Will adults convey messages to other adults in the community?

Some school-community agents have suggested that reliability of the child as a common messenger varies with age, the younger being less reliable. However, others observe that perhaps very young and teen-age messengers are less reliable than children of middle-range age. In general, the more the child has a positive stake in the message, the more likely he is to deliver it, regardless of age. For example, a message concerning the child's misbehavior is less likely to be delivered than a message about a reward he will receive; a message inviting the parent to a school play in which the child has a part is more likely to be delivered than one announcing a PTA meeting. In addition, the stress put by the teacher or community agent on the message is very important in determining whether it is delivered. If the teacher passes out messages in an offhand way, they will probably not get home; if great stress is put on the importance of delivering the message, it probably will. Other techniques used to increase the reliability of the child messenger include: (a) pinning the message to be delivered to the very young child, so he won't lose or forget it on the way home; (b) having a portion of the written message signed by the parent and returned by the child to the teacher; and (c) having the child himself compose or write the message so he values it as his own.

The reliability of the adult messenger has been found to be influenced by the prestige he attaches to his membership in the school as an organization. This may work in either direction. In some instances, parents will not convey information they regard as a basis of their own prestige and do not want to share. We have previously mentioned the women planning a protest at the state capitol who would not publicize the trip generally to the local community but only to their friends whom they felt had high prestige. In other cases adults strongly identify with the school, and may welcome the chance to enhance their prestige by transmitting messages to the community-at-large. This is related to the acceptance of the common messenger by the community group.

3. *Degree of acceptance of the common messenger by the community group.* The degree to which the messenger is accepted by the community group may influence the group's readiness to read, listen to, or otherwise respond to the messages delivered. For example, in neighborhoods where there is a tradition of parental nonparticipation in school activities, a parent who works in the school lunchroom or who teaches an evening class may become alienated from his community group precisely because of his participation. In such cases, his effectiveness as a common messenger is greatly reduced. However, it may be possible to build up the acceptability of the common messenger, in part by having him carry messages that have community value in themselves, such as information about job training or other salient activities.

## When to Use the Common Messenger Approach

In light of the previous analysis, we may briefly indicate some of the considerations that should govern the choice of the common messenger procedure.

The community agent should be cautious about using the

approach when family or group solidarity is so great and so exclusive that a member who uses his position in the school on its behalf is likely to be viewed as disloyal to the group. This is more likely to be the case with the adult than the child common messenger, but it applies to both. At the opposite extreme, when families or community groups are already so overly identified with the school that the separate characteristics of school and primary group are blurred, the common messenger approach should be used with caution. If used in these circumstances, formal (usually written) communications of a factual nature are to be preferred and may, indeed, help to increase distance.

The common messenger approach is most useful when families and community groups have a fairly well established pattern of cooperation with the school and need information about specific activities or aspects. Because the common messenger is a member of specific groups, he can deliver messages tailored to those groups.

## Special Problems for the Community Agent in Using the Common Messenger Approach

For the most part, the common messenger approach does not require much technical knowledge on the part of the community agent. However, several special problems should be noted.

1. *Access to common messengers.* When the child is used as a common messenger, the community agent usually has to obtain access to him through the teachers. Therefore, if the procedure is to be effective attention must be paid to informing teachers of the purpose and character of the message and securing their cooperation. In some schools so many communications—safety leaflets, announcements from the principal, school newspaper, etc.—are sent home with the child that they become routine, and neither the teachers nor the children take the communications very seriously. In other instances, teachers may be reluctant to have the child used as a messenger. In either case, the community agent should establish a relationship with the teachers that facilitates his

purpose and fashion his use of the approach to that relationship. Sometimes the preparation and conveying of information through the child can be made into a very useful educational experience and is welcomed by the teacher. Some teachers will be interested, also, in trying to find ways by which more complex information— such as their methods of motivating a child or of handling discipline—can be conveyed, and will participate in experiments with the community agent to develop ways of doing this.

Some adults who can serve as common messengers will be directly accessible to the community agent because they are in activities of the after-school program or other school-community activities. With them the community agent is in a position (when conditions in the community are appropriate) to work out more informal as well as formal ways of carrying desired messages. Other adults, such as teachers' aides, lunchroom assistants, etc., will not be so accessible and will have to be reached through other school staff.

2. *Preparation of the messages.* If the message is in written form, attention to its presentation, language, format, and content will be required, as in the case of messages using mass media. The salience of the message to the messenger should be considered since, in contrast to the impersonal mass media, its delivery is affected by it. General messages or those expressly fashioned for one or a limited number of families or groups should be distinguished.

If the message is to be delivered orally, making sure that its essential meaning is understood is more important than its form. This may require considerable interaction with the children or adults who are to carry the message so as to clarify what is intended and help them find comfortable ways of expressing it.

However the message is to be communicated, it should always be prepared with full awareness on the part of the community agent that the common messenger is not merely a means of transmission but also an active participant in the communication process.

3. *Assessment of effectiveness.* The community agent should try to assess each phase of the process involved in communication

through the common messenger approach. Was the message appropriate for the messenger to deliver and the groups to receive? Were the right children or adults used as common messengers? Did the message reach the intended destinations? Was it understood as intended? Did it have any effect and, if so, was it what was wanted?

There are no simple ways of assuring adequate assessment without allowing enough time to follow the process through. The community agent may, however, seek feedback from the children or adults involved, from teachers and other staff members, and from members of community groups. He will want to listen for indications that the common messengers have been put into difficult positions unintentionally. He will try to see if parents and community persons communicated with by this means appear to participate more positively and meaningfully.

## Community Use of the Common Messenger Approach

As noted in chapter 1, a form of common messenger approach has been reflected in demands by some militant community groups that community members be employed by the schools (for example, black teachers from the neighborhood), taken into positions of power on local school boards, or permitted to monitor school performance through parent watchdog committees. We have pointed out that in the extreme this can be tantamount to denying the necessity for any expertise in the educational enterprise. The counter position, equally extreme, has been taken by those who reject all participation in the school by community members. This controversy is mentioned here to warn against overstatement of the long-range value of the highly placed common messenger even if it is possibly of immediate benefit. In either case, the common messenger is best used with respect to nonuniform, nonexpert tasks. These are not, however, to be thought of as trivial. They include inputs in decisions regarding personnel, curriculum, and distribution of resources.

The implications of our theory suggest that low-powered

common messengers may be of value to the community when there is fundamental agreement on goals and when information needs to be conveyed more personally than other mechanisms of fairly wide scope allow. This is particularly useful when groups of parents convey to teachers through their children either supporting or corrective information. The general principle seems to be that the common messenger mechanism is of most value as a continuing two-way channel when agreement is sufficient to prevent much stress from developing. The mechanism shades into preliminary phases of other approaches—such as demands to open up the possibility of advocate expert participation—when the community uses high-powered common messengers.

## Conclusion

The common messenger approach when used appropriately can be a valuable part of the school-community agent's deliberate procedures for affecting a fruitful relationship between the school, families, and other groups. Children and participating adult family members will necessarily, if unintentionally, act as common messengers, and the community agent should try to see that their effect is, at the least, not contrary to the purposes of the community program and, at the best, a positive contribution to it.

In addition, the community agent should recognize the potential value of the common messenger approach as a source of information about the community. He should remember that families and other groups, if in less deliberate ways, will use the common messengers to communicate their viewpoints and information to the school. The possibility of two-way communication is potentially a valuable asset for the community agent when he uses the common messenger approach.

# 11 ✦ Formal Authority

When a school uses the power it possesses through law or through the quasi-legal force of position and tradition to influence families and other groups in its community, it is using formal authority as a linking procedure. A clear illustration of this procedure is the use of the legal power of the attendance officer to require (or set in motion processes that can require) the parent to send the child to school. The power of the principal to suspend or expel a pupil is another example rooted in the legal position of the school. The capacity of the principal to "compel" a parent to come to school to discuss a problem about a child is an example of a formal authority often so firmly established by local tradition as to be viewed as "quasi-legal." In our society most legal power is vested in "law enforcement authorities," such as the police and the courts, and it is officially circumscribed by constitutional and judicial protections. Even the limited legal power of the school carries great weight and its use in the linking procedure we call formal authority can be very influential. It can have both positive and negative effects in a school-community program and it must be used with special care.

Because of its own legal power, the school can mobilize secondary legal power more readily than many other organizations, such as hospitals, social agencies, and private businesses. It can call on the police to back up its authority as well as to give it protection. This potential force makes the school a significant instrument of formal social control even though its more central purpose is the education and socialization of children. The school, on its side, is under an equally severe legal requirement to provide education. The compulsion of law can be invoked by parents as well as by the school, but the school is obviously in a better position to wield its legal power because it is an organization and because it has institutionalized agents of enforcement. Possessing this character, the school acquires still greater authority from the way both children and parents are likely to view their relationship to it. The school often appears to them to back its demands with a force that cannot be directly resisted. When we speak of the use of formal authority by the school, we refer to both legal and secondary sources of power. The wielder of such authority may seem to possess overwhelming power, no matter how trivial the issue involved may be. The apparent imbalance of power creates special problems when used in a school-community relations program whose purpose may be to narrow social distance from the community. It is difficult for this sense of overwhelming power not to pervade all school-family relations.

Considerable formal authority of the school over the child is exercised directly by control over the child's educational career through evaluation of academic work and behavior and determining whether or not he will pass on, to the next grade each year. Controlling the educational career of the child, the school exercises considerable indirect formal authority over his parents, most of whom are concerned about their child's success in school. The threat of poor grades or expulsion is an implicit and powerful force that school personnel always possess. Thus, when a teacher requests a meeting with the parents of a child who is doing poorly in school, this is an implicit command to the parents if they want the child's grades to improve.

Because of this indirect formal authority, communications to parents from the school often take on a mandatory tone. This can be quite overt, as when the principal or the visiting teacher requires the parents to come to the school to talk about a child whose behavior is disruptive under threat of expelling the child if they do not come. However, routine communications can also take on a mandatory tone, simply because they come from the school. For example, in one school with a history of poorly attended PTA meetings, the principal decided to send out a letter at the beginning of the year announcing the first PTA meeting. There was no statement that attendance was required, but the parents interpreted the announcement to mean that attendance was mandatory and the meeting was crowded. For the most part, the formal authority exercised by the school is of this implicit nature. Suggestions are often taken as half-commands, for example, that parents obtain certain kinds of medical help for their child, or get the child glasses, have dental work done, or have the child evaluated by a child guidance clinic. Parents are periodically reminded of the indirect formal authority of the school when the child brings home his report card. This is not to say that the commands of the school always achieve the results intended, but they are sure to have some effect on parents.

In general, the school makes comparatively less use of overt than of indirect formal authority. When it does use overt power, it is usually to deal with an extreme situation, for example, the child's behavior is so bad he will be expelled unless there is improvement, the child is so inadequately dressed or grossly undernourished that his school work is affected, or the parents are allowing or encouraging the child to miss school. In these cases the school may frankly warn the parents that unless they cooperate in improving the situation the child will be expelled or legal proceedings instituted.

Formal authority is one of the major means of influence at the disposal of school-community agents. Simply by being a school "official," a certain amount of formal authority becomes attached to them in the eyes of parents. The worker can use this formal authority to gain access and cooperation. He can also either emphasize or mute the amount of formal authority he wields, depending on the situation. He can borrow selectively from the formal authority of teachers and principals by indicating he has their support. He can do this verbally by sending communications cosigned by them or appear with teachers and principals at school events. The community agent can work with direct formal authority by routing some of his efforts through the attendance officer. By delegation, the community agent can enlist the power of the police, public health officers, court personnel, and other enforcement agencies. (See chapter 12—Delegated Function.)

## Formal Authority and Forms of Influence

*Reward and punishment.* We have noted that formal authority carries the overt or indirect force of threat, but it also carries promise of potential benefits. Compared to other linking mechanisms, power to reward or punish is most evident in the use of formal authority. As already noted, the power to punish is often associated with control by school officials over the conditions of acceptance of the child. Power to reward is evident when a principal lends the prestige of his office at public meetings to acknowledge cooperative efforts, to imply special advantages for attendance at meetings, and the like. Punishment and reward are obviously intertwined, since the withholding of punishment may be viewed as reward, but our concern is with the more general meaning of this form of influence, which is easier to express in terms of punishment.

One question is the extent that punishment can be used without antagonizing people so much that relationships will be broken. Among the therapeutic professions there is a feeling that when the helping person has the power to punish, it is difficult to develop a relationship of trust. Thus, if a mother is on welfare and the worker would like to offer therapy, the client and the worker both face the dilemma arising from the worker's enormous punitive powers (for example, the right to withdraw income from client). The client may want to discuss with the worker a serious problem concerning her husband, whose presence she cannot acknowledge without risking loss of benefits. Under such strain the success of therapy becomes doubtful. The dilemma is similar to that of the street worker with delinquent gangs. If the gang breaks the law and the worker tells the police, rapport with the gang is damaged and influence reduced; if he does not tell the police, he is an accomplice to an illegal act and puts himself and his agency in jeopardy. Therefore, many therapeutic practitioners decline to accept any kind of formal or legal authority which might be viewed by clients as punitive. This reluctance of therapists is buttressed by studies of effects of punishment on crime which suggest that there is little relationship between the severity of the punishment (for example, the death penalty) and the frequency with which the crime occurs.[1] In short, the argument is that formal authority and the use of interpersonal therapeutic techniques are frequently contradictory.

However, complete rejection of the use of punitive power is probably not necessary to create a condition for therapeutic influence. There are many occasions when forms of help take place under duress. Most treatment of juvenile delinquents occurs under the threat of punishment by the court if the juvenile does not cooperate. There have been therapeutically-oriented programs that claim success under such circumstances.[2] One agency in a large city claims success in its use of a detached worker approach to gangs, although it recruits the gangs in police headquarters and thus has strong backing from formal authority. The literature on extreme forms of coercion shows some evidence that compliant behavior and personalities may evolve from the use of force.[3] Such results are said to differ, however, from those intended by therapeutic approaches in that the latter are more likely to be integrated into the

---

1. See Sheldon Glueck, "Predictive Devices and the Individualization of Justice," in Sheldon and Eleanor Glueck, *Ventures in Criminology: Selected Recent Papers* (Cambridge, Mass.: Harvard University Press, 1964), pp. 175-93; Thorsten Sellin, "The Death Penalty Relative to Deterrence and Police Safety," in Norman Johnston, Leonard Sanitz, and Marvin E. Wolfgang (eds.), *The Sociology of Punishment and Correction* (New York and London: Wiley, 1962), pp. 74-84.

2. L. T. Empey and J. Rabow, "The Provo Experiment in Delinquency Rehabilitation," *American Sociological Review*, 26 (October 1961), pp. 679-95; B. Bettelheim, *Love is Not Enough* (Glencoe, Ill.: The Free Press, 1949); also see Jules Henry for a discussion of The Orthogenic School in "Types of Institutional Structure," M. Greenblatt, D. J. Levinson, R. H. Williams, *The Patient and the Mental Hospital* (Glencoe, Ill.: The Free Press, 1957), pp. 76-84; H. A. Weeks, *The Highfield Experiment* (Ann Arbor, Mich.: University of Michigan Press, 1959).

3. E. H. Schien, "The Chinese Indoctrination Program for Prisoners of War," *Psychiatry*, 19 (1956), pp. 149-72; R. J. Lifton, "Thought Reform of Western Civilians in Chinese Communist Prisons," *Psychiatry*, 19 (1956), pp. 173-95; Bruno Bettelheim, "Individual and Mass Behavior in Extreme Situations," in Theodore M. Newcomb and Eugene L. Hartley (eds.), *Readings in Social Psychology* (New York: Holt, 1947), pp. 629-39; A. Kardiner and L. Ovesey, *The Mark of Oppression* (New York: Norton, 1951); D. C. McClelland, *The Achieving Society* (Princeton, N. J.: Van Nostrand, 1961); Hortense Powdermaker, "The Channeling of Negro Aggression by the Cultural Process," *American Journal of Sociology*, 58 (1943), pp. 750-58; T. E., Pettigrew, *A Profile of the Negro American* (Princeton: Van Nostrand), pp. 13-14, 46-47.

person's own value system and the former to require external support and surveillance.[4]

The apparent contradiction between these two viewpoints—that the power to punish is self-defeating for the therapist and that extreme coercion can significantly change people—may be resolved if we recognize that there may be different degrees of force and different degrees to which deviant behavior is maintained. Brutal, overwhelming force sufficient to induce changes in persons—as in a concentration camp—may be effective, but it is rejected by the values of democratic and humane society. Force of such magnitude is clearly beyond the reach of the school. Deep-seated or strongly defended behavior would seem to be resistant to fairly weak force, and this situation often faces therapists. The school, however, may be said to possess relatively strong formal authority, if by no means approaching totalitarian power, and the behavior it often seeks to influence is sometimes only moderately sustained. These are the circumstances that appear to allow the most effective use of formal authority.

Three types of situations illustrate this point. The first supposes a form of behavior so strongly held, either by an individual or a group, that the punishment will be suffered rather than the behavior abandoned. Some people would "rather fight than switch," or like Patrick Henry choose "liberty" or "death." In behavior relevant to the school such an extreme is uncommon but it does occur. There are religious sects that refuse to send their children to school beyond a certain age regardless of the law; religious conviction against vaccination may override the threat of the unvaccinated child's exclusion from school; racial segregationist attitudes may be equally strong.

A second, more familiar, kind of situation is illustrated by deviant behavior related to emotional or other psychological factors, such as acting-out behavior of child or parent or psychopathological conditions. A child may not be able to control his temper tantrums and aggressive actions; the parent may be incapable of giving positive emotional support to the child. Force is

4. See Herbert C. Kelman, "Processes of Opinion Change," *Public Opinion Quarterly*, 25 (1961), pp. 57-78.

not likely to work in such cases; it may actually aggravate the condition. Consider the probable consequence of threatening to fail a child who is already so fearful about his school work that he cannot learn; or using force on a person who is not sufficiently rational to perceive the meaning or consequence of punishment; or punishing someone when the punishment itself may provide gratification. Conceivably, massive punishment over an extended time might even in these conditions effect changes, but this is neither possible nor suitable for use by the school. We believe that the threat of moderate but available punishment can have both a deterrent and a socializing effect for most children and parents because most of them show only moderate degrees of deviance. The fear of getting caught stealing and being punished, or being humiliated by threat of expulsion, or summoning the parents for not getting the child to school are likely to carry some weight. Under these circumstances, conforming behavior may be facilitated, and this in turn may create the condition (which psychologists call dissonance)[5] in which the individual seeks to bring his attitudes into harmony with his behavior.

A third kind of situation where the effectiveness of punishment is limited gives more specific recognition to the sociological context of deviant behavior. If the deviant behavior is strongly buttressed by the person's primary groups, punishment may even strengthen that behavior by making him a martyr. In studies of delinquency, it has often been observed that the prestige gained from being arrested, or even committed to a correctional institution, may outweigh for a gang member the negative effects. If the extended family supports parents in the belief that their high school child should work rather than attend school, threats of punishment against the parents may bring them even more support from their most salient primary group. Such situations do not, in our opinion, commonly prevail in most school communities; most parents and peer groups of children support the general objectives of the schools. There-

5. Jack W. Brehm and Arthur R. Cohen, *Explorations in Cognitive Dissonance* (New York and London: Wiley, 1962).

fore, the school is often in the position where its use of formal authority can reinforce tendencies to conform which can be found in the primary groups of the population it is trying to influence.

To summarize the discussion of reward and punishment as a form of influence most characteristic of formal authority, the schools, unlike the police and many therapeutic agencies, often have a fairly conforming and psychologically normal population to deal with. School personnel can expect the use of formal authority to be effective within limits, but it should not be expected to be very effective among most deviant populations. Whenever formal authority is used, the school-community agent should be alert to side effects on the relationship between the school and client groups.

*Legitimate, expert, and reference power.* It has been noted by workers in the schools that the prestige of some of the staff in the eyes of the local community is increased by the amount of formal authority they can wield. A person, such as a school principal, vested with the capacity to reward and punish, should also have other bases of influence.

The wielder of authority is sometimes influential because he is thought to be expert. According to Max Weber's theory of bureaucracy, authoritative people at the top of the organization are also said to be the most knowledgeable.[6] There is some evidence that the authority of the principal and the teacher leads some parents to believe them expert in child rearing practices. This may not actually be so, but the belief that it is may mean that formal authority is accepted. This is further enhanced when the school personnel are viewed as professionals.

Some parents may respond to use of formal authority by the school staff not because of punishment or reward or because of

---

6. Weber implicitly assumes that knowledge is the basis for making decisions. *From Max Weber: Essays in Sociology,* Hans H. Gerth and C. Wright Mills (trans. and eds.) (New York, Oxford University Press), pp. 196-244. Gouldner makes the point that there is a difference between knowledge and status, and that where they conflict there will be organizational tensions. Alvin W. Gouldner, "Organizational Analysis," in Robert K. Merton, Leonard Broom, Leonard S. Cottrell, Jr. (eds.), *Sociology Today* (New York: Basic Books, 1959), p. 413. Weber assumed that knowledge and status did not conflict.

superior expertise, but because they accept the staff as a legitimate source of influence. From their own childhood experiences at school they learned to accept as legitimate the authority of the school in certain areas of life. Orders or requests made under this authority are viewed as coming from those whose positions give them the right to expect compliance. The principal wields authority as the head of a substantial enterprise, and in that status possesses considerable legitimate power even over those who have the indirect relationship of parents to the school organization.

With respect to referent power, it might be noted that in social-psychological literature there is some evidence that many people seek to identify with high power figures, and that low power people seek to mix with and emulate high power figures.[7] People wielding formal authority frequently become positive reference points to others. Some of their effectiveness emerges from this aspect of their role rather than the mere use of punitive power. As a consequence, the person wielding formal authority is not always feared and avoided but has the ability to attract and provide by his mere presence a sense of reward.

*Kinds of Client Groups Most*
*Susceptible to Formal Authority*

The previous discussion suggests that the use of formal authority by the school is not so useful when behavior results from deep-seated personality disorders or is the result of tightly-knit deviant groups. For families and other client groups of this type other linking mechanisms are more appropriate for a long-term effort. In the contrasting circumstance, where client groups are generally well integrated and support the school, the deviation of one or a few of them is likely to be modest and the ordinary use of legal authority can be very effective.

Most families will usually fall between these two extremes. In low-income areas in particular, there may be families who

7. Eric Fromm, *Escape From Freedom* (New York: Holt, Reinhart and Winston, 1941), pp. 163-64; A. Zander, A. R. Cohen, and E. Stotland, "Power and the Relations Among Professions," in D. Cartwright (ed.), *Studies in social power,* (Ann Arbor: Institute for Social Research, University of Michigan, 1959), pp. 15-35.

want their children to get ahead in school but are not organized to help them do so. Lack of organization may result from an adverse employment situation or a reversal of family roles (for example, the mother works but the father is unemployed). It might result from a marriage in conflict or a broken, fatherless home. It might result from illness that absorbs the energy of the family. A very important possibility is that well-intentioned parents are often simply uninformed. Thus, a mother might be using inadequate forms of discipline because she has never had experience with better ones. She might not know what study habits need to be developed in a good student. Parents might not realize that their other interests (having a good time, necessity to support needy relatives, involvement in social groups) prevent them from supervising the child adequately.

In such cases the use of formal authority might serve as a useful first step. In all of these cases the parents are sufficiently concerned so that if they are formally requested by a school official to participate in a corrective program they will probably comply. Moreover, they will have a receptive attitude when efforts are made to find out what is wrong and to do something about it. To deal with lack of knowledge in such matters as discipline, some mechanism other than formal authority is needed, for example, services of a settlement house or detached worker. However, procedures might be more acceptable and salient because they are backed by formal authority. It is quite clear that people will frequently agree that they have transgressed some legitimate norms, and within that context will accept a threat of punishment as just. The practitioner who deals with people brought in under formal authority need not assume that the clients will be invariably or deeply hostile.

## Considerations of Policy and Values in the Use of Formal Authority

The exercise of formal authority should be viewed primarily as a distance-creating or maintaining device in relating the school to primary groups in its community. The basis for this conclusion rests on the values of a democratic society in which formal authority is expected to be used impersonally and formally rather than in ways that allow personalized interactions that create intimacy with the primary groups.

It should not be assumed that the power to use legal means and ultimately police power to affect persons and groups is invariably associated with alienation and separation. We have suggested that other forms of influence in addition to punishment often accompany the use of formal authority. When punishment is viewed as just, it may draw the punished closer to the source of punishment. This may be the case, for example, when a family wants a child to go to school and feels that the authority of the attendance officer is on their side. Such an achievement depends on the use of authority in an impartial, impersonal, and formal manner because the values of our society insist on strong safeguards against the arbitrary and personal use of legal power. Its exercise is delimited by a priori rules, with clear specification of lines of authority and conditions under which it can be used, with avoidance of all elements of favoritism by stressing the impersonal character of justice, and with minimal discretion given to any member of the organization that has the legal power. In other words, to protect the civil liberties of those who might be subject to it, the exercise of formal authority is usually located in an organization whose administrative style is rationalistic.

It is sometimes argued that agencies vested with great formal authority and legal power should be given greater discretion and freedom from some of the restraints that now keep them from becoming therapeutic agencies. Some propose that the determinations of the juvenile court be based on diagnostic and therapeutic considerations and the matter of guilt or innocence play almost no part. Similarly, in domestic relations cases and even adult criminal cases the court could require the varied services deemed desirable rather than be limited by legislative and judicial restrictions. A different position—with which we agree—is that the risks to the civil liberties of citizens are too great to allow a human relations approach when powerful legal authority can be used.We do not argue that therapeutic efforts should not be made for those who by virtue of their actions become subject to legal control. We suggest as an alternative that where professional discretion and human relations types of organizations are necessary to solve social problems, they be separated from the legal system or legal authority. Rather than change the police force into a human relations organization to deal with problems of delinquency, it might be better to develop an independent youth board. Rather than give judges more discretion to deal with divorce, agencies separate from the courts might be developed and their diagnostic conclusions and treatment recommendations used as part of the testimony presented to the court.

It is our view that in a democratic society, the large-scale organization which has the right to exercise legal control must be bound, when doing so, by the demands of rational social relations. For this reason the exercise of formal authority should be viewed as a distance-maintaining device in relating bureaucratic organizations such as a school to external family and neighborhood groups.

Several other points are pertinent. First, the school should restrict the kinds of tasks for which it undertakes legal responsibility to those that can be dealt with uniformly. Second, the schools should as much as possible seek to delegate to other agencies the use of legal power. Where the school must itself use its legal authority—as in some severe cases of deviancy—it is wise to employ specialists whose job it is to handle such matters, and who work independently of the rest of the staff, and who are guided by a different system of organizational constraints. This is the usual arrangement for attendance officers.

As pointed out earlier, there are relatively mild forms of legal authority that are quite effective in dealing with mild forms of deviance. In such cases the problem of safeguarding civil liberties is correspondingly reduced. Our position is that the use of formal authority in a school should, in general, be restricted to relatively mild forms of deviations, and when more authority is required its use should be delegated to other organizations. When formal authority is exercised it should be used within a rationalistic organizational context. With these points in mind, formal authority may usefully influence many families and groups.

## Some Practical Points
## in the Use of Formal Authority

As school-community agents have discussed practice problems in the use of formal authority, the following pragmatic suggestions have been made:

*The threat of authority is sometimes more effective than its use.* It has been observed that there are times when the threat of punishment is more effective than the actual punishment. As a consequence, the practitioner should be careful not to put himself in a position where he must actually exercise formal authority. For instance, it may be more effective to remind parents that their child *can* be suspended than actually to suspend him. The parents might readily conform to avoid the public disgrace associated with having a child removed from school. Moreover, when the child has been suspended once and the family has faced the effects, further threats might not have as much effect.

*The separation of the wielder of authority from other personnel.* Many practitioners sense the fundamental contradiction between attempts to win the trust of the client population and the capacity to control them through legal authority. Yet, they feel that both are necessary for the total school-community program. As a consequence they suggest a division of labor among school personnel so that one person wields formal authority and another works with other linking procedures. Some discussions in small group research and family socialization bear on this. It is pointed out that the role of task leader should be separated from that of social-emotional leader.[8] If trust relations are a function of the latter and

8. R. F. Bales, "Task Roles and Social Roles in Problem-Solving Groups," in Eleanor E. Maccoby, T. M. Newcomb, and E. L. Hartley (eds.), *Readings in Social Psychology* (3rd ed.) (New York: Holt, Rinehart and Winston, 1958), pp. 396-413; R. F. Bales and P. E.

authority relations are a function of the former, the sort of division of labor that practitioners have suggested is backed up. This must be balanced against the view that the wielder of authority accrues prestige, legitimation, and the air of authority that causes even those who are targets of punishment to seek him out.

*The use of passive and aggressive forms of formal authority.* It should be recognized that formal authority can be exercised in a passive or an aggressive way by the organization. Sending a truant officer or a principal to tell parents what they must do is a more aggressive procedure than sending a note to them about the situation or asking them to come to the school to discuss it. The first procedure gives the family much less option to alter its behavior on its own decision but it does provide the formal authority with much more opportunity to observe what is going on. It may place the family in the difficult position of feeling spied on and coerced, thereby discouraging cooperation. However, where there is real suspicion of serious deviancy (such as child neglect or parental brutality) that cannot be assessed except by a home visit, formal authority may have to take this aggressive form. In general, when there is no other way of assessing the consequence of deviant behavior, the more aggressive use of formal authority should be undertaken. By contrast, when the formal authority involves behavior that can be otherwise assessed, the more passive form of formal authority can be applied. There are often reasonable alternatives to aggressive formal authority, alternatives which might be better employed, for example, by detached workers.

*The use of formal authority in emergency situations.* One of the chief values of formal authority is its capacity under many circumstances to provide emergency relief for a situation. By virtue of having legal authority, the school can, if necessary, cause people to be removed from the situation. Thus, if parents are charged with child brutality, it might be very important to remove the child from the parents' care in order to protect its life. This short-

---

Slater, "Role Differentiation in Small Decision-making Groups," in T. Parsons, R. F. Bales, *et al., Family, Socialization and Interaction Process* (Glencoe, Ill.: The Free Press, 1955), pp. 259-306.

term solution has great virtue even though it does not provide a solution because the basic problems of the family are not attacked.

It should be borne in mind that short-run solutions may actually make for long-term problems. For example, some principals tend to deal with very difficult children by expelling them from school. This solves the short-term problem of a given teacher in a given class. However, the problem of educating the child still remains. If the number of expelled children increases, their influence may affect other children. The capacity of formal authority to deal with emergency situations must be used in recognition of long-term consequences.

*Stages in the use of formal authority.* Since formal authority has several different potentials, it can be used at different stages of a school-community program, depending on which functions are to be used. For instance, because of its emergency power formal authority might be used as a first step where extreme deviation is a threat to life or property. In case of child brutality, formal authority might be used to remove the child from the family. In most cases life or property are not immediately threatened, and formal authority may solidify the deviant group, not change it. Under these circumstances an alternative procedure, such as use of the detached worker, should be used. In general, even when dealing with moderately deviant groups, other procedures might do the job as well, and with fewer negative effects than formal authority.

# 12 ✤ Delegated Functions

Many other organizations in addition to the school are involved in the community, and they can and will play a part in linking the school and its outer community. Generally, there are three circumstances under which the schools should take account of other agencies. First, the services of other agencies may overlap or compete with those of the school. For instance, if a community center in the area has a fully developed after-school program, it would be sensible for the school to lodge this aspect of its school-community effort with the ongoing program of the center. The school might also find itself related to another organization which provides complementary services necessary to the school but quite different from those the school can provide. For instance, if the school finds that its night programs are affected by fear of street violence, it might seek cooperation from the police department for closer supervision of the area. In the case of an inadequately clothed child whose parents are on welfare, the school might seek the cooperation of the welfare agency to provide additional clothing or to help the mother with budgeting. If the school finds there is a hostile ethnic group in its community, it might seek through the churches or other associations to gain access to the people. In all these cases the school seeks to coordinate its efforts with those of other organizations.

Finally, the school might find it desirable to stimulate organizations to perform jobs it cannot do but which must be done. For instance, it is difficult for a school to succeed in its educational tasks when it is located in a neighborhood where there is much crime or racial disturbance, or where there are no recreational facilities. Dealing with these ills is not the specific job of the schools—at least in the short run. To strengthen the neighborhood, it may be necessary to encourage organizations such as churches, block clubs, local political clubs, local branches of social service agencies, and the like to pay attention to local problems. These organizations can bring to the neighborhood the resources of the larger community as well as provide an organizational base to combat crime, delinquency, and social intolerance. The development of powerful grassroots organizations seems particularly necessary in low-income areas where there are high rates of mobility. It is generally observed that where neighborhoods have strong organizations which adhere to the norms of the larger society, the task of the school becomes easier. The school might encourage the development of independent grassroots organizations which, when developed, need not have direct ties to the school.

To sum up, in working in the community through other organizations the schools might merge activities with these organizations, seek to cooperate while maintaining organizational independence, or seek to develop other organizations independent of the school to serve its objectives. The latter two procedures have been most often used by school-community agents.

We use the term delegated function to refer to the procedure of linking the school to the community through other organizations for the purposes of its school-community program. Since the community agent does not work in these organizations, the school is in effect delegating some of the functions it might otherwise need to perform. Another organization may have greater access to the population, greater competence than the school in carrying through some tasks, or greater recognition to legitimately engage in a certain activity. In some instances, the school can accomplish its purpose only by delegating functions.

The capacity of the school to exercise forms of influence by delegated function may be enhanced or restricted to the extent that the other organizations themselves are using (deliberately or without conscious plan) the linking mechanisms previously discussed. To gain the cooperation of a social agency may mean that professional social workers become available as detached workers or workers in a settlement house type activity. The formal authority of the police and the courts may serve the purposes of the school. The church bulletin may be a medium for communicating to residents. The clinic can provide medical expertise. When it uses the delegated function mechanism, the school may lose the benefit it might derive from direct contact with client groups.

The school is inevitably involved with other organizations that work in the community and must pay attention to its relations with them when seeking to accomplish some of its own objectives, just as other organizations must pay attention to the school in seeking their goals. An extended discussion of interorganizational relations—that is, the relations between formal organizations—is beyond the scope of this book.[1] Such relations for the school may involve the school-community agent but they more often concern responsibilities centered in the principal's office. The community agent usually has more limited responsibilities for relating the school to the primary groups of the school's community.

## The Decision to Delegate Functions: Some General Criteria

Whether or not a school-community program should delegate a function to another organization can often be decided on a pragmatic basis. Is there an agency in the local community that can and will work with the local primary groups (that is, to encourage relations with the school that approach the balance believed to be optimum for achieving the school's goals)? Will that agency work effectively on behalf of the school (not necessarily in its name)? Will the delegation of function deprive the school of an important avenue of community contact that would be important in other aspects of the school-community program? Can the school gain resources by delegation (for example, serve more peo-

1. For an elaboration of a theory of interorganizational relations, including bibliography pertinent to delegated function, see Eugene Litwak and Jack Rothman, "Toward the Theory and Practice of Coordination between Formal Organizations," in William R. Rosengren and Mark Lefton (eds.), *Organizations and Clients* (Columbus, Ohio: Charles E. Merrill, 1970) pp. 137-87.

ple), or will it take resources from the school that may be needed for other purposes? Will an activity contemplated by the school threaten another organization's place in the community and adversely affect community relations through competition? Are community groups already so dependent for service on some other organization that the school would be viewed as going beyond its legitimate functions?

The question is whether or not delegation of some function will strengthen or weaken the school as an organization and thereby its capacity to conduct an effective school-community program. To deal with this question we will first consider the nature of organizational integrity, then some effects of various relations between organizations on organizational integrity.

*Organizational Integrity*

One of the more obvious reasons for an organization to exist is to apply resources—financial, physical, and especially those of coordinated personnel—to some purpose that may be called the organization's goal. Organizational integrity, in the sense of maintaining the organization for the purposes of its goal, is an obvious concern of all organizations. This integrity involves conceptions both of goals and of means by which the organization pursues them. Personnel, whatever their private commitment to the organization's goals, tend to develop occupational interests that attach them to the organization. The maintenance of organizational integrity will be more difficult when there are conflicting goals or means, and joining with another organization may or may not introduce conflicting goals or means. On this we may base a major criterion for deciding if and how two organizations should relate to each other, that is, how different relationships will affect their organizational integrity.

A school's organizational integrity can be said to be greatest and least threatened when it takes responsibility only for the limited goal of "educating" children. When it takes responsibility for broader aspects of socialization, such as citizenship training, inculcating appropriate social behavior, and the like, it complicates its organizational requirements and affects its organizational integrity with respect to its primary goal. The fact that this may be necessary or desirable, or that education cannot be achieved without acknowledging and pursuing other goals, does not alter the general conclusion. When the school delegates to another organization—for example, to a community center or a church—some of the responsibility for educating school children, it may weaken its organizational integrity to the extent that the goal of the other organization differs from that of the school, even if such delegation is necessary.

Additional factors may affect the decision to delegate functions and the kind of delegation that may be most useful. Before considering them, we shall discuss the theoretical effects of interdependencies between the school and other organizations in terms of the consistent or conflicting character of their organizational goals and means.

*Extent of Interdependence and of Delegation*

Although there is, in the broadest sense, interdependence between all organizations in the community, it is possible to recognize degrees of interdependence. Complete interdependence, means that organizations cannot operate effectively without continous exchanges in all significant areas such as staff, clients, funding, goals, and housing. Such cases often require mergers for effectiveness. An example would be two public elementary schools in the same area, where there were only enough children for one and where surplus teachers can be reassigned. Without merger, neither school can be operated effectively. Partial interdependence refers to situations where each organization has other goals or means which are not directly relevant, or sometimes contary, to those of the other. For instance, schools and health authorities must exchange information ans share responsibility for immunization of young children. However, they require little exchange over adult illnesses or funding. Independence is the term used to describe organizations which require virtually no major exchanges. Primary schools and professional football teams are generally a case in point.

For the purpose of exposing the underlying principle that may serve as a criterion, we argue that organizations having complete interdependence can maintain organizational integrity with maximum delegation of functions, even to the point of merging. Partially interdependent organizations can delegate functions through coordinating procedures that protect each organization while allowing cooperation. When organizations are independent or conflicting in goals-means, delegation of functions would be harmful to organizational integrity.

The principle is stated in an abstract and compressed form. It can only sensitize the community agent to underlying issues. He must, in the real situation of his school and community, analyze the nature of organizational interdependence as he finds it and make judgments considering the factors involved.

*Complete Interdependence: Organizational Merger*

Schools often perform functions that are distinct from those of education, such as provision of food services, social work, nursing functions, and so forth. Why have these functions been merged with the primary functions of the school? Further questions arise as to whether the school should merge a parent education program of some agency into its operations, or delegate some activity of its school-community program to another agency.

We may explain the first illustration generally (ignoring, of course, local historical circumstances) by noting that the functions of teaching children and of feeding them in school are greatly interdependent. The school draws from a large geographical area, the school day is long, neighborhood restaurants are not available or cannot accommodate the children at prices they can afford. Although supplying food is not a school function, it is absorbed into the school organization with little difficulty. Two different but consistent goals—educating children and supplying food— usually found in different organizations can be merged without damage to the integrity of the school. Of course, there are many other reasons why children are fed in school—nutritional, economic, the need for parental freedom from child care during the day, and so forth. We are concerned here only with illustrating how complete interdependence of goals can readily sustain merged functions.

In a similar manner the schools have found themselves involved in social work. Schools are required by law to provide education for children up to a given age—generally sixteen— regardless of any personal difficulties of child or family that may affect educability. They must provide education for difficult children and also assure that they will not interfere with the education of others. School systems often incorporate social workers to identify disturbed children and provide them with some forms of service. This service may take the form of referring children and families to suitable social agencies for treatment. The consistency of goals makes this delegation of function appropriate.

A similar situation may obtain with respect to school-community relations. The school may find it necessary to develop a community program and employ school-community agents. In some low-income neighborhoods the entire student body might be below the national achievement norms, most of the children systematically underequipped in terms of conceptual ability, attention span, knowledge, and achievement motivation. In the case of a single child, the problem may be dealt with by available special services. If the entire student body is involved, a community program may be needed for which there are no agencies available. The school may take on the job of diagnosing and building up the necessary organizational base of the area. If some aspect of this effort—for example, conducting parent education groups on child rearing—can be undertaken by a community agency having the same goal, the school can delegate this function entirely to that agency.

*Partial interdependence: coordination.* When the school and some other organization have goals and/or means that are both consistent and conflicting, or where the function is such that it is partly consistent and partly in conflict with the goal of the school, there is partial interdependence. Such situations call for coordination rather than merger. The school wants to be sure that the function is performed but it would weaken its organizational integrity if it were incorporated in the school.

Suppose that the school has concluded that its neighborhood needs strengthened grassroots organizations such as block clubs, political groups, churches, and the like. While the school should encourage the development of such organizations, it should not attempt to control them. To the contrary, the values of our society require a clear separation between religion and the school, between the school and the activities of political parties, or voluntary social and ethnic organizations. The school is supposed to respect diversity of our cultural values within generic views on democracy, religion, citizen responsibility, freedom, and so forth. The schools are not supposed to favor Democrats over Republicans, one form of religion over another, one ethnic group rather than another, one position on an issue by a neighborhood block club. If the schools sought to control the grassroots organizations, they might introduce conflicting values that would affect their primary organizational goal of education. However, as previously noted, to achieve their goals the schools may need the support of strong (if diverse) grassroots organizations in their neighborhoods, and it cannot ignore the effects these groups may have. For instance, in one area a local church promoted racial prejudice which had highly visible effects in a school that served both blacks and whites.

If the school must be kept separate from the grassroots organizations but at the same time is dependent on them, coordination is called for while each organization retains its organizational autonomy. The school's interest is best served by finding some other organization or agency that can appropriately encourage and influence the local grassroots organization and delegating to that agency the function which the school needs performed. This makes it necessary that the school make known its purpose and interests and conduct its own activities that might affect the grassroots groups so as to complement the work of the other agency. This is neither merger of function nor entire separation but coordination.

Situations of partial interdependence calling for coordination will also occur when resources of the school are inadequate to pursue a particular goal without neglecting another. Some other organization or agency may be in a position to perform the function. The school may want to have an after-school recreation program for the children but may have to decide whether to spend its money for this or for a detached worker program. If a local community center can provide the recreation program, the school can coordinate its interest with that of the center by forming groups of children and sending them to the center or permitting representatives from the center to recruit children during school classes. In this situation, lack of means prevents merger of function although goals of the school and the community center are entirely consistent.

*Independence or conflicting goals: no delegation of function.* It may seem unnecessary to mention that the school should not delegate a function to an organization whose goals conflict with its own. It would not delegate parent education to a business whose purpose was to sell home freezers, even though in selling the freezers the business professed to educate families about economies of quantity buying. In some instances, however, goals may appear consistent when they are in fact conflicting, as when a sporting goods company offers to sponsor an athletic team in the school but expects the children to buy its equipment. Or, a religious group may offer to work with families for the school while actually proselytizing for its church. In general, the recognition that there is "conflict of interest" prevents conflicting goals or means.

*Other Factors Affecting*
*the Decision to Delegate Functions*

Although we believe that consistency of goals and means is the most important factor to consider when deciding to delegate functions, there are other factors as well. Traditions of separate activity may prevail regardless of consistency of goals, as, for example, between public and parochial schools, or nonsectarian and sectarian social agencies. Vested interests of personnel—both in the school and in other agencies—must be considered, for example, delegation of some treatment functions may threaten the professional role of the school social worker. Associated with such a factor may be the rigidity of the school organization or of another agency, making delegation difficult if not impossible. In short, the application of the general principle of goal consistency must be applied with recognition of the particular circumstances and traditions of the school and the other available agencies.

## Forms of Influence and Delegated Function

The organizations to which the school may delegate functions vary widely and may exercise forms of influence in different ways. When using delegated function as a linking procedure, the community agent will want to select agencies in part for the appropriateness of the particular kinds of influence sought. Often it will be the superior capacity of another agency to affect the families and other groups that will encourage the delegation of function. Let us consider each of the forms of influence we have previously identified in terms of the bearing on delegated function.

*Expertise.* The school will frequently turn to other agencies for help in achieving a given objective because the other agencies have trained expertise the school does not have. As an obvious example, the school may refer sick children to a clinic or hospital since these organizations have the trained personnel to deal with illness. The school may turn to the police to curb crimes that keep people from attending evening programs. The school might seek the advice and help of a community center or social work agency to deal with a gang that is disrupting the neighborhood. It might seek university researchers to help diagnose neighborhood problems that affect the education of the child.

*Referent power.* The school may turn to other agencies because they have strong bonds of trust with the populace, that is, they have referent influence over certain families or other groups. In a highly religious community the churches may have greater influence than the school, so the school might work through the churches. Suppose, for example, that the school has a problem with vandalism after school. If the school can get the ministers or priests to speak to their congregations, the clergy might have more impact than a direct appeal from school personnel. It might be more appropriate for the school to appeal through local ethnic clubs or recreational associations. Sometimes this appeal can make use of popular nonlocal organizations. A given school might invite a well-known athlete to speak to the children about the importance of education even if the athlete is a member of a sports organization that is not local.

*Legitimation.* The schools might turn to an agency that has greater legitimacy for the particular purpose among the population to be influenced. The development of "front organizations" may be intended to legitimate obvious self-interest of an organization among people who are suspicious of it. If the schools ask citizens to pay higher taxes in order to provide salary increases and better school services for the child, there may be suspicion of self-interest. In such a situation the school might seek some other organization which is ostensibly free from charges of self-interest to promote the goals of the schools. Such established organizations as large business, real estate associations, unions, and churches may be approached. Special organizations might be founded to provide greater legitimacy, such as a citizens' committee. A housing authority may have more legitimacy than the school to promote a desired clean-up program. The medical association or the health department can exercise more legitimate influence with respect to some objectives. A council of churches may be more effective with some groups when teen-age codes of conduct are proposed.

*Reward and punishment.* Finally we consider the delegation of authority to utilize reward and punishment power. The school might turn to the police to use legal power to eliminate illegal businesses that are demoralizing the children. It might urge a block club association to pressure city building inspectors to condemn property not being kept up by its owners. It is the building department's legal force that the school seeks. Using the influence of reward, the schools might ask various civic organizations to offer prizes—such as tickets to a ball game or a weekend at a recreational camp—for students who do well in school. Civic groups may be asked to recognize families that cooperate.

## The Use of Delegated Function
## to Open or Close Social Distance

Delegation of function in itself has little effect on whether groups in the community will come closer to the school or be moved farther from it. However, delegation can be used deliberately to affect social distance. A school might delegate a function to another agency as a means of increasing the school's initiative and narrowing the gap. It might want to develop an after-school community program for a population with very strong ethnic ties, people who might not understand, might be fearful of, or might be indifferent to the school. The school might systematically establish contact through ethnic associations willing to urge parents to go to the school or to invite school personnel to attend meetings. By this means the school increases its ability to reach parents and closes social distance.

In contrast, when a school seeks to widen distance with the community it might also request aid from outside agencies. Suppose a parent group uses the PTA politically with respect to various civic and political issues. The school might insist that this is not the business of the PTA and recommend civic and political organizations that might more properly handle such issues. Moving community problems outside the sphere of school interest is to some extent increasing distance between school and community. Similarly, a mother who is overly concerned with the schooling of her child might be encouraged to discuss problems with a family agency instead of with the school staff, thus decreasing the family's involvement with the school.

## Training and Costs

We briefly summarize some of the costs of using a delegated

function approach. First, it takes time and energy to coordinate activities with other organizations. In terms of training, this means that there must be knowledge of and sensitivity to other organizations in the community and what they do. Furthermore, dealing with personnel from other agencies requires different modes of interaction than dealing with families and other primary groups directly. Problems of status and prestige become magnified. A lower-status member of one bureaucracy may have limited access to a high-placed member of another bureaucracy. Not only must the community agent know what organizations are available and what they are doing, but he must also know the proper channels through which they can be reached.

The kind of training required for community organizers to deal at the grassroots level with low-income families differs from the kind of training required to deal with other large-scale organizations. Without specific training in approaches and techniques for working with other organizations there is a tendency for professional persons to seek to deal with other organizations using professionals, and to avoid other community organizations. It is not uncommon for a community agent to seek to reach the outer community by becoming active in a community council made up entirely of professionals from social agencies. In this way, he does not have to learn a new language, does not have to understand different values, does not have to mix with people of lower status. Given the real need to actively involve other agencies and given the expected hesitation of some community agents to become involved with low-income families, this is not surprising. In the training of community agents there should be special efforts to acquaint them with the procedures for direct access to nonprofessional organizations.

In addition, where the emphasis is on the interorganizational problems of coordination, the agent should be trained to detect and appraise the extent to which organizations are in partial or complete interdependence with the school and the extent to which they are independent. He must also be able to assess the competitive position of these organizations as well as the forms of influence they can and do use.

## Community Use of Delegated Function
## to Reach the School

The community needs to consider a delegated function approach when it must deal with the school bureaucracy on matters requiring technical knowledge or where large-scale resources are called for. The neighborhood might be involved in a long-term complex court case over school districting policy. It must retain a law firm. Alternatively, it may seek to develop an organization which can put pressure on schools by withdrawing children and enrolling them in private schools until the parents' demands are met. In general, local groups need to resort to delegated function when the school refuses to cooperate with them, thus limiting their access to the expertise of the school.

The community may use two kinds of delegated function. One kind allows community groups to "borrow" a bureaucracy from the larger society and use its experts to influence the school. The other calls for community groups to develop their own bureaucracy with which to influence the school.

Delegating functions to "borrowed" organizations may be accomplished by community primary groups without developing a high degree of local community cohesion or forming numerous active voluntary associations. This assumes that there is an organized segment in the larger community that is friendly to the local groups. Thus, a few black families living in a largely disorganized neighborhood might nevertheless appeal to the NAACP for legal help in fighting against local school discrimination. A local black family might appeal to a city commission on human relations. As a consequence, the "borrowed" delegated function possibility is an important alternative to building local voluntary associations and advocate bureaucracies.

The use of the "borrowed" organization for a delegated function by community groups is limited by the degree to which there are friendly external sources of support. Furthermore, unless there is high congruence or overlap between local group interests and goals of the "borrowed" bureaucracy, the local community may have to compromise to get the service it wants, or it may find that the organization used is less vigorous than desired. An outside civil rights organization may be interested in appealing a case to set a judicial precedent, whereas the local community may be more interested in an immediate change in a situation affecting their children. Local parents may have to abandon tactics they prefer in order to get the support they want from an outside organization.

The process described may lead the local community to recognize that it cannot "borrow" an organization but must build its own. This involves a long, slow process, as in the case of labor unionism. Sometimes help in organizing a local advocate bureaucracy can be obtained from a "borrowed" organization, as older unions have helped organize newer ones.[2] Sometimes voluntary associations created for one purpose can be converted to another, as when a recreational club takes on political functions. Even associations promoted by the school itself may be used to function as advocate bureaucracies to which local groups can delegate their purposes. Thus, block clubs stimulated by the school to combat neighborhood apathy and increase control over delinquent youth might, under some circumstances, become vehicles of demand on city government for better community services, including more resources for the local school. The sustained effort and organizing skill required, as well as the need to develop economic support, make it difficult for local community groups to build their own advocate bureaucracies except under the most favorable conditions.

To summarize, the use of delegated function for local primary groups is very important when the community seeks to affect technical aspects of the school and the school is unfriendly or resistant. The local community is most likely to be able to delegate functions when it can "borrow" bureaucracies from friendly sectors of the larger community. To do this may entail compromises, but nevertheless gain most of the local objectives. Where longterm differences with the school exist and the community can muster sufficient resources, it may try to build its own advocate

2. See the history of the CIO in Irving Bernstein, *Turbulent Years* (Boston: Houghton Mifflin, 1970).

bureaucracy as its delegated agency, thus gaining greater control but sacrificing speed of action. Usually a local advocate bureaucracy requires the establishment of a voluntary association, which in turn becomes an established bureaucracy. This is so difficult that one may say, for all intents and purposes, that the local community can use the delegated function approach to influence the school only through a "borrowed" advocate bureaucracy.

# ✤ INDEX

297

## DATE DUE

| | | | |
|---|---|---|---|
| | | | |
| | | | |
| | | | |
| | | | |
| | | | |
| | | | |
| | | | |
| | | | |
| | | | |
| | | | |
| | | | |
| | | | |
| | | | |
| | | | |
| | | | |
| | | | |
| | | | |
| | | | |
| GAYLORD | | | PRINTED IN U.S.A. |